Stages in Prayer

J. G. Arintero, O.P.

Stages in Prayer

Translated by
Kathleen Pond

SOPHIA INSTITUTE PRESS
Manchester, New Hampshire

Nihil obstat: Andreas J. Moore, L.C.L., *Censor deputatus*
Imprimatur: E. Morrogh Bernard, Vic. Gen.
Westminster, March 25, 2957

Sophia Institute Press
Box 5284, Manchester, NH 03108
1-800-888-9344
www.SophiaInstitute.com

Sophia Institute Press is a registered trademark of Sophia Institute.

paperback ISBN 978-1-64413-720-8

ebook ISBN 978-1-64413-721-5

Library of Congress Control Number: 2022934342

First printing

Translator's Note

This work, by Fr. J. G. Arintero, the distinguished Spanish Dominican who died in 1928 with a high reputation for sanctity, has been translated from the fifth Spanish edition. The preface is that to the second edition, the fifth edition being prefaced with a mere note. In the original Spanish, certain chapters are followed by an appendix, and these are placed at the end of each chapter, but it was thought that the continuity of the text would be better maintained by placing all the appendices in order at the end of the book. This has accordingly been done.

Direct quotations from Scripture are given in the Douay version; indirect quotations have been translated from the original Spanish. Since the works of St. Teresa and St. John of the Cross are so well known, *The Dark Night of the Soul* has in certain instances been abbreviated to *Night* and *The Ascent of Mount Carmel*, to *Ascent*. Of the extracts given from the works of both St. John of the Cross and St. Teresa, I have made my own translations.

Kathleen Pond

Oxford
Vigil of St. Andrew, Apostle, 1956

Preface to the Second Spanish Edition

This little book first saw the light when it formed the seventh and last of the author's *Cuestiones místicas.* It was written for the purpose of completing the questions by showing which are the true phases of the progress of the spiritual life that normally figure in the lives of the saints and of great servants of God—however rare, on account of our want of fervor, weakness, and unfaithfulness, some of them prove to be in actual fact among the generality of those who are termed "devout Christians." Such phases thus come to be considered, quite unjustifiably, as *extraordinary*, whereas they are really, of their own nature, *ordinary* in the perfect Christian life.

As, with this end in view, we had been trying to sum up and synthetize what there was to be learnt of greatest importance concerning prayer, its true progress and ordinary manifestations, it seemed the opportune moment to publish a separate book, under the title of *Stages in Prayer*, for the benefit of the many to whom, on account of lack of time or the high price of the larger work, such a compendium might prove useful.

In point of fact its success has shown that the publication of this small work filled a pressing spiritual need, with the consequence that in a very short time it was out of print. A large number of devout persons all say that they have found great comfort in it, and the light they needed.

This encouraged us to re-edit the work in a more convenient format, improving it as much as possible by the correction of small points and with certain additions so that, in accordance with the wishes of good friends, the result may be both a concise treatise on prayer, in which light is thrown on the chief difficulties that the devout and even their directors generally find in it, and also a genuine handbook of the spiritual life—which in a certain sense can be wholly reduced to the interior life, that is, to the life of prayer; for as one's life of prayer is, so will the whole of one's Christian life be.

As St. John Climacus so aptly says:[1]

> Prayer is the union of man with God, ... is the work of Angels ... a foretaste of joy to come, a work which never comes to an end, a source of virtues, the means of obtaining graces, hidden profit, the support of the soul, the light of the understanding ... an indication of the measure of one's virtues, a declaration of one's state, the revelation of things to come and an indication of the divine mercy.... All this is said of prayer, for it helps man in all things.... What can there be higher than to unite oneself to the Lord and persevere in this union with him?... No one can learn perfectly from another man's teaching how great is the beauty of prayer, for within itself it contains God for master and he teaches man wisdom.

This divine wisdom will teach us all things, the whole of what we need to know to be happy in this world and in the next. Thus, striving in all sincerity to attain to this, in the end we shall be able to say with the Wise Man: *Now all good things came to me together with her, and innumerable riches through her hands.*[2]

This is what I most sincerely desire for you, fervent reader. If you should happen to light upon anything here that serves you as light and sustenance, I ask that you will bless the Giver of all good things for it, asking His mercy for this unworthy instrument of His, so that he too may share to some degree in your devotion and fervor and, when he has preached to others, may not become a castaway.

Fr. J. G. A.

Salamanca
Feast of the Espousals of Our Lady,
February 1918

Contents

Chapter 1

Mysteries of the Christian and of the Mystical Life

The stages of prayer form, so to speak, a résumé of the mystical life as a whole; and the mystical life, it can be said, in a certain sense takes in the entire spiritual life and even the whole Christian life in the strict sense of the term[3] — since every faithful Christian, by the mere fact of being baptized into Christ, which is equivalent to stripping oneself mystically of self and putting on Christ,[4] symbolizes his own death to all things, his spiritual burial and resurrection, and his new life hidden with Christ in God.[5] The mysterious life thus hidden in God is the mystical life, a life that, if he is to be perfect and like another Christ[6] — *christianus alter Christus* — must reproduce over again in every Christian, as we shall now see, all the wonderful mysteries of our Savior.[7]

By Baptism, indeed, we are engrafted into Christ[8] so as to form with Him one single body — His Mystical Body.[9] We are given life by His very Spirit. His divine sentiments enter into us in ever-increasing measure, in proportion as we strip ourselves of our own.[10] That is how we receive the adoption of the sons of God, by means of the pouring into our souls of the Holy Spirit, who, by His gift of piety, moves us to address

Almighty God by the sweet name of "Father," and to serve Him, love Him, and honor Him as such, praying in the manner we ought.[11]

Thus He dwells in us, not only sealing us with the living image of Christ, whose features He imprints upon us,[12] but also anointing us and illuminating us with the gentleness, sweetness, and splendor of His grace, which is in substance the whole of mystical life and eternal life itself, hidden and immanent within us.[13] We receive Him as the fount of living water that, by divine impulse or instinct, makes us rush forward toward eternal life.[14] He dwells in us not only as the life-giver who purifies, fortifies, and renews us, destroying in us all the elements of death,[15] but also as Lord,[16] with full right to dominate, direct, and govern us,[17] imposing upon us His sweet laws of love that give us the glorious spiritual liberty of the sons of God and free us from the tyranny and slavery of the world and of the life of routine.[18]

All our good consists, then, in cleaving to God[19] until we have become one spirit with Him;[20] in being truly docile and teachable toward Him,[21] never grieving His loving Spirit, not resisting, much less extinguishing the Spirit,[22] or letting Him call to us in vain; striving, on the contrary, to be very attentive to Him, interiorly recollected that we may catch every sound of His voice, and desiring faithfully to accomplish that which the Lord our God deigns to speak within us, for He speaks words of peace to His saints and to all those who are converted to the heart.[23] Then, dwelling in us, as St. John of the Cross says,[24] "with pleasure," He will not tarry in making Himself the sweet Master, Director, Consoler, and Lord of our souls, moving and governing us in all things as if we were perfect sons of God, causing us to proceed, not according to flesh and blood—*non secundum hominem*—but in a manner that is supernatural, superhuman, and truly divine—that is, mystically, or *secundum Deum*. To this end all the intimate, loving, and familiar intercourse with God by means of prayer and contemplation is ordained, to the copying and imitation as perfectly as possible—allowing the divine Spirit to imprint them in us "supernaturally"—of the adorable perfections of the heavenly Father, striving to this purpose to become configured to His only-begotten Son, the splendor of His glory and our exemplar and model.[25]

In order, then, to understand the stages that this divine life offers and the phenomena that it presents from the time it is received in Baptism until it is fully unfolded in glory, it is essential to keep well before the mind all the mysteries—joyful, sorrowful, and glorious—of the life of our Lord. To that end, it is good that we should meditate on them deeply at the side of Mary, Mother of Divine Grace, in the holy Rosary; for all of them—from the Incarnation itself, by the Holy Spirit, of the Virgin Mary, and from the birth of Christ to His Passion, death, Resurrection, and the sending of the same divine Spirit, in which sending the marvels of the Christian life are consummated—have to be reproduced, each in its own way, as in so many other Christs, in all perfect Christians.[26] Those in whom they have not been reproduced in any way will always be very imperfect and puny followers of Christ, as St. Bernard warns us (*Serm.* 44).

Chapter 2

The Different Stages of Prayer and of the Spiritual Life

In reality, it is the reproduction of the mysteries of Christ that we have just been considering that forms the true substance of the mystical life. Our progress will thus consist in growing "in grace, and in the knowledge of our Lord" (2 Pet. 3:18). All this, however, is brought about in a special way in prayer, which is the school of the spiritual life for, as St. Augustine said (*Serm.* 90): "He who prays well, lives well." Hence, to recognize the different stages of the spiritual life—which ought to show continual progress[27]—it is sufficient to know the stages of prayer that serve it as norm; for the life is an echo of prayer itself, an unceasing conversation in Heaven.[28]

The different stages or modes of prayer, then, are like the different spiritual talents that God gives us for the purpose of treating and negotiating with Him the *unum necessarium*, namely, the pursuit of His kingdom and His justice. Every man should pray according to the special manner of prayer that God gives and shows him, and not in some other way, for that would be to go outside the divine order and plan.[29] But he who employs the talents he has received well will at once find them doubled and even multiplied one hundredfold (Matt. 25:14, 29).

To pray is to converse with God Himself, honoring Him with the virtue of religion and entering into intimacy and familiar company with Him by means of the three theological virtues, which, since they cause us to share in the mutual knowledge and love of the three Divine Persons, unite us with Them in ever-increasing measure[30] — and by means of the seven gifts of the Holy Spirit, which put us under the loving direction and influence of this divine Comforter, and which are the mystic eyes with which the Lamb who is slain enables us to penetrate the marvels of the book of His mysteries (Rev. 5:6).[31]

This is how, through fervent prayer, we obtain those blessings from on high that are necessary to enable us to set a ladder in our hearts and mount it, ascending from virtue to virtue until we come to practice them all with full perfection and heroism and thus deserve to be recognized by the Eternal Father as His faithful children and counted in the number of those in whom He is well pleased, for He sees how such souls, in imitation of His Only-begotten Son, already proceed in all things under the impulse of His divine Spirit. To such, then, He will manifest Himself and will even now allow them in some sort a glimpse of the summit of Zion, that is, of the heights of contemplation and true sanctity.

This full holiness or perfection, which does not stop short even at heroic virtue, has to be communicated to the soul by the seven most precious gifts of the sanctifying Spirit.[32] By means of these gifts, if we strive always to be responsive to the divine inspirations, we shall come to be wholly possessed by this most sweet Guest, consoler, re-fashioner, and guide of the soul, and shall be not only thoroughly purified and enlightened by Him, but in all things animated, governed, moved, and directed, as by the true Lord and Giver of life.

Then we shall work, not in conformity with our own human standards but in conformity with His, which are divine; not on our own initiative but passively, in a sublime manner that is no longer human, but superhuman and divine. This becomes souls that are truly spiritual, that is, *perfect* Christians, the faithful sons of God; for, as the apostle says (Rom. 8:14), only those are such in the full measure of perfection who find themselves moved and possessed by the divine Spirit in all things: "Whosoever are led by the Spirit of God, they are the sons of God."

When it is accomplished actively, as we proceed in human affairs, our way of prayer, and in general our manner of practicing virtue, will, then, be "ordinary and natural," that is, ascetical, the way appropriate to beginners. It will be, so to speak, "extraordinary and supernatural," that is, mystical, the way appropriate to proficients and perfect, to interior and spiritual souls, when it is accomplished passively, not according to our mode, nor on our initiative, but as it is continually given us by Him who, having taken possession of us and accepted our surrender, incapacitates us for what is not according to His pleasure and gently moves and urges us to what He requires of us in each case, which is always that which is most fitting for His glory and our profit.

Thus, although He is ever the life of the soul—giving us sanctifying grace in the communication of Himself and in the same act diffusing charity in our hearts, at the same time enriching us not only with the infused virtues but also with His seven most precious gifts—nevertheless, except on rare occasions, He does not usually work in us by means of these gifts until they have been considerably developed and consolidated with the practice of the virtues that we call normal or ordinary.

By means of the latter alone, although it is in reality God who is working, He does so so secretly under the veil of charity that it appears as if we had done all ourselves on our own account: for strictly speaking, it is our reason that governs and directs, but reason now enlightened and strengthened in greater or less degree. Hence this process can be reduced to rational and fixed rules, as in the case of the rules of asceticism, which every Christian can easily understand.

Hence also it occurs that, knowing by faith that our good actions are accomplished in the power of God, we yet often appropriate them to ourselves, imagining that we have done something by our own efforts. But when, with the good exercise of virtue thus practiced in the ordinary, human mode and with faithfulness to grace and the divine inspirations, the gifts have developed, the Holy Spirit wants to manifest Himself through them, with great frequency, as absolute master of the soul, and the latter begins to realize that it is no longer itself working but God in it. Thus, it attributes nothing to itself.

As the divine Spirit inspires us when He wills and as He wills, without subjecting Himself to our evaluations and standards, similarly the true process of the mystical life cannot be confined to fixed rules, and one has to go almost entirely by the fruits, judging by them if things are from God or not. Hence comes the difficulty that so many generally find in the study of mystical theology (the key to which is the treatise on the gifts of the Holy Spirit), for they want to discover fixed rules in it, like those of asceticism, which are based on the ordinary conditions of virtue, whereas the one and only rule is to be attentive to the inspirations of the Spirit of sanctification, who is not content merely with the good but ever urges us in each single instance to what is most perfect, best, most in conformity with God's pleasure.

When the divine Guest gives no inspiration, the soul should continue to "travel on foot," as it is usually expressed, returning to the ordinary way of asceticism. This is very frequent in the beginnings of the mystical life. For this reason, as we shall see, different modes of procedure and of prayer are to be used to a greater or lesser extent. In the period of transition from the life of asceticism to that of mysticism, the two are associated together in such a way that they come to constitute certain intermediary forms.

Thus throughout, a long series of progressive stages will come to be noted.

Chapter 3

The Stages of Ordinary or Ascetical Prayer

The first stage is that of *vocal* prayer, in which conversation with God is maintained with the usual signs of articulated language. It can thus be seen that this is always within reach of all, and it will be so long as that external language is not replaced by the heart's silent expression or by the completely supernatural language of the Spirit who is all-pervading: "For the Spirit searcheth all things, yea, the deep things of God" (1 Cor. 2:10). There are many simple persons who, unless they use words, can scarcely manage to express their humble feelings before the Lord, so that, when they close their lips, as St. Teresa noted, it seems to them that they are also closing the eyes of their mind.

But these very persons, as the saint adds so expressively, although they feel incapable of *meditating* all their life long, are not thereby excluded from entering in due course into mystical repose, that is, into the royal mansion of contemplation.[33] On the contrary, if they persevere faithfully in this simple manner of prayer of theirs, even though they confine themselves merely to repeating, but with all their heart, the short petitions of the Our Father, in them alone, and especially in the first three, they will find inexhaustible treasures, such that, when they are least thinking of it, they will thereby be raised to the highest degree of contemplation and union.[34]

But the ordinary way, particularly in persons with a certain degree of education, is that they maintain their fervor and recollection better if they keep their lips closed and pray only in mind and heart (1 Cor. 14:15); God understands their thoughts, desires, and affections very well, without there being any need for them to express them verbally. This interior conversation, or conversation from the heart, which at this stage is generally carried out "in spirit and in truth," is *mental* prayer, which can take on many different forms and constitute numerous stages, as will be seen.

To the second stage of prayer belongs what we call *meditation*, that is, consideration of the mysteries of God, or discursive prayer, to which almost all those who embrace the spiritual life[35] with a certain amount of religious knowledge devote a shorter or longer period, and in which ordinarily, and particularly at the beginning, it behooves us to proceed methodically and step-by-step, in order to learn to use that precious time well and with profit. Hence almost always one has to begin by the acts of preparation, namely by composition of place, reading, meditation, reflection, and so forth, which are, so to speak, instructions for learning how to converse with our Lord and His saints, by means of the affections, petition, praise, offering, thanksgiving, practical resolutions, and so forth, in which the essence of prayer consists and which, therefore, should never be lacking, even if the rest should be lacking. Thus, when the soul succeeds in doing this with a certain skill, and ceases to be an apprentice, it ought then to suppress certain of the acts of preparation, which now become useless, and confine itself to the principal part of its prayer, that is, the loving conversation and petitions.[36]

However, almost always the movement of the affections must be acquired through considerations that force us to make strong resolutions by which, aided by the lights and helps that we therein beg God to give us, we can day by day correct ourselves of some particular vice or defect and make progress in virtue, in order to serve God with more fidelity and fervor, which is what we go to prayer to learn and accomplish. But the light, fervor, sweetness, and devotion that we thus derive, and the very firmness of our resolutions, although produced in a human way, that is, after the manner of other ordinary resolutions by means of considerable reflection and consideration, with a labor—to use St. Teresa's attractive image (*Life*, ch. 11–18)—comparable to that of a man drawing a little water out of a well by the strength of his arms—all this, I say, does not depend so much on our own efforts, although they are normally indispensable, as on God who deposited there, with the abundance and depth needed, that mysterious spiritual water—the water of the wisdom of salvation—that we seek for our cleansing and refreshment, that it may fortify us and heal us of our soul's diseases. Like every precious gift, these virtues and precious qualities depend exclusively, as does also the very abundance and right proportion of this water of life, on the most high Giver of all good things and Father of lights.[37]

Thus it may happen that, in spite of all our efforts, at times we may not succeed in drawing even a single drop of that mysterious water, because the Owner of it has willed that that day it should not flow, or has willed to leave the well quite dry; while on the following day, perhaps at the first effort—and even without any effort—He will provide water in abundance.

Thus it is that although we may be able as a general rule to use this method of discursive prayer, that is, meditation, whenever we will and at the hour we will—for at all hours, with the ordinary grace that is, as it were, to our hand, we can reflect upon the mysteries of our faith and exercise ourselves more or less successfully in the acts and affections of faith, hope, and charity, which will be an excellent mental prayer[38] — yet we cannot have it as we will, but as it is given to us, with the fervor, sweetness, tenderness, and other feelings that the Lord deigns to bestow upon us together with a certain hidden inflowing of His gifts of fear, piety, knowledge, counsel, and so forth. This inflowing of the gifts already gives this prayer a certain "supernatural" or mystical aspect.

Thus we see that, although meditation (because in it all our faculties concur, working to the fullness of their capacity) is the form of prayer most characteristic of the ascetical life, for it is so even more than vocal prayer itself (which is wont at times to become mystical and wholly in the spirit, without our knowing how), yet with all this there can be noted in it, in the midst of our ordinary activity and all our own initiatives, a certain *passive* quality, a certain superhuman mode, which is proper to the gifts with which the Holy Spirit deigns to intervene to refresh our thirsty souls and give them, even here and now, some rest.[39]

At times He intervenes so quickly and in such a way that we have only to begin to prepare ourselves, or to begin the reading or the consideration, to feel ourselves already filled with an abundance of affections and without the inclination to exercise ourselves in anything else but in following the sweet movements and inspirations with which the divine Comforter then so lovingly forestalls us, so that almost without any labor, we may the sooner succeed in enjoying His sweet fruits. Then, obviously, we ought not to go on painfully seeking what, without labor, we have already found.[40]

If this occurs frequently so that we are seldom able to remain in meditation or even to attend to what we read; or if, forcing ourselves to do so, we become dryer instead of more fervent and end by not understanding what we read or by immediately forgetting it so completely that we cannot think of the point prepared or of anything, nor even reflect—then we ought to content ourselves with offering to God the affections that He Himself deigns to put into or suggest to our heart, and keep Him company in sweet and loving conversation and petition.[41] This is what constitutes the third stage of prayer, in which something "supernatural" or infused can already begin to be noted.

Chapter 4

Transitional Stages from "Ordinary" to "Supernatural" Prayer

The Third Stage of Prayer and the First Stage of Transition: Affective Prayer

In this manner of prayer, to use St. Teresa's simile, we shall be able to say that the water, although it is still drawn in a way that is apparently natural, almost when we will, now comes with very little effort and in much greater abundance, as when water is drawn using a pump or, again, not from a well where the water is deep down and in scant supply but from one where it is high and so full that it almost overflows.

Thus, although the manner still appears to be human (and that is why the saint considers this prayer as ordinary, "natural," or ascetical), yet the greater facility in conversing with God, and the abundance and diversity of the affections that we then come to feel—at the same time as a growing difficulty or real incapacity for discursive prayer—are proof of a certain mysterious supernatural influence that, for our greater good, puts us in that happy state of passiveness, bringing it about that much more fruit is gathered with less labour.[42]

In this case, since the purpose of meditation is thus achieved sooner and more successfully than if with much scrupulosity we continued to use the ordinary methods and procedure, it is obvious that the latter ought to be done away with, for they now cease to be useful and instead of being means become hindrances.[43] Thus we see how the stroller is done away with as soon as the child has learned to walk properly and it can then only serve as a hindrance; and how one should not lose time either, in thinking out and learning by heart the way to talk with some personage when one already knows how to do so easily and naturally and much better, as the heart, or the opportunity of the moment, dictates.[44]

But if the soul in all sincerity imagines that it ought always to follow these methods that were taught it when it began, then the Holy Spirit Himself, as the interior Master of all truth and most especially of this science of the ways of God, will mercifully undeceive it, if through bad advice, or obstinate presumption, it does not resist Him. Practically speaking, He will teach it by binding its faculties, the exercise of which would then be doing it harm, and by gently persuading it to surrender to what is most fitting for it, which will sometimes be conversations and affections that give great delight, at other times the breathing forth of unutterable groanings, in which it recognizes its own nothingness and longs for Him who is its all. Thus, sometimes He blinds the understanding so that it wanders about meditating to no purpose on what it will have to do, when He Himself brings it about that all it had to do is already done. He only wants it to be responsive and pay good attention to all He is suggesting to it in secret, and that it should no longer speak to Him in formulas but from the abundance of the heart.[45] At other times He Himself will check it and send it dryness so that it may not let itself go in

His presence with affections that are too tender and too much of the senses, when it should be listening in silence, or when He wants to imprint in it, in the midst of the suffering, dryness, and anguish—and it then finds itself incapable of everything—other purer, more sincere, and spiritual sentiments in full conformity with those of Jesus Christ, with whom, though it does not know how, it comes to be united and configured.[46]

It is in this way that the divine Spirit begins to incapacitate the soul so that it does not lose time in vain preparations, which are now useless or a hindrance—when they are not ridiculous—just as would be the case of anyone who wanted to go in search of a fountain when he was already there; for by his going he would not attain his object, which was to collect water, but would be frustrating it by moving further away; or, again, as in the case of someone who, having water at hand, would nevertheless give himself the trouble of drawing it out of a well with great efforts.

When this incapacity for certain things and this greater facility for others begin to be habitual, they may immediately be taken as the clear indication of a beginning of mystical life or of some sort of incipient mystical state, in the sense that what is produced is really a mystical act, even though it only occurs at fairly long intervals, for it is produced in a supra-human mode through some one or other of the gifts, just as, in a general way, the feeling of fervor that comes when the Spirit breathes upon us, kindling our love and moving us to pray and work as He pleases, may be called mystical.[47]

Since these affections and petitions are what is most essential, there is no true prayer if they are wanting; and one of them well persevered in, even though we do nothing more, will constitute a very good and profitable prayer.

Such is, in fact, what we have just been describing under the name of affective prayer and what others—the author of *Espinas del alma* (colloq. 7) and Fr. La Figuera (*Suma espiritual*), for instance—call acts of virtue, in which meditating is generally very difficult and at times even impossible. They therefore constitute in the strict sense of the term, in our opinion, the first clearly transitional stage.

When in this state, in which the understanding is left in darkness and the heart oppressed and dry, we experience such aridity and difficulty in everything that we can think of nothing and no good affection or resolution occurs, then we should sometimes try to elicit such affections by making new reflections, if this is possible, and if not by reading from time to time for a few moments. If what we read is forgotten or not understood, we shall have to content ourselves with reading over and over again some particular affective act that suits us best, which we can have already prepared, or else take the Our Father, making use chiefly of the second and third petition, asking the Lord God with all our soul to deign to come and reign in our hearts and take full possession of our will, so that His will may always be fulfilled in us. In order to be able thus to glorify His holy Name, we shall ask Him to nourish and renew us, purify and comfort us with the Bread of Life.[48]

But if this distracts us and we find ourselves out of tune with it and, generally speaking, unable to express or even feel anything at all in particular, yet at the same time have a certain mysterious desire to remain in silence before God, hoping, as it were, to see what He wants of us—this is a clear sign that it is really He Himself who is not only clouding our mind but making our heart dry, and even binding our will, so that we may not be able to move of our own initiative but only at the good pleasure of His Spirit, who now wants to make us captive and to come and take possession of us, in order then to be able to govern and direct us in all things Himself, as our sole Master.

"O, then, spiritual soul," warns St. John of the Cross (*Night*, II, ch. 16),

> when darkness comes over your desire and your affections are dry and forced and your faculties of no avail for any interior exercise whatsoever, do not be troubled on that account, but rather count it as blessing; for God is detaching you from yourself, taking your fortune and your resources out of your hands—since however useful they seemed to you, you would not work so well, so perfectly and securely as now, when God, taking your hand, guides you in the darkness as one does a blind man, where you do not know, nor would you ever, however well you walked, manage to travel along the road using your eyes and feet.

The Fourth Stage of Prayer and the Second Stage of Transition: That of Simplicity or of Simple, Loving Regard and Trusting Surrender

When the soul thus finds itself, as it were, dry and in darkness, it should remain in God's sweet presence, to which it finds itself so magically attracted, and not shatter its peace vainly trying to exercise the faculties that the Lord wishes it to keep in subjection. In this frustration it should be resigned and should rejoice to see how God is already beginning to reign in it, reducing it to this helplessness. It should offer itself, so far as lies in its power, with the keenest and purest desires, since it cannot do so with words, that God should do in it and with it whatever may please Him most. In its affliction let it hope against all hope and continually trust that the divine compassion and mercy will come to its help in due time. Let it set its eyes upon the Lord like a poor man in great necessity asking alms, or like a sick person in the presence of the sole physician from whom he hopes for life and health. Thus it will find peace, refreshment, and consolation, whereas if it does otherwise it will afflict itself in vain and each time will remain dryer and more incapable of spiritual things.[49]

The heart should be left in silence and alone to speak to God in its mute but completely sincere language that pleases the Lord so much. It should listen to what the God of its heart and its everlasting inheritance is speaking within it, the God in whom it has placed all its hope and in whom it finds all its good, its pleasure, and its sole rest (Ps. 72, 26, 28); for He is there, delighting the soul and uniting it intimately with Himself, speaking words of peace to it in secret, suggesting all truth and teaching it to remain in that tranquility of the senses and passions, on which He has imposed so much silence, in order that the soul may thus attend solely to what He wants of it, may enjoy His loving presence and learn to do in all things what is most in accordance with His divine pleasure.

This state, as will be seen, already has much in common with infused contemplation—in other words, with supernatural prayer—and is quite different from meditation or from ordinary simple mental prayer.[50] For then it ought rather to be said that grace is working in and through the soul, and not that the latter is working with grace. Now what is working in and directing us is not so much the proper initiative of our own mind as the divine Spirit who is in us as Lord and Master, working, moving, teaching, inspiring, and directing through His gifts of fear, piety, knowledge, fortitude, or counsel.

But for these gifts to develop and work freely, and that the two highest—intelligence and wisdom—may be able to manifest themselves clearly—the complete purgation of the night of the senses and even part of that of the spirit is necessary. The lesser lights must be extinguished if the greater ones are to shine or be perceived, just as we cannot see the stars of Heaven if the ordinary light is not withdrawn from our eyes.

That illumination, which, by means of the gifts of the Holy Spirit, purifies, vivifies, raises, and strengthens the powers of the soul so that it enables it to converse with God in a mode that is truly superhuman, celestial, and divine, will very soon begin to be noted in the infused prayer of recollection, and much more so in that of quiet and of union, and eventually, better beyond compare and as it were continuous, in that of transforming union.

Here, then, is the mystical repose to which we are all invited. There and there alone will it be given to us to find true rest for our souls.

As soon as we enter fully into the mystical state and show perfect docility, the Holy Spirit constitutes Himself so to speak our permanent director, governor, and master. By His unction He teaches, directs, enlightens, purifies, and gives strength and facility in everything, filling the heart with light and purity, with strength and life.[51]

But as on no account whatever ought we to resist the Holy Spirit when He calls us to enter into mystical repose, and the director who, upon some specious pretext or other, tried to put difficulties in the way would be greatly to blame, so no one should anticipate the divine action, leaving his present gift for another he has not yet received.

The certain signs that a soul ought not to weary itself in meditation, obstinately persisting in exercising its faculties, but should make room for the secret action of God, are these three: (1) the very difficulty it experiences in discursive prayer, without having given special cause for this by distractions; (2) the pain felt at the involuntary distractions it suffers and the distaste for vain conversations and frequent contact with creatures; and, most important, (3) the persistent attraction to remain quiet in some single feeling or thought that continues to engage the attention, or else in complete silence before God. In this, although there is some fear of self-deception, that we may be wasting time in idleness, there is no real remorse on this account, for we see that this is a good thing, that we cannot do more, and that if we try to move out of that spiritual idleness by making distinct acts, far from our fervor being increased, it is scattered to the winds, and we are filled with trouble.

Finally, then, it will be noted that the soul comes out of that apparent sleep with greater fruit, more recollected and with much more love of virtue and disposition for everything good than if it had exercised itself in lengthy considerations and made many fine resolutions. If, on the other hand, it had remained in culpable idleness through sloth, without wanting to exercise its faculties, by grieving at this fault and trying to conquer the sloth with specific acts—that is, by reflections, affections, or petitions, and so forth—it would gradually recover its fervor; or, if not, it would end by gaining no fruit and with real remorse at not having done what lay in its power. And if, being deceived, it gave a false appearance of the prayer of quiet or some other kind of infused prayer, instead of increasing in solid virtues—in humility, obedience, charity, peace, patience, kindness, discretion, fortitude, and constancy—it would, on the contrary, gradually increase in vanity, presumption, obstinacy, harshness, inconstancy, disorder, and cowardice for whatever does not flatter self-love.

Chapter 5

The Different Stages of Clearly "Supernatural" Prayer according to St. Teresa

In her *Life* (ch. 14), St. Teresa compares the first two stages of the prayer that is known as "supernatural" or infused to the watering of a garden—that of our own souls—carried out not with the poor result, difficulty, and labor of the man who draws the water from the well by the strength of his arms alone, as happens in meditation, but with the facility and abundance obtained when the garden is watered by means of a good bucket and windlass.

This is what happens, she says, in the two ways of prayer known as infused recollection and quiet. For although these are given to us by God with scarcely any labor on our part, and even at times when we are least thinking of them or disposing ourselves toward them, yet a certain carefulness in recollection, and, above all, in not exposing ourselves to losing that grace too soon and in using it in the best possible way, is still generally necessary. So that, although it is clearly the same Holy Spirit who produces the watering, yet, in order not to break the continuity of the whole, He generally leaves a large part to our industry and initiative.

The *third stage*, that of simple union, the saint compares to irrigation with water that now needs no kind of effort or industry to draw it[52] but comes to us freely as if from the bed of the river or a spring, and the human labor of the gardener is reduced merely to distributing and directing it where it is most wanted.

In full or ecstatic union, which constitutes, so to speak, the fourth stage, the saint points out that this very carefulness is now superfluous and even turns out to be impossible, for it is God who does everything, as when He sends us abundant rain from Heaven. It is sufficient for the soul to let itself be thoroughly saturated, like a sponge, by that living water from Heaven, which bathes, satiates, refreshes, and purifies it, flooding it within and without and leaving it full of vigor, joy, and life.

But in her second relation to Fr. Rodrigo, Teresa, the holy doctor of mystical life, discovers or seems to indicate another kind of supernatural prayer, namely, that which could not in any way be acquired by our industry and diligence alone—and one earlier than recollection. It consists in a certain presence of God that comes to be almost continual so that it is sufficient to recollect oneself a little to obtain it.

It would not be difficult to identify this prelude to contemplation with the prayer described above, called by others that of simplicity, of spiritual idleness, or of a simple loving attention to God. This, if it is prolonged throughout the day and becomes, as it were, habitual, becomes a presence that gives delight, while later, in the dryness and desolation of the night of the senses, it is changed into a sorrowful presence or vision in which the soul is wonderfully purified.

Here the mystical act—which at the beginning was so infrequent and then was so much interrupted by those acts that are proper to the ascetical state—each time becomes more frequent, and even gradually habitual, although it, too, is always being more or less interrupted by numerous acts that are not mystical, that is, acts performed, as they were previously, in a human mode and on our own initiative, even if each time with greater perfection and deeper recollection.

Thus we shall see how—from the prayer of simple loving regard—the indications of mystical life already begun in affective prayer are more deeply accentuated each time, and how in this way one passes almost imperceptibly or by gradual transition, from a state purely and simply ascetical, like that of laborious considerations or meditation, to one so clearly mystical as that of union and above all of abiding union, where all one's own initiative ceases, as does all effort that is not simply cooperation with the gentle movements of grace. Meanwhile, so long as the ascetical state is predominant, it is broken into by mystical acts and then by mystical states of brief duration. These will eventually be predominant, and it will then be the short ascetical acts that break in, though only from time to time. These are now routine acts, but always full of fervor and life. In her important work, the *Interior Castle*, in which the great doctor of mysticism sets forth her thought, now definitive and mature, more clearly, we can see how she leads souls in order, without any interval, through her seven famous halls or mansions, which represent so many stages in prayer and the corresponding stages of perfection or progress in the spiritual life—from the first steps, or as soon as the abyss of sin is left behind, until the fullest union and transformation attainable in this life are reached.

She devotes the first three mansions to souls who are still quite imperfect and cannot yet enjoy intimate converse with God. The first is for newly converted sinners who not only need much active purgation and many penances to cleanse their souls thoroughly but also great means of preservation if they are not to fall again. For this reason, it is very good for them to ponder over the last things and to be well grounded in self-knowledge. But this does not mean that they should not at the same time prepare themselves for entering the other mansions in turn.[53]

The second[54] is for those who can already refrain from grave sins without difficulty but still take little heed about falling into light ones. It is good for such persons to meditate on the Passion of our Savior and on the incredible evils that tepidity causes, that they may be encouraged to serve God with full fervor and fidelity and be responsive to the divine inspirations.

Into the third mansion enter those who are already "blessed" in another way, those who truly fear God and who, desiring truly to please and serve Him, begin to live a recollected life and to devote themselves to all kinds of works of piety. Thus, with the fear of God, which is the beginning of mystical wisdom, and with that piety that "is profitable to all things, having promise of the life that now is, and of that which is to come" (1 Tim. 4:8), they come to deserve that God should treat them as faithful sons and thus bring them into most intimate communion with Himself.

Thus, there is no complete separation or lack of communication between one mansion and another, and thus, the saint says, there is no reason why those who are faithful to what is asked of them in any particular mansion should not be allowed to pass on in due course to the second and so on until they reach the final one.

The fourth mansion is for proficients, that is, souls of experience who, entering fully into the spiritual life, begin to taste the sweetness of infused contemplation through the prayer of recollection and of quiet.

The fifth belongs to the prayer of union.

In the sixth, ecstatic union, the mystical espousals and the great favors—together with the corresponding sufferings and purifications that precede and follow them—are described; as are also, on the one hand, raptures, flights of the spirit, and the wounds of love, and on the other, the unbearable absence, dereliction, and annihilation of the terrible night of the spirit.

The seventh is reserved for the spiritual marriage, in which abiding union is obtained with the true transformation of the soul into God and, accordingly, the full perfection in the real sense of the term, to which "we are all called."

In *The Way of Perfection*, the saint treats not only of vocal and discursive prayer but also of that of quiet and of infused recollection. Her full explanation of the simple petitions of the *Pater Noster* is in no sense a deviation from this, without which true and solid perfection cannot be conceived. To that she adds some explanations about union and rapture, as of things not very rare or "extraordinary" in souls that are truly fervent and faithful.

In her *Life*, following on from the prayer of recollection and quiet, she describes, together with that of union, ecstasies, raptures, and flights of the spirit.

In the relation to Fr. Rodrigo Alvarez already mentioned, she speaks of recollection and quiet, then of the sleep of the faculties, of union—which can be *simple*, of the will alone, or *absolute*, of all the faculties of the soul—of rapture or suspension (ecstasy), of transport (*rapto*) and the flight of the spirit, the impulses and wounds of love.

Chapter 6

Comparison of St. Teresa's Classification
with Those of Other Writers

This classification of St. Teresa's, particularly as it figures in its
full development in the *Interior Castle*, clarifies most vividly what
appeared to be a chaos, and has thus come to serve as a norm
and basis for all later writers who have tried to penetrate the inmost secrets of supernatural psychology and to set down the true
progress of the mystical life, which before seemed an indecipher-
able enigma. For the stages that were formerly established corre-
sponded only to certain special phenomena, or at the most to
certain virtues, but not to the spiritual life as a whole. Thus, St.
Teresa's clear and masterly classification has finally come to be
commonly admitted in its essence, even if certain writers eliminate
or add something, and others, with more skill, try to simplify it,
reducing it to the fundamental stages.[55] Thus Philip of the Most
Holy Trinity (*Summa theologiae mysticae*, pat. 3, tr. 3, d. 3, a. 5)
enumerates six principal stages, namely: recollection, quiet, ordinary union, impulses or flights, rapture, and spiritual marriage.

St. Francis de Sales (*Traité de l'amour de Dieu*, bk. 6, ch. 7–15;
bk. 7, ch. 1–3) is satisfied with only three of the most notable
stages pertaining to conforming union. He ignores transforming
union altogether, doubtless because there are so few who attain to

it. These stages are recollection, quiet, and union, although in the latter he distinguishes simple union from ecstatic, which is the supreme stage, and in the prayer of quiet he distinguishes various phases such as, firstly, simple repose, silence, and inebriation, and then liquefaction, the wounds of love, and the languor of love.

St. Alphonsus Liguori (*Praxis*, n. 132–137) recognizes five stages beyond spiritual idleness, namely: recollection, quiet, simple union, the espousals, and the spiritual marriage. This classification seems to us the most suitable and practical, provided one distinguishes clearly between these last two stages, which belong to transforming union, and the previous ones, which merely pertain to conforming union; for it is not to no purpose that the long and terrible night of the spirit is set between these two kinds of union.

Scaramelli, however, preferring to go into greater detail, enumerates and tries to distinguish as many as eleven stages (*Direc. mistic.*, tr. 3, ch. 1–23), namely: recollection, spiritual silence, quiet, inebriation of love, spiritual sleep, longings and thirst of love, divine touches, simple union, ecstasy, rapture, and solid, abiding, and perfect union, that is, spiritual marriage.

Somewhat similar, and perhaps based on this, is the following classification that we saw in a certain manuscript by someone who claimed to write what they had actually experienced. Thus, it goes no further than the wounds of love and, moreover, gives three stages prior to recollection. We set it down, with a few explanations, for the interest it may perhaps offer:

- First stage: Purification and newness of life.
- Second stage: Enlightenment (inspirations and so forth).
- Third stage: The writing on the heart—there God engraves His law, which is the grace of the New Testament,

so that the soul may discover, meditate, and correspond to it. Trying thus to set God Himself as its seal, the soul will come to feel His loving presence.

- Fourth stage: Recollection—from now onwards it is the Holy Spirit who directs; He gives light by which to recognize the ugliness of our faults and at the same time consolation, strength, and a spirit of moderation in all things.
- Fifth stage: Spiritual silence—suspension in God's presence without being lost in Him. A great vacuum of everything is felt, and this is the sign that God wants to fill us.
- Sixth stage: Quiet—in which the soul feels much peace, rest, and interior sweetness, and from which it comes forth with great affections of love and desires to praise God and to establish itself in humility and the other virtues.
- Seventh stage: Inebriation of love.
- Eighth stage: Spiritual sleep.
- Ninth stage: Longings and restlessness of love.
- Tenth stage: Touches of God on the soul that kindle its love, give light to the understanding, and communicate virtues.
- Eleventh stage: Fires and languor of love.
- Twelfth stage: Union—in which the use of the senses is not lost—imaginary visions—ecstasy.
- Thirteenth stage: Rapture and impulses of love.
- Fourteenth stage: Espousals—exchange of hearts—intimate union.
- Fifteenth stage: Wounds, with great longing and thirst of love.

Before St. Teresa, as we have said, only a very few variations of phenomena that may figure in one particular stage of prayer, or that at most indicate the progress of some particular virtue, were known.

Thus, Richard of St. Victor (*De quatuor gradibus viol. caritatis*) says: "When I examine the works of vehement charity, I find ... some souls wounded, others bound, others languishing, others fainting.... Now in the first stage, God enters into the mind which turns in upon itself; in the second it rises above itself and is raised to God; in the third, when the mind is raised to God, it passes wholly into him; in the fourth, on account of God the mind goes out of itself...."

The short work entitled *De septem gradibus contemplationis* says:

> Seven stages ... I conclude are to be deduced.... The first, then, let us call fire, the second unction, the third ecstasy, the fourth speculation, the fifth savour, the sixth quiet, the seventh glory. For in the first the soul is set on fire, once set on fire it is anointed, anointed is rapt, being rapt it speculates and contemplates, contemplating it tastes the joy of experience, so tasting it attains repose. These things can be acquired in our earthly pilgrimage, not, indeed, suddenly, but gradually. A man, however, experiences these things more quickly, if he exercises himself more frequently in spiritual things. The seventh stage is bestowed in our heavenly home and more abundantly on those who have practiced the earlier stages.

St. Lawrence Justinian, again, indicates six genuine stages of contemplation or prayer, by perseverance in which its summit is reached. It is particularly to be noted that in the first four, considerations or discursive reasoning still intervene to a greater or lesser degree. "Let those," he says (*Lignum vitae*, tr. 13, *de Orat.* ch. 10), who desire to cleave to God and become one spirit with him, and who have chosen to become one with him through the power and practice of prayer, give no rest to their spirit and never grow weary of the purpose they have conceived until they obtain their heart's desire. Lest, however, such souls should be deceived through ignorance,... I have thought it worthwhile to set down the different stages of prayer, moving gradually through which, they will in very truth arrive at the summit of contemplation, which is the end of prayer.... For there are six stages of contemplation, by passing through which the soul is led to the haven of true quiet. The first stage consists in the imagination alone ... when we observe in a spirit of wonder the corporeal things we know by our senses, and consider how great, how diverse, how beautiful and pleasing they are.... The second stage takes place in the imagination but makes use of the reason, for it probes into the order, disposition, cause, manner and usefulness of any given thing. In this consideration a certain spiritual light from the divine goodness illuminates him who contemplates.... The third stage is when a man is lifted up through speculation upon visible things and is led to a consideration of invisible things which holds him spellbound. The mind of him who contemplates is enlightened by a certain wonder and filled with sweetness; and, permeated with this sweet joy, it breaks forth in praise of God. Thus the understanding of the thinker becomes the contemplation of the lover, leading him to certain spiritual consolations which both fill the heart with delight and inflame it with the desire of heavenly joys. The fourth stage is when, wholly separated from the works of the imagination, the mind focuses its attention solely on things unknown to the imagination, but which the mind gathers by discursive reasoning or understands rationally.... Then souls experience how great is the abundance of the sweetness of God, hidden from those who are governed by fear. For those who come within this category contemplate the glory of the heavenly kingdom, the abundance of its delights, the magnificence of the King.... Filled with such considerations, and filled to their depths with the fire of charity ... by which they are made worthy, their affections enkindled by love, they say in spirit (Ps. 83): "How lovely are thy tabernacles ..." The fifth stage is when we are able to see into the depths of those things which we know by divine revelation but which we are utterly unable to search out by our reason.... For to those living in the flesh and in this life, growing in this inestimable virtue, the eternal brightness of God can be seen in the intensity of contemplation and, enlightened by the sentiment of love can be attained by them.... The sixth stage of contemplation is when the soul, through that divine irradiation of light ... transcends all human reasoning and effort. Emanating hence, the mighty flow of the stream makes glad (Ps. 45) the mind of him who contemplates. In this sweet experience in which God's power and might and glory lead man to love him with his whole heart, the lover (man) is carried away to the Beloved, though even now, in the depths of his being by faith and hope, he experiences the bliss of the Beloved ... so that he cannot call himself back until he is made one spirit with him. When this has been perfected in him, then only the veil of the flesh separates him from ... that highest bliss of heaven. Here is the end, here the reward, here the rest from one's labours, consolation for sorrow and suffering, perfection itself, and the true wisdom of man seeking, and occupying himself with God and clinging to him through the desire of prayer and through the leisure of contemplation.

Gerson (*Myst. theol. spec.*, p. 7, consid. 35), basing himself on the properties of love, reduces the stages of contemplation to three: ecstasy, union, and quiet, which are thus here mentioned in inverse order: "Love," he says, "seizes with rapture, unites, satisfies. First, indeed, love carries the soul off to the Beloved, and thence arises ecstasy. Secondly, love joins the soul with its Beloved and makes them as it were one. Thirdly, it is sufficient to itself and seeks nothing else except love."

The mystics later than St. Teresa who did not take their inspiration from her, continue to suggest stages that are unacceptable. Thus, although he does come close to the saint in some ways, Álvarez de Paz (*De gradibus contemp*, I, 4, p. 2, Introd.) takes into consideration as many as fifteen stages, basing himself on fifteen classifications he found in various authors. He says: "I find fifteen names assigned to contemplation in ascetical writers, and these seem to me to designate so many *stages* of contemplation. Now these are: 1. Contemplation of the truth, 2. Withdrawal of the powers of the soul to inward things, 3. Silence, 4. Quiet, 5. Union, 6. Hearing God speak to one, 7. Spiritual sleep, 8. Ecstasy, 9. Rapture, 10. Physical visions, 11. Visions of the imagination, 12. Spiritual investigation, 13. Divine blindness, 14. Manifestation of God, 15. Intuitive vision of God."

Godinez bases himself on the general division of contemplation into cherubic and seraphic, which no one any longer admits today, for it only indicates the predominance that the gifts of understanding and wisdom may have, respectively, at one particular stage. Thus, the first has to be subdivided almost solely with regard to the divine mysteries or attributes to which it relates, there being included in it, however, the prayer of silence and of quiet. In seraphic contemplation, he distinguishes ten stages, namely: fiery, flaming, conformative, resigned contemplation, abnegation or self-stripping, affective solitude, soliloquies of the soul, spiritual cloud, liberty of spirit, obscure contemplation and wounding love (*Práctica de la teología mística*, I, 5 and 6).

Chapter 7

Fundamental Stages

Leaving aside such classifications, so lacking in solid foundation and order, and confining ourselves to the simplification given in St. Teresa's masterly descriptions, we shall be able to reduce the different stages that are generally recognized today in contemplation to these five fundamental ones: recollection, quiet, union, espousals, and mystical marriage. The first three, as we have said in *Evolución mística* (p. 491), belong to conforming union, and the other two (among which obscure contemplation might well be inserted) to transforming union.

We believe that the first time, all souls go through these five or six principal stages in strict order, not passing on to any one of them without having stayed a longer or a shorter time in the one next below, and, usually, not without experiencing a fresh crisis in which one's faithfulness is tested and this ascent to a higher stage earned. But once the soul is established in a certain stage, it can receive almost indifferently either the prayer proper to that stage or that belonging to any of the lower stages, as is best fitting for it, without excluding even meditation or discursive prayer. To the latter it ought to have recourse in order not to be idle—like the Quietists—but journey as it can on foot, or using oars, whenever its mystic wings fold up or the divine inspiration ceases (cf. St. Teresa, *Life*, ch. 18).

However, it seems that certain souls arrive gradually at the stage of union by an imperceptible transition, or else amid such continual trials and darkness that, since the moments of light pass swiftly, they do not succeed in recognizing themselves in any of the preceding stages, and it may thus perhaps appear to them that their only state is that of perpetual night, only interrupted or cut through by brief flashes of light and consolation that they cannot succeed in explaining. But when they arrive at union and have been established in it for some time, while the night of the senses gradually disappears to give place to that of the spirit, as they return from time to time to the previous stages or come across a description of them in some book, they begin to realize that this is not new to them, and that, even without being aware of it, they had already really had that manner of prayer several times.

Thus, as they can very well recognize, recollection preceded the prayer of quiet. Many mystics, however—and at times St. Teresa herself—associate the former with the latter or perhaps describe it afterwards, doubtless through not being properly aware of it or through considering it only as a sudden flash in the midst of the dark night of the senses, or again as a simple ray of clearer light amid the habitual presence of God that they were already enjoying. But when the rest and repose of the soul in the prayer of quiet are clearly perceived and souls see how their will remains captive in it, they realize they had been preparing themselves for this by acts of infused recollection that came upon them more or less unexpectedly.

Since the other kinds of prayer that the mystics mention—such as that of silence, spiritual sleep, inebriation, jubilation, and so forth—as Fr. Poulain points out (*Grâces d'oraison*, ch. 3, n. 8), are only, as it were, certain modes of being of these five principal kinds—or else phenomena that usually accompany them or effects that may follow at times—we shall now endeavor to indicate, for the sake of greater clearness, in what the essence of those stages that we consider as the principal ones consists, and what are the phenomena that usually accompany them. We shall then complete this brief account with a few examples, or rather with descriptions given by souls of much experience, from which the reader will be able to form a more complete idea of these wonderful workings of grace.

.

Chapter 8

The Principal Stages of Conforming Union and the Phenomena That Usually Accompany Them

The first stage of mystical union—or of clear contemplation (and the fifth of prayer)—is constituted by infused recollection. This is the simple union of the understanding with God, who with His infinite beauty and splendor attracts and delights the mind from without, that is, objectively, while within, by His omnipotent power, He possesses and holds it captive and strengthens it, enriching it with the precious gifts of knowledge, counsel, and understanding, by means of which He causes it to penetrate like a flash into that higher world resplendent with His ineffable wisdom.

In this way, uniting it each time more intimately with Himself, although it is only for brief moments, He leaves it purified and enlightened so that it may "never sleep in death" (Ps. 12:4) but now lives renewed and, as it were, deified with the splendors of God's effulgence.

This infused recollection is generally preceded, as we have said, or sometimes followed by, a lively sense of the presence of God, likewise infused, by which the soul comes to feel a certain all-pervading impression of the divine immensity, at times in joy, as when it is gently drawn by certain attributes or by the mysteries of the faith;[56] at other times in sadness and sorrow, as when it seems to it that it is in darkness and far away from God and that all things are asking it: Where is thy God?[57] This presence or that of the supernatural light that is inviting us to contemplation is frequently shown in the continued persistence with which a single holy thought haunts the soul, or in the deep impression that some phrase or spiritual maxim comes to produce in it. For many days it will have the heart fixed on this thought, finding in it all the light and strength it needs.[58] This and the painful presence are noted particularly in the night of the senses.

With recollection there are associated at times as quasi-phenomena, or as simple effects, a delightful wonder of admiration that uplifts the soul and fills it with joy and gladness, as it discovers in God so many marvels of love, goodness, and beauty; at other times a certain suspension[59] or a deep spiritual silence in which it remains astonished, absorbed, humiliated, and, as it were, annihilated before so much majesty—whence come the sentiments and effects of solid humility and deep respect for divine things that this prayer produces.[60]

In this way, in a moment and without any labor, the soul acquires light so great that it would not have been able to obtain it with whole years of study and meditation—whence we see how valuable, desirable, and precious this heavenly wisdom is proved, even from its initial manifestations.

With this light the will itself is supernaturally stirred, attracted, inflamed, and purified and thus also comes to remain captive.

The second stage of contemplation and the sixth of prayer is that of quiet. This is the union of the will with God who, as highest Good, attracts it forcefully so that in Him alone it may find its rest. Infinite power, goodness, gentleness, and sweetness, with God's gifts of fear, piety, fortitude, and wisdom, overwhelm it and at the same time take it captive, set it ablaze, fill it with caresses, and, drawing it near, so to speak, to the "breasts of his consolation" (Isa. 66:11–13), strengthen and satisfy it, inebriating it with unspeakable delights.[61] There the soul finds for a time every now and then—times that seem to it short however long they last—its full rest, its refreshment and strength, its peace and happiness.[62] And it frequently enjoys this delight, though the fact is scarcely realized by the sensitive faculties, or even by reason itself. Thus at one time the sensitive faculties may, as it were, wander and try to disturb the will, and at another they may appear frightened, without knowing why. But on other occasions the spiritual joy overflows on to the faculties themselves and so does all that peace, holiness, and sweetness, by which they too are purified and prepared for remaining, in due time, captive and united with God.

The effects of this mystical rest are a great increase of spiritual health, of peace and joy and facility for everything good. The soul comes out of it greatly improved in every kind of virtue and ready to labor for God.[63]

With the prayer of quiet is associated the inebriation of love, which in the beginning is a thing more or less of the senses, and it is necessary to moderate its manifestations somewhat. They generally take the form of cries, groans, songs of praise, leaps of joy, and other great follies of love. Afterwards all this becomes more and more spiritual, and the resultant "follies" are full of prudence and Christian wisdom that those who are not spiritual are incapable of understanding, and in which we begin to enjoy the true and glorious liberty of the sons of God.[64] At other times this inebriation, instead of expressing itself in utterances and canticles and other outward forms, does so in the mystical spiritual sleep, in which the soul is like the child sleeping on its mother's breast, enjoying the good it possesses, while the heart continues to watch and burn with love (Song of Sol. 5:2). To this are added certain divine caresses or touches of love with which God continues to attract the soul increasingly and to prepare it for true union.[65]

The third stage of contemplation (the seventh of prayer) is that of union. What is simply called union is that manner of prayer in which all our faculties remain more or less united with God, and where He indeed takes them captive and takes full and complete possession of them in order to handle them at His pleasure without their resisting Him in anything. Thus, the soul comes to know that it is now no longer itself that works, but God in and through it. For all its activity comes to be so much in harmony with the divine that it appears, as it were, fused and identified with it, without its being possible for it any longer to doubt of this tremendous intimacy.[66] On this account this stage is called par excellence that of union, because it is the union of all our faculties together and not of some of them alone—of the intelligence or of the will, or of these two only—as happened in the previous stages.

But although all the faculties of the soul are thus more or less already united with God, and, as it were, overshadowed and full of awe in the presence of such majesty, in simple union, in which the captivity of love is not so great, the latter is chiefly concentrated in the will, leaving the sensitive powers, although in some measure captive, not so bound that they cannot perceive their respective objects and even attend to them if this is conducive to the greater service of God. At times the understanding itself is in this case, a person thus being able to be occupied in external holy works, whilst his soul or rather his "spirit," or the highest point of his soul—rejoices in that intimate union of the will. In this way the contemplative life is joined with the active, a thing that was scarcely possible in simple quiet.

But when the divine attraction is very intense, as happens in what is called full, or ecstatic, union, the sense faculties themselves fail, not being able to bear so great an excess of light and fire. The use of the senses is then lost, and the body remains, as it were, dead, in order not to hinder the soul from enjoying the ineffable delights with which it finds itself flooded, and the inestimable lights that are communicated to it.

In this stage, the sweet touches and divine caresses are changed into intimate embraces so penetrating that the soul melts and remains, as it were, dissolved in God's love alone. At other times they are blows, intense and penetrating, like darts of fire that wound to the quick and sweetly consume and set ablaze, making the soul sick and faint and causing it to burn and languish with love; at times also they make it burn with pain and grief at seeing God so offended and, so to speak, obliged to send forth darts of indignation and anger.

Hence the unconsciousness and raptures or ecstasies—delightful or painful—in which the soul remains, so to speak, outside itself, lost and dispersed in the sea of infinite Goodness, or dissolved in that of Sanctity and Justice. Hence also the mysterious wounds of love—and of pain—that heal as they wound, and as they slay appear to fill one with life and vigor.[67]

To this must be added the great impulses of love, raptures and flights of the spirit, in which new worlds of wonders are shown to the soul. Such phenomena are sometimes wont to be accompanied by levitation or bilocation, the body thus sharing in the movement of the spirit.[68] In this way also the wounds of love, although directly produced in the heart or in the soul itself, may in their turn be expressed outwardly in stigmatization, that is, in the imprinting of the sacred wounds.[69]

Thus, the effects of this prayer frequently come to be truly marvelous, and clearly they are always better beyond compare than even those of the prayer of quiet; for they leave the soul, so to speak, renewed and different, already sharing in a certain way in the divine attributes and giving forth in all it does the good odor of Christ (2 Cor. 2:15).

Into each one of the three stages of union mentioned, it is absolutely necessary to enter through the narrowness, darkness, crushing, and privations of the dread night of the senses. "When the Lord allows this to extend its black shadows, then the wild beasts, that is, temptations and tribulations, come forth from the woods and penetrate everywhere." But, tested by them as in a crucible, then "at dawn, man will go forth to his labour"—which is principally the contemplation of the divine marvels—and to his ordinary work, with the faithful practice of the virtues, until the evening (Ps. 103:20, 23), in which, with the new darkness, will come new trials that prepare the soul for further progress in the way of perfection and sanctity.

This first night is intended before all else to reduce the sense faculties to reason and to prepare reason itself in order that in its turn it may quietly come and submit in all things to the Holy Spirit, who henceforward will take charge of it and direct it with another prudence, unknown to worldly and carnal men. But for this it is necessary to correct and repair thoroughly, by means of the different kinds of crosses or passive purgations, the defects and imperfections that could not be sufficiently corrected by the active purgations.

This mystical night consists, then, of a total withdrawal of light, support, and sensible consolations, through which the soul comes to remain in darkness, afraid, arid, dry, and, so to speak, in the air, without feeling the least pleasure, protection, or support in anything, nor any attraction for anything.[70] Yet an imperceptible light and wholly spiritual interior force make it more faithful and diligent than ever, and it thus walks along the secret path that has been traced out for it "in darkness and secure—without other light or guide—except that which was burning in the heart." This light guides the soul and causes it constantly to remember God and to rejoice in Him spiritually, without wishing to find consolation in anything else, desiring Him ardently and with the whole heart and always longing to see and enjoy Him.[71]

But the more the soul desires God and seeks Him, the more difficult and even impossible it seems to it to be able to find Him, as it sees that everything comes to conspire against it and set itself against it: the passions to humiliate it, enemies and false friends to try it, and its very directors to disconcert instead of encouraging it, together with sicknesses and misfortunes that test it in a crucible like Job and Tobias.[72] But he who remains faithful in all these trials and perseveres to the end will find all he desires and incomparably more.

To sum up, this night, as Fr. Poulain says, "is a tendency of the soul to orientate itself, in the midst of the darkness and dryness, solely towards God alone, through desire and memory."

But if, through misfortune, it should lose that happy orientation, or, weary of waiting or ill advised, should seek comfort from creatures, it will be incapacitated for finding mystical repose and, through cowardice, will not come to taste the sweetness of the hidden manna that is thus reserved for those who truly fear God and conquer the world and themselves

(Ps. 30:20; Rev. 2:17). Such souls will exclaim with St. John of the Cross (*Spiritual Canticle*, 3):

Seeking my loves
I shall go through mountains and banks:
I shall not pluck the flowers,
Nor shall I fear the wild beasts,
And I shall pass through strong places and cross frontiers.[73]

It is here, then, that the segregation of those who, through weakness, turn their glance backward and become inept for entering into the kingdom of heaven that is within them (for they have not the great violence that is necessary) chiefly occurs. Thus, contenting themselves, as they say, with being "good ascetics," following a path that they call common and ordinary and shunning "singularities" and rough and little-frequented tracks, they lead a tepid life, full of innumerable imperfections and venial sins of which they take little account. By so doing, not only are they preparing a terrible Purgatory for themselves, but—because they do not wish to enter upon the "narrow path" of Christ and leave the broad way so well trodden by worldlings—they place their very salvation in grave danger.[74]

Fr. Godinez affirms that 99 percent of those who begin to enter upon the night of the senses do not succeed in passing beyond it, chiefly through the fault of bad directors who, instead of encouraging them to overcome their cowardice and stimulating them to go on and persevere, on the contrary, with the vain fears that they put into them, cause them to go backward and lose their way.[75] And of the very few who do pass beyond, almost another 99 percent come to a standstill in each one of the numerous crises, through the same causes.

Nevertheless, in spite of this, the courageous and valiant always triumph.

Very much the same as this is affirmed by St. Teresa (*Life*, ch. 15), who saw many souls, relatively, who attained to the prayer of quiet and very few who, always remaining firm, merited to pass beyond and did not turn back.

"Let us fear therefore lest the promise being left of entering into his rest, any of you should be thought to be wanting" (Heb. 4:1).

Chapter 9

Transforming Union: Its Stages and Principal Phenomena

We have just seen in what conforming union consists and what are the stages and phenomena it shows. In this marvelous union, God progressively takes possession of our faculties, each time more fully and more perfectly, uniting them intimately to Himself as they become more purified, beginning, in recollection, with the intellect, the faculty that is least impure and vitiated, continuing with the will in the prayer of quiet, and then, in full union, taking possession even of the sensitive powers and faculties. These He also floods with His sweetness, in order thus to make Himself master of all our operations. He Himself, working in us, communicates to all our actions—with participation in His infinite power—an inestimable virtue and value. But although this union is so wonderful and so desirable, presupposing such a divine manner of operation, and is a true deification of all our powers, yet it may perhaps be considered more moral than vital and for that reason is simply known as conforming union. God, who wants to carry His marvelous love to incredible extremes (John 13:1), is not content with that but, after giving the hidden manna and the new name (Rev. 2:17) to these valiant souls who overcome, if they respond to His generosity will cause them to be configured to His suffering image and will perfect their rebirth to the full, clothing them once more with the garment of innocence and even confirming them in grace.[76] He will then make them firm pillars of His holy temple (Rev. 3:12) and finally will set them on His very throne so that even in this life they begin to reign with Him.[77]

Thus God wants to pursue His conquests of love in us much more extensively. He wants, if we are faithful to Him, to take possession not only of all our faculties but also of our very life and soul and of our whole being, to identify it in a certain manner with His own, setting it ablaze with love, absorbing it, renewing it, and, as it were, transforming it into Himself, thus deifying it so completely that it already seems to be in every way one single thing with God, in imitation of the sublime manner in which the Divine Persons are one—"that they may be one, as we also are one: I in them, and thou in me; that they may be made perfect in one" (John 17:22-23).

This is already not only union but a certain true unity and, as it were, identity of life, so that already God not only works but lives in us, and "our new life is now Christ," for it comes wholly from His very Spirit, as from our true Lord and life-giver, "soul of our life and life of our soul."[78]

This, then, is what this supremely marvelous and deifying transforming union, to which we are all called, consists of: *all* are called, for our Lord Jesus Christ asked that it should be so when He said (John 17:21): "That they all may be one, as thou, Father, in me, and I in thee; that they also may be one in us."

But this requires, if we are to receive that same glory that Jesus receives from the Father and promises to give us (John 17:22), a prolonged and terrible series of purifications and rebirths that very few are firmly resolved to undergo; for such things are painful in the extreme (though at the same time they give joy) and must penetrate to the very marrow of the bones, down to the very depths of the soul, reaching even to the division of soul from spirit (Heb. 4:12) and reproducing the mysteries of the sacred Passion.

This incomparable union consists of two principal stages, sufficiently clear and distinct in themselves—in spite of the fact that there is a certain imperceptible transition from one to the other[79]—namely, the mystical espousals and the spiritual marriage, apart from other stages, very important but obscure and difficult to define, which succeed one another throughout the deep darkness of the night of the spirit, in which all this rebirth is effected and among which figures the obscure contemplation in which the soul is allowed to enter the sea of light inaccessible where God dwells. Then purified through and through and perfected in the highest degree with the three theological virtues, it will become directly united with the Godhead itself and with each one of the three adorable Persons, becoming transformed into them, as it shares, as far as is possible, in the divine attributes.

In the espousals, between ecstasies and raptures, are experienced the meetings of the Word made flesh with the soul whom He comes to take as His bride, after having configured her to Himself and clothed her with His virtues, feelings, and thoughts.[80] This is where this highest union begins, is established and confirmed with mutual solemn promises of love and fidelity, and with a total exchange of interests, at times symbolized or confirmed by that of hearts, just as the promises are often guaranteed by the mystic ring, which vanishes from the soul's view when the latter becomes less fervent or falls into some neglect.[81]

In the immediate preparation for these divine espousals, the most Blessed Virgin generally intervenes, imprinting in the soul, as it were, her own virtues and perfections and clothing it with the mysterious white mantle of her purity and innocence, so that thus, following in her train, it may be able worthily to appear before the King of Glory (Ps. 44:15).[82]

In the spiritual marriage, this union is completed and consummated in perfect unity of life and sentiments and becomes abiding and permanent. Thus, by a most singular grace, the soul remains irrevocably united and made one thing with the Word made flesh, presenting His divine image in so lifelike a manner that it will seem to be Jesus Christ, the Son of the living God Himself, still living upon earth and perpetuating His mission of redemption.

Hence the great marvels that, although in a mysterious way that the world is wont not to notice, are continually being wrought for the good of the Church and of souls.

Outstanding Phenomena. Apart from the genuine intermediate stages that—like the obscure contemplation already mentioned—might perhaps be instanced as occurring between the espousals and the spiritual marriage, figure, either as causes or as effects, very many highly interesting phenomena that serve to throw into relief the sublimity of these states. Among them we should mention the complete raptures and flights of the spirit, which are increasingly marked after the espousals, in which the soul is wholly raised above itself and led to contemplate the glory and riches of the Bridegroom, by whom in the midst of its sufferings it will be greatly consoled and filled with delight. Thus also it will be able to take charge of His sacred interests and watch over them, being zealous for the honor of its Beloved. It is thus that it comes to discover ineffable marvels unknown to the rest of mortals—*altiora mysteria, quae sunt perfectorum* (S. theol., 2-2, q. 171, prol.)—and which it is not possible to relate, for they are the intimate secrets of Bridegroom and bride.

To this should be added the mysterious divine darts with which God calls and awakens the bride, enkindling in her the most ardent desires and penetrating the heart, causing those painful but delightful wounds of love that kindle and test faith and hope to the utmost possible extent, perfecting charity and giving life as they slay.

In addition, there are the unbearable, yet refreshing and dei-fying flames of the fire of the Holy Spirit, whose living flames of divine love penetrate to the very marrow. They cauterize and burn away all the stains and imperfections and every trace of the old man, leaving the body, so to speak, dead—indeed, buried and destroyed. It then rises again, made spiritual and thus capa-ble, like the glorious body, of flight wherever the impulse of the spirit may bear it away. There often occurs, too, the "transforma-tion in suffering," the mortal agonies of the Garden and of Cal-vary, the participation in and living anew of all the torments of Christ, of His loneliness and abandonment, of His scourging and crowning with thorns, of His falls that crushed Him under the terrible weight of the Cross, of His Crucifixion and the dis-location of His bones, of His being raised between Heaven and earth on the holy wood, His thirst, His cries of anguish, His giv-ing forth His last breath, His death itself, finally, and burial, and then—the happy renewal and transformation—His glorious Resurrection, Ascension, and the sending of the Holy Spirit. And amid all this, the palpable touches "which savour of eternal life," and which, imprinting on the soul the most perfect and ardent charity, give it eternal life.

From these most important phenomena and effects, which are usually chiefly noted throughout the extremely prolonged night of the spirit, in which the desired rebirth of the soul is prepared and effected, we shall now be able to see how momentous, and also

how lovely and delightful, that night must be in the midst of
its horrors, and how well it deserves to be called "lovely, happy
and delightful"; for it illumines the soul with ineffable delights
(Ps. 138:11-12; Isa. 58:10) and leaves it united forever with the
divine Bridegroom.[83]

In its first phase, which usually begins during simple union,
the soul, in the unbearable excess of divine light, remains darkened, blinded, and lost to everything earthly and of the senses,
completely annihilated in the presence of the divine.[84] In the
midst of a total stripping and, so to speak, destruction of one's
own nature, even of what appeared to be virtuous and good in it,
it will now be able to see only its nothingness, sins, vileness, defects, imperfections, stains, duplicity, ignorance, darkness, and a
thousand other miseries that crush it, causing it to feel most
keenly the radical opposition to infinite sanctity, purity, justice,
divine simplicity, and truth that it finds in itself. On the one
hand, these things attract it irresistibly, and on the other, by their
sublimity they crush and annihilate it, and at times seem to drive
it away as a thing contrary; and they make that full union for
which it so much longs impossible for it. This causes such great
and inexplicable suffering that it can only be compared with the
pain of loss of Hell or Purgatory—for it really constitutes Purgatory in this life.[85]

The soul, thus thoroughly humiliated, empty of self, free
from all attachment and purified to its depths with that most
intense fire that burns and consumes it, now enters upon the
second phase. This occurs particularly after it has celebrated the
mystical espousals in which, amid ecstasies that are alternately
delightful and acutely painful, it sees first the adorable beauty of
the divine Bridegroom and then the ignominies and affronts He
suffered for our love, and the poor return that is made to Him

today. Then, when it is least thinking of it, it is brought into the unfathomable abyss of the great darkness, where, losing sight of that sacred humanity that served it as consolation and support, as way and as guide, the traces of everything earthly now obliterated and destroyed, the soul is submerged and lost in that bottomless immensity in which it finds itself—while it seems to it that it is deprived even of faith, hope, and charity. It receives very gradually the impression of and participation in the divine attributes, in the goodness and mercy of God, His purity, sanctity, truth, and justice, and finally even His very majesty, wisdom, and immensity. Whereas it had but recently been lost, it now comes forth truly found, enriched with the graces and most singular mercies that the three Divine Persons show it continually[86] and adorned with all the virtues and with faith, hope, and charity wholly confirmed and purified and charity so wonderfully established and so ardent that it will now triumph over death and Hell itself, for it cannot be extinguished by the waters of any tribulations whatsoever.

Thus, the soul comes forth now fully purified, illuminated and perfect in all things, as far as is possible in this life, and particularly in those three great theological virtues by which it is wholly united to God. Thus, gradually becoming fully configured to the divine Word, it can now be admitted to the eternal marriage, consummating the espousals before contracted "in faith, in justice and in judgement," in that tremendous and delightful kiss of God that is the full communication of the Holy Spirit, and in the most close and ardent embrace of His inextinguishable charity.

There the sweet bride,
Transformed and changed into her Beloved,

In him lives and rests,
From him receives life,
Her own being now consumed.
(María de San Alberto)

Through this most sublime state of spiritual marriage, the soul comes to experience such intimate and wonderful society with the Divine Persons that it now almost habitually enjoys this ineffable vision, catching from it the reflection, with the delight of glory, of the eternal processions of the Word and the Holy Spirit, hearing the voice of the Eternal Father, who says, "This is my beloved daughter in whom I am well pleased," and thus receiving the mystical kiss of the Father and of the divine Bridegroom.[87]

In a word, as true daughter and bride, the soul merits to penetrate the secret judgments of God and rejoices to see how true and just they always are. It adores and loves and praises equally the terrible rigors of His inviolable justice and the incredible excesses of His infinite goodness and mercy (Rev. 19:1-2), thus identifying itself in all things with the divine views and dispositions.

Through living thus deified, so that only very rarely and for a short space does it suffer absence or dryness, it usually no longer now experiences ecstasy or raptures, for it is strengthened after the manner of the saints of Heaven to receive the greatest excesses of light without shrinking.

Thus it comes to remain, according to St. John of the Cross (*Spiritual Canticle*, 22), confirmed in grace and even exempt from the pains of Purgatory (*Dark Night*, II, ch. 6). Its life is a beginning of eternal happiness.[88] Frequently the just in this sublime state begin to show forth the splendors of glory or odors of celestial fragrance.[89] At times they spend long periods with scarcely any sleep or without any other food than the Eucharist; yet they enjoy sufficient strength to work with inexpressible zeal and activity for the glory of God and the good of their neighbors. For this at times, as if dispensed from the law of gravity and the condition of these earthly bodies of ours, they fly or are suddenly transferred to the most distant places and to the highest and most inaccessible regions. At times they even recover the primitive domination over wild beasts and over nature, finding themselves, so to speak, back again in the state of innocence and associated with the work of Christ risen and glorious.

Such is the inconceivable height to which even in this life souls faithful to grace are raised. And such is the ideal that can be realized by all true Christians who aspire to be configured with Christ: deification.

"Oh souls created for and called to these splendours," St. John of the Cross says to us (*Spiritual Canticle*, 39), "what are you doing? Over what are you wasting your time?"

Chapter 10

Examples of Various Stages: St. Teresa and Ven. Ana María de San José

In order to make the outline we have just given about the stages and degrees of progress in the mystical life clearer and to support it with concrete data, it would seem desirable to quote as practical examples first the summary that St. Teresa gives in her most interesting second relation to Fr. Rodrigo; and then another account, very little known though it well deserves recognition—that given by a humble Franciscan nun of the seventeenth century, the Ven. Ana María de San José. To complete the evidence, and also to show that God's arm is not short-ened and that He can just as easily do in our day what He did in days of old, and even more if it were desirable, we could easily indicate other recent or present-day examples;[90] but it is better to leave these until they have come to their full development and can thus give proof of due maturity and certainty.

Account Given by St. Teresa

Recollection:

> The first supernatural prayer of which I had experience, in my opinion (for so I call that which cannot be ac-quired by industry or diligence despite all our efforts,

although we can certainly prepare for it and do much to have it), is an interior recollection which is felt in the soul, so that it seems to acquire new senses corresponding to its exterior ones, and seems to want to withdraw from outward bustle and noise. Thus sometimes it carries the external senses with it and wants to close the eyes and neither see, hear nor understand except that in which the soul is then occupied, which is to be able to hold converse with God alone. Hence there is no loss of any sense of faculty, the use of all is entire, but it is so that it may be employed on God.

Quiet:

There sometimes comes from this recollection an interior quietude full of happiness and peace, so that the soul is in the state of seeming to lack nothing. Even to speak wearies it (I refer to vocal prayer and meditating), it only wants to love. This state may last for a short time but may sometimes last for long periods.

Effects:

From this prayer usually comes a sleep which is called the sleep of the faculties. But the latter are neither so completely absorbed nor suspended that it can be called rapture, nor can it in any sense be called union.

Simple union:

Sometimes and even often, the soul understands that the will alone is in union.... It is wholly set on God and the soul sees that it cannot attend to or do any other thing. The other two faculties are free for the business and work of God's service. In short, Martha and Mary go hand in hand.

Full union:

> When there is union of all the faculties, things are very different, for they can do nothing, because the understanding is, as it were, dazed. The will loves more than it understands; but the understanding does not know if the will loves, nor what it does, in any way it can explain. Memory, it seems to me, there is none, or thought, nor even for the time being are the senses awake. The soul is like someone who has lost the use of its senses in order that it may be more fully employed in what gives it joy. This passes quickly.

Effects:

> From the wealth of humility and other virtues and desires which remain in the soul, it understands the great good which came to it from that grace, but it is unable to say what it is.

Raptures and suspension of the faculties:

> In my opinion these are all one, but I usually speak of suspension in order to avoid the term "rapture," which frightens people. This union we are discussing can also correctly be called suspension. The difference there is between that and rapture is this—that rapture lasts longer and is more perceptible outwardly, for it interferes

with respiration so that one cannot speak or open the eyes; and although this occurs in union, in rapture it takes place with greater force, for the natural warmth vanishes, I know not where. When the rapture is deep (for in all these ways of prayer there is greater and less)—when it is deep, as I say, the hands become icy cold and sometimes remain stretched out like sticks and the body, if the rapture comes upon it when it is standing or kneeling, remains so. The soul is so deeply absorbed in the joy of what the Lord shows it that it appears to forget to animate the body, and abandons it. If the rapture lasts, the nerves are affected.

It seems that here the Lord wants the soul to understand more clearly what it is enjoying, than in union. Thus it is most usual for His Majesty to reveal certain things to it during rapture. The effects left on the soul are considerable, as is the self-forgetfulness which only wants so great a Lord and God to be known and praised. In my opinion, if it is from God, the soul cannot remain without a knowledge that it can do nothing, and an awareness of its wretchedness and ingratitude in not having served him who, of his goodness alone, shows it such great mercies ... and thus it comes to hold all things of the world as of little account.

Rapture or transport:

The difference there is between rapture and transport is that in rapture one gradually dies to these external things, losing the use of one's senses but being alive to God. Transport comes with a single warning that His Majesty gives in the very depths of the soul and so swiftly that it seems to it that he is carrying away the higher part of it, and it feels as if it is leaving the body. Thus courage is necessary at the beginning to cast oneself into the Lord's arms that he may bear the soul whither he will; for until His Majesty establishes it in peace where he is pleased to take it ... the poor soul does not know what is going to happen.

Effects:

In my opinion the virtues are all the stronger on account of this, because the soul's desires grow, as does the knowledge of this great God, leading to fear and love of him. Thus without our having any control over the matter, God bears the soul away in transport, for he is the Lord of it, and it remains filled with deep repentance for having sinned against him, dismay at having dared to offend so great a Majesty, and very great longing that no one should offend him, but that all should praise him....

The flight of the spirit is—I know not how to describe it—something which springs up from the deepest part of the soul ... and goes where the Lord wills. It cannot be further explained, but it seems a flight.... I know that it is realized very clearly and cannot be prevented. It seems as if this little bird of the spirit has escaped from the wretchedness of the flesh and the prison of the body and, not concerned about that, is now better able to devote itself to what the Lord gives it. It is such a subtle and precious thing, from what the soul understands, that it does not seem there can be any illusion in it—nor even in any of these things when they occur. The fears came afterwards, because the one who received these favours is so wretched … although in the innermost part of the soul certainty remained.

Impulses:

I call impulse a desire which God sometimes gives to the soul without its being preceded by prayer, and which is generally, indeed, a remembrance which comes suddenly of the soul's absence from God, or of some word it hears to this effect. This remembrance is sometimes so powerful and of such great force that in an instant the soul appears to have lost the use of reason. It is like when some very painful news is given to one suddenly.… Such is the case here, except that the pain comes from a cause for which the soul knows that it is well worth while dying. The fact is that it seems that all the soul then understands makes for its greater distress, and that the Lord does not want it to draw profit from anything, nor remember that it is his will that it should live, but it seems to it that it is in very great abandonment and deprivation of everything, an abandonment which cannot be described—for the whole world and everything in it cause distress. Nothing created gives it companionship, nor does the soul want anything but the Creator and this it sees is impossible unless it dies. As it cannot kill itself, it yearns for death in such a way that it is truly in danger of dying and sees itself as it were hanging between heaven and earth, and does not know at all what to do with itself. From time to time God gives it a knowledge of himself, so that it can see what it is losing, in a manner so strange that it cannot be expressed. For there is no experience in the world, at least of those I have passed through, which equals it, and ... leaves the body dislocated ... and with very great sufferings. Of this the soul feels nothing until that impulse has passed away. It has enough to do with its consciousness of what is happening within it, neither do I think it would feel severe physical pain. It has all its senses and can speak and even observe, but it cannot walk, for the great assault of love unsteadies its gait. Even if one were to die of longing for this, it would not profit, for it only comes when God gives it. It leaves very great effects and benefits in the soul....

The *ordinary impulse* consists in a desire of serving God and brings with it great tenderness and tears of longing to escape from this exile: but the soul has liberty to consider that it is the will of the Lord that it should live. With this it consoles itself and it offers him its life, begging him that it may live only for his glory. With this, the suffering passes.

Another sufficiently ordinary way of prayer is a kind of *wounding*, which truly seems to the soul as if an arrow had pierced the heart or pierced the soul itself. This causes great pain which makes it complain, but it is so delightful that it would wish never to be without it. This pain is not in the senses, nor is it a physical wound, but it is in the depths of the soul without any sign of bodily suffering.... It is impossible to understand it unless one has experienced it, that is, to understand the extent of its penetration, for the pains of the spirit are very different from those of this world. From this I conclude how much more the souls in hell and purgatory suffer than can be realized by comparing their suffering with bodily pains.

At other times it seems that this wound of love springs from the soul's inmost depths: the effects are great. When the Lord does not give it, there is no means of having it, despite all one's efforts, nor, on the other hand, can one prevent its coming when he is pleased to give it. It is like desires for God, so keen and subtle that they cannot be expressed. As the soul finds itself helpless and cannot enjoy God as it would wish, this gives it a great hatred for the body, which seems to it like a great wall preventing the soul from enjoying what it then seems to understand that it would enjoy within itself, if it were not for the body's hindrance. Then it sees the great evil which came to us with Adam's sin, which deprived us of this liberty.

Remarks:

This prayer came before the raptures and the powerful impulses which I have said were experienced. I forgot to say that generally those powerful impulses do not leave one, unless the Lord gives a rapture and great joy by which he comforts the soul and gives it courage to live for him....

All this that I have said cannot be fancy.... The effects and how the soul is left so much better, cannot fail to be understood....

Another prayer I remember which comes before the first I mentioned consists in a presence of God which is not a vision of any kind. It seems that whenever (at least when there is no aridity) a person wants to commend himself to His Majesty, even though it be only in vocal prayer, he will find him.

Ven. Ana María de San José

After this definitive account given by the great mystical doctor, let us examine the full and clear story of the wonderful life and progressive stages of prayer of the Ven. Ana María de San José, abbess of the Discalced Franciscans of Salamanca.[91]

Prayer of recollection: After the total surrender of herself to God that Ana María made at the beginning of her novitiate—"I was left," she said (*Autobiography*, nn. 14-15),

> with a way of prayer which consisted in placing myself [in spirit] at the gates of mercy, and I asked for a kiss of peace. This manner of prayer was supernatural and God himself set me in it..... My practice was to speak to God and then to recollect myself with him within me. In this recollection I found great satisfaction and I had only to close my eyes to find myself in it immediately. I never understood [the use of] discursive reason [in prayer] and it seemed to me that I knew nothing of prayer nor had I [the grace of it].... Questioned by the Novice Mistress, I said: "Mother, I do not seem to have [the grace of] prayer: what I do is to speak to God and then I am aware of his presence within me. I listen to him, although he says nothing to me." And she said, "Ah, Anica! there you have the better part; that is what you should do, for that is the best." With that I was consoled, and I took courage despite my incapacity....

Returning, then, to the gates of mercy, I did not reason about these gates, nor did I imagine them, but simply remained as if I were a poor person who is at the gates of a great lord who has much to give and likes us to ask, and to expect him to give even more than we ask.

Prayer of quiet:

The help [I received] was so great, that not even for an instant did it seem I could withdraw from it.[92] [In this prayer] I sang in the choir, went my way in the daytime, ate, slept and woke again: and in this way I found so many matters of doctrine and divine teaching, that I had no need of books or of anyone: fervour and desires left no room for idleness.... This way of the prayer of the gates of mercy lasted for some months and I found it so good that I said: "Lord, here I shall live, here I shall die, here shall be my rest ...," always hoping for that kiss of peace.

Union:

When I was at prayer one night, on the eve of a Communion day, and my senses and faculties were deeply recollected, I felt the presence of God close to me. He said to me: "Give me an embrace.... You are to receive me tomorrow and now you do not want to give me an embrace?" When this was said, I felt myself locked in God's embrace and filled with his Majesty and greatness. I experienced union with God and such great benefits that it seemed to me there was nothing more I could desire upon earth. This union remained perceptible to me for many days and brought with it a very great suspension of the faculties and a love of gratitude felt deeply in the senses. When I found myself in God's embrace and felt his presence, it was not a corporeal vision but [took place] within me; as also did the realization and knowledge of what it was, without a full overflowing on to the senses. With this I forgot about the gate and sometimes when I wanted to return to it, it eluded my memory. This kind of forgetfulness is quite usual when souls go where God leads them and where he himself puts them, only to remove them again when it is his good pleasure.

Renewal of the soul and exchange of hearts:
"A few days afterwards," she added (n. 17),

> when I was at prayer, I felt within me a very great noise, as if they were pulling down a house, but I knew that "that was the work of God." After they pulled down that house, leaving neither stone nor nail, so that all the old structure disappeared, I felt that God was building a new house for himself, and was casting away everything that had made the first a house of vermin and other such pests.... Then I felt God within me and, as he had made a house for himself, so he made himself master of all. He said to me: "From now onwards, you no longer have soul, heart or senses, or anything [of your own], for you are all mine: the soul is mine." And he took my heart away from me and gave me his: "In order that henceforward you do not use the gifts I have given you so badly as hitherto ..., I shall take care of you and you will go where I take you, for if you want to give me the glory of your sanctification

and discipline you must follow me and give me my whole house without anyone else entering it...." From that point until now, I have never failed to feel God within me ..., neither for dryness nor for distress of heart...; and from that point until now I have never been able to say – "*my* soul, *my* heart, *my* senses," but I always say when I speak to God: "this soul of yours, this heart of yours" and so on.

The interior Master: "After this favour," she continued (nn. 18–19),

I always had a Master with me and to listen to his teaching was as natural as breathing; and that not only occurred to me interiorly, but I went about like a novice with his Master. Continually he taught me perfection in thought, in word, in deed; and if I did some external thing that did not show all the requisites of perfection, he made me do it again. How many times did this happen to me! At the same time he took books away from me ..., all was to be learnt interiorly. I had so much, and found within me continually so many new things and so much teaching, with the desire of suffering so close at hand, that I heeded nothing else and remembered nothing. Everything became a wish to resemble my Master: I found it all in the crucifix. That was my book; there I found all I could desire; and I called the virtues which were resplendent in Christ on the Cross the chapters of the book....

The fervent desire of not stopping until I reached the mount of perfection grew, and it seemed to me that this mount was a transformation into Christ crucified.

Of the joy of communication with God (n. 21):

> I said within myself: if there were no other reward than
> this gladness, joy and jubilation that one has within
> oneself, the gaiety and delight one has on the occasions
> of mortification and withdrawal from creatures would
> be generous payment; whereas to those who have no
> experience of it, it seems a source of sadness.

*Configuration with Christ; the glory, power, and
riches of the bride; the fire of love (n. 26):*

> The desire of resembling God in all things—in trials, con-
> tempt, sanctity, in life and in death, increased in me and
> I desired to live and die in the greatest contempt. I was
> filled with this desire and very many times he said to me:
> "Daughter, I make you heir of all I suffered as if you your-
> self had suffered it. I make you heir of my wounds, of all
> my virtues and of my life and death." Although I valued
> this greatly I said to him: "Lord, I want to suffer in my
> body and feel in it for your love what you suffered for love
> of me." ... Finally there came the overflowing desire to see
> myself transformed by love and grace into my Master,
> Christ. Being in deep prayer and in rapture I saw myself
> made wholly one thing with him; and I saw that what he
> had by nature was in myself through grace.... At this tre-
> mendous grace I said in all sincerity: "I live, yet not I, for
> I no longer live except in Christ, and he is I for I am no
> longer myself." I saw the likeness of Christ in myself more
> clearly than the day, and it seemed to me as when riches
> come forth from the womb of the sea, for there came
> forth outwardly the perfection of the virtues, all together

and each one separately, with the perfection of the eight beatitudes; and finally I was made one spirit with that of Christ and the mysteries that were hidden in the spirit of the Church. I had the keys of hell, as mistress of it, and of all the things of earth. I saw myself as Queen in heaven through the perfection of poverty of spirit; the perfection of this virtue was remarkable. In my heart I had Christ crucified and with him all the company of the virtues; patience, which was the one most dear to me, was a support for the head of Christ, for with patience every virtue is crowned and made glorious. Finally there was the flame of love corresponding to that state of transformation, and as it grew and waxed mighty I was given a certain fire from that same love. I had many thousands of reasons for love the least of which could have torn away my soul.

Mystical death, the terrible judgment, and
the glorious resurrection (n. 27):

> There was given to me in this fire of love a rapture, or rather spiritual death, in such a way that I can say I died and it seemed to the nuns that I was dying.... In this rapture or death I was carried away to judgement and in the presence of that Judge and of many friends of his whom he had with him as witnesses, my whole life was revealed, each sin, each imperfection with all its circumstances, all the benefits and graces I had received up to that time: the Judge ordered me to judge myself and pass sentence; and I judged myself as if ... this soul were not mine and I gave sentence that I deserved to be cursed by God and was unworthy of his presence ... that the fact

that justice should be done ... was more important than the salvation of my soul. This was a very great experience, and only he who has been through it will know the value of it, for it cannot be measured. There I was pardoned, there it seems to me I was confirmed in grace and there I could understand how certain effects of original sin were removed from me: at any rate this truth remained with me some time and it seemed to me certain that ... thus I was restored to original justice and remained established in it and in self-knowledge: there in the midst of nothingness, I was in a vacuum, with the crushing experience of seeing myself just as I am and of giving to God what is his; and it seems to me from that time onwards, not only have I not had to confess pride and vain glory but not even [have I had] the first movement of them, and even it almost seems I have remained incapable of entertaining them.

Mystical ascent and hidden life in God (n. 28):

I left all things, with utter detachment from every-thing, as if there had been nothing for me in heaven or on earth, save God alone. In this solitude I experi-enced no aridity, rather I enjoyed a tranquillity, peace and serenity of soul beyond compare.... I was raised above everything created and found myself outside the body, very far from myself and plunged in God. In *these flights of the spirit* ... I was shown that in order to be a spiritual being, it was fitting that I should be weaned from the love of all that was not God and God alone, to rise to the knowledge of the Father and then move, as it were, without support, but in order to seek

him in spirit and in truth. There were infused into me
esteem, gratitude and love of my Master and of having
him as Redeemer, example, friend, brother and Lord.
But I was not to take his Humanity as my principal
aim, as I had been doing.[93] Thus I was left with only
one desire of which I was promised fulfilment if I gave
the love that I had in my heart. This was the desire to
see God in the Majesty of his Glory. This was not only
a desire, but an effect of grace, that with it I might
pursue my course in hope ... of seeing him in that
Majesty, without image, without figure, and of being
transformed into him — for as from the beginning all
my desire was to be transformed into Christ, how it
was like the beginning of another and more spiritual
life. Thus it seemed to me that there was no higher
place to which to ascend, judging by the perfection I
found in the state of transformation into Christ. No
comparison is possible. This is another and a new
spiritual life, with renunciations, purifications, cir-
cumcisions, abnegations of the faculties and senses,
moving on the wings of faith, stripped of every attachment to feeling, with the faculties purified, journeying
in pure faith with the desire to see God and to be
transformed into him, which I was given; and thus, as
I was saying, to resemble him in the virtues, in sanctity, in trials and contempt; here, in the way I have
been explaining, to be transformed into him, to resemble God in his goodness and in our sharing in his
attributes: to be like him in purity, to be full of that
eternal light; and finally, all that is after the mode of
God and makes us one spirit with him.

Transformation in God; the all and the nothing; the divine glance upon the humble soul, raising it up; heavenly humility; the divine attributes; the secrets of Providence; vision and peace; God all in all (n. 29):

The time of the promise that had been made came, and once when I was in the deepest contemplation, desiring to see God in the majesty of his glory and to be transformed into him, heir to his spirit, goodness, purity and light, there came the fulfilment of this state ... and, submerged in the depths of my littleness, far[94] below hell itself..., from this deep lowliness and emptiness of my being, I gazed upon God's most sublime Majesty in the height of his greatness, where all the blessed were, so to speak, as nothing; and finally all that is pure creature, even the most Blessed Virgin — for she alone has more than all together — in the end is at an infinite distance from God, for it is creature. From that most sublime Majesty I gazed at myself and in that glance I was raised up to become one spirit with him. Being raised, I yet found myself in greater lowliness, and out of that lowliness of mine which, in my awareness of that most sublime goodness I surrendered to him, I sank down to where his glance set me; I gave myself to him and he raised me up. The splendours which he communicated to me were the love and very deep knowledge I had in this vision of God, as far as is possible in this life — there heavenly humility which arises from the knowledge of God was given to me and it remained a living spirit of the praise of God. Till then, although it seems deep humility, it is more self-knowledge, but this is the kind there is in heaven. There I understood the mystery of the most Blessed Trinity and the distinction of the Divine Persons, and all three and each one wrought in me great and wonderful things. Certain splendours, which were his attributes, came forth from that divine Being. I penetrated the works of these attributes and in particular, that of his power and wisdom, that of his mercy and the others. All were so different and so mighty that they cannot be expressed in human language. This caused in me certain effects of glory and bliss, a languor and annihilation, but glorious joy that God is who he is. In a certain manner his riches became mine, as if I were God by nature. There knowledge, love, esteem and appreciation of the mystery of the Incarnation were given to me. And I saw the blessed who, after singing to God for his glory, were giving thanks to him with wonder and praise that he had gone forth from himself to communicate his divine Being to us and raise our dust to such a dignity. There I understood the dignity of Christ and rejoiced in his immense riches as if they were my own. The love of the Master and gratitude that through his love, teaching and merits, I had come to such a state, were a great support to me; and my divine Lord, Master and Redeemer continued to look at me and rejoice that the Father (to whom he had brought me) had favoured me so much. He continued to give me to understand that just as I rejoiced in his goodness, so he rejoiced in mine. There faith and hope seemed to disappear, for all was as it were *possession* and *sight* of God.... This looking at God and with this contemplation, my glorification, abasement, being raised up, surrender, the attracting him with my glance of self-annihilation and an infinity of other effects, were lasting. But my transformation henceforth into his divine Being and being made one spirit with him, and always loving and understanding without interruption, were also permanent. The spirit of contemplation and the judgements of God and his intentions in regard to creatures filled me with delight.... Not only is everything plain to me, but the more God does through his power, goodness, justice and mercy, the more his judgements delight me; and when on certain occasions he reveals his intentions to me, the more remote they seem from me, the more they satisfy me, although they may appear to some, severe and very great punishments. Fears left me, and I can never think of anything with premonition nor is there a thought which gives me any kind of care or trouble about anything, or despondency, or dryness or fervour, for though it has not (sensible) fervour, the spirit is made one with God and loves. It is full of meekness, the senses are subject to the faculties, in love, the faculties to the spirit and the spirit to God, and finally all is in God and God is the mover of this creature, and it is not in itself, but in him.

Hunger and thirst for God; rivers of glory, peace, and grace; intercession and reconciliation; the soul made all things for all; victim of love (nn. 30–31):

From this great grace two effects remained to me as was usually the case with other graces, for from one particular state there remained within the soul a new effect or promise. And that I might be given what His Majesty had determined, he [first] gave me the desire for it and made me know its effect so that I might [be moved to] ask for what he wanted to give me. From this came an insatiable thirst and hunger for God. The thirst was to know him more and more and the hunger was to love him.... I was always receiving [him], and that left me with a greater hunger and thirst, for I had a void in my mind and will impossible to satiate, and thus I asked to drink up all that river of glory ... but everything increased my hunger and thirst.... A heavy shower of water began to rain down on me ... and from the abundance of this water, rivers came forth from my soul and senses... these rivers spread through the Church, and ... I felt that all I had desired and asked for, there I was seeing fulfilled. And God said to me: "All you have desired you possess: only one thing you have asked me for, I do not grant you, that is, to leave the flesh and come to me. I have my Mother in heaven and you on earth to make supplication to me, propitiate me, surrender to me; for the future, you will be dealing with angels, saints and with creatures. Hitherto all I have wrought in you has been for your sanctification: now you have to be all for all." And with this he infused into me a love for my Mother the Church and her children both far and near, and for the souls in Purgatory.... I say that he left me a different, a new creature, because I was now *all for my neighbour*....

I had compassion for all, and with this I became so clothed with all the needs of the Church that I bore them all on my shoulders.

The fruits of life in the Church;
cooperation in the work of Jesus;
mysterious and important apostolate:

> Sometimes our Lord confers this grace upon me. After I have received him sacramentally, he bears me away to certain cities and kingdoms …; I feel that he carries me in himself in spirit, and at other times I feel that he bears my heart [away] and when he takes my heart, he first says to me, when I have just received him, "Now let them all ask me, for I am in the heart of Ana. Let them all ask me for graces, for here I shall allow myself to grant what is asked…." Sometimes he says to me: "Now we are going to Japan, for I have many friends there working at the conversion of souls and we have to visit and strengthen them…." And then it is given me to understand an infinity of things about the errors of the Indians and of the fruit which the presence of our God brings, the darkness which exiles those blind souls and the spirit which he pours into those who labour…. At other times I felt myself carried away, I knew not by whom …; many times it has happened to me to go through the air as if flying, and sometimes I find myself among a crowd of Indians of different nations, with the book of *Christian Doctrine* in my hand and they on their knees listening to it…. At other times, after Communion, it happens to me to be carried away, and I bear the most Holy Sacrament on my breast; and then I see that very many adore it. On these occasions, too, the Lord gives very great graces.

State of the soul consummated and transformed in
love; continual divine communications; living according
to a divine mode; peace and happiness:

This love and knowledge, union and transformation, prepare me for the continual reception of receiving the divine communications. I am always receiving the divine Word in my mind, and finally, God as he is in himself, without image, without figure, in spirit and in truth. And this working in me gives me life, not in myself, but it gives me divine being. Mine [i.e., my being] is not in itself, but in this Most High Lord who works according to his nature, doing the same work as in the blessed and leaving the same effects. Although all his mercies are worthy of praise, yet all are inferior to this work. Before souls reach this state of contemplation, God shows them very great mercies and all fit themselves to prepare for this. Sometimes he causes them to cleanse and detach their minds from everything that is pure creature, to arrive at perfect detachment. This is in the state of highest contemplation, where it is God alone who works. The spirit receives and hearkens, not understanding in such a way as to be able to express it afterwards, for as all is according to the mode of God, it has no language. In this state there is no danger of being deceived.

In this state (of spiritual marriage) it is impossible to have vain glory or pride or doubts or fears to which one adverts, for one is not in oneself, neither has the soul sufferings, or fervour, but an actual joy that God is who he is, a calm love becoming gently inflamed, a very great candour of soul, sweet peace and abiding tranquillity. The divine will is always clear to it as regards what concerns the spiritual common good of the Church and as regards particular things. The soul continues to live without reasoning things out beforehand through its forgetfulness, without any noticeable manner of exterior comportment, but with sincerity, goodness and simplicity: with the same effects proceeding from its inmost being, which are sufficient and most certain. For he who has the senses, as they are in this state—and I experienced it—subject to the faculties, the faculties to the spirit, and the spirit to God, is finally wholly possessed by God; for the creature is not in itself, but in God himself, and it is clear that the exterior has to be modified according to the manner of the work which is always going on in the interior.

Conclusions

I. The Meaning of "Ordinary" and "Extraordinary" in the Mystical Life

.

From what has already been said it will now be abundantly clear that in the case of the saints and true mystics many things that are usually thought extraordinary are not really so. For, although such things are very rare among the generality of Christians—for the majority of them are not what they ought to be—yet they are either quite ordinary or at least very frequent in perfect Christians who are pleasing to Christ. Christ sees such Christians resplendent with the glory that He merited for them, and He gives them power to do what He did and even greater things. To them, as to His true and faithful friends—however much the fact may astonish worldly people and the undevout—even here and now He wants to manifest Himself in a certain way and communicate His secrets.[95]

Let us leave for the time being the power of working different kinds of wonders, which, although it is very frequent in one form or another in almost all the saints—who, says Fr. Weiss, are followed by miracles as the body by its shadow—yet since it is obviously a grace *gratis data,* being ordained primarily to the common good and varying according to the mission entrusted to each servant of God, it cannot strictly be called *ordinary*. Thus, as regards the external glory, there can be and usually is great danger of vanity in desiring this. Almost the same can be said of the gift of discerning spirits in its more important manifestations, although in others it is wont to be very common in great saints and very useful to all those who are entrusted with the direction of souls, who, if they are what they ought to be and ask for it sincerely, will never lack it in the measure in which it is necessary and fitting for them.

But among things that are truly ordinary in substance, although not so in their external manifestations, which are startling and which may vary and even disappear without harm to the spirit (I mean among the things that generally and normally figure in the soul's progress as an integral part of it, or as causes, or ordinary effects, and that therefore, although at times they may perhaps appear startling in certain of their manifestations, may, however, as to their substance be constant and normal features in the complete development of the mystical life), it seems to us that, in conformity with the different classifications indicated, and the examples given, the following phenomena, together with what is characteristic of the principal stages, should figure: *silence* and even to a certain extent *spiritual sleep*, the *inebriation of love*, if not to the extent that it resembles that which the first disciples showed when they had received the Holy Spirit, at least sufficiently to cause a certain intoxication, not so completely repressed that in some eyes it might not pass as madness. It seems to us that the same and more ought to be said as to the substance of the *raptures* or *ecstasies* and of the *transports* and *flights of the spirit*. For if in many servants of God who have passed through the corresponding phases, such phenomena are not much shown outwardly or are not so clearly noted, it is because God withdraws them from the public eye, perhaps giving them time to hide themselves, or again the facility, even during ecstasy, of moving and performing the same ceremonies as others, thus walking, for example, in processions or going to communicate;[96] although at other times they move as best they can, leaning on or clinging to some object in order not to fall on the ground when they feel themselves fainting away in ecstasy or transport, or not to find themselves raised from the ground with the impulse of the spirit in raptures and flights. But all will feel the essence of the thing that is that tendency either to fall or be raised from the ground and will observe that for a certain time they have lost the use of the senses, either completely or partially, even if God gives them the grace of awakening or returning to themselves at the opportune moment in order that, when it is time, they may get up without being noticed, as used to happen in the case of Madre María de la Reina de los Apóstolos, who died in the odor of sanctity in 1905.

Neither are the keen longings and thirst of love, the impulses, and even the wounds of love ever wont to fail to occur in their due season, even if the fact of such things being expressed externally in visible wounds, as of raptures and flights being accompanied by levitation and above all by bilocation, is now a rare and truly "extraordinary" thing.

Visions, or *exterior locutions*, that is, those perceptible to the senses, might also with justice be classed as extraordinary, for they do not always cause sanctity or even presuppose it. This applies even to imaginary visions, insofar as at times they may also be had by sinners and be absent in great servants of God; but what are not extraordinary are some that are purely *intellectual*—always of the greatest utility—and still less so others even more intimate and spiritual, which manifestly presuppose and involve the state of union, and which are normally present in any perfect mystic. These appear, so to speak, indispensable for the completion of the true and full illumination and most spiritual instruction that the Holy Spirit, as the Master of all truth, gives interiorly.[97]

Thus, strictly speaking, these belong to the order of sanctifying graces and thereby may be the work of the principal gifts of this divine Guest; for, although secondarily they are ordained to the good of others, primarily they always serve for the greater sanctification of him who possesses them.[98]

This happens above all in the case of substantial words that, after the manner of sacramental words, bring about immediately what they express and thus, as St. John of the Cross remarks, are of inestimable value. The same should be said of the deep knowledge communicated by means of the *substantial touches.*

Thus, then, whatever directly contributes to one's own sanctification, even though it may partially differ from certain servants of God to others, in accordance with the special form of sanctity that the Lord requires of each, is up to a certain point ordinary, in its corresponding form, and in the measure that, for this particular manner of sanctity, it is essential. This can be said of the special preponderance of some particular gifts over others, of that of wisdom or of that of understanding, that of counsel and that of fortitude or knowledge, which make the supernatural physiognomies of the great saints so beautifully varied. These forms taken severally are not ordinary in each servant of God; but some particular one is in each one, and all considered in the collectivity, that is, in the Holy Catholic Church.

Even certain gifts gratuitous in themselves—because at times they are wholly indispensable for certain of the great functions that God entrusts to His servants, and that the latter could not fulfill, or, therefore, sanctify themselves in them, if they did not possess them in a greater or lesser degree—can be said, in view of this special mission and a particular stage of progress along the mystical ladder, to become, as it were, ordinary with respect to such a state or to that particular form of sanctity. This is why in great saints the different gratuitous gifts usually abound exceedingly;[99] and inasmuch as they see that they are very fitting for them in order that they may be the better able to discharge their particular mission, they do not hesitate at times to ask for them or desire them, not for their own glory but for that of God.

We may consider, then, as *extraordinary*, in general, all those lights and graces or special favors that neither proceed from union itself nor tend principally and directly to produce it. Thus, although such grades often help and foster union, they can very well manifest themselves without it, because they are ordained directly to other holy ends.[100]

On the contrary, it should be said that those graces that produce or favor union in themselves or that always accompany it or result from it, however rare they may come to be in reality, or however startling they may at times appear in some of their most notable manifestations, belong in substance to what is *normal* and are therefore *ordinary* in the full development of mystical life. They are therefore desirable in themselves in everything they have of the normal, although perhaps in their abnormal or accidental aspects they may present certain inconveniences.

This is, then, what there is to say of ecstasies and raptures, with the great supernatural lights and other phenomena that accompany them.

To understand, indeed, that such things ought in a certain measure to be ordinary in the mystical life, it is sufficient to recall that ecstatic union forms a stage notably higher than that of simple union, or may merely be the latter raised to greater height and intensity, as St. Francis de Sales declares, basing himself on St. Teresa.[101] Therefore, what such union has that is most essential is the effect of the same love raised to a higher stage, as Fr. García de Cisneros remarks.[102] For God is accustomed to *inebriate* His many friends or lovers in that way with the torrent of His delights, from which at the same time He fills them with marvelous lights, satisfying them with the "water of the wisdom of salvation."[103] Consequently, in contradistinction to *prophetic* ecstasy—which certain souls who are wholly beginners can have and sometimes even sinners such as Balaam—*mystical* ecstasy, regarded not in its outward manifestations but in its intimate depths where all is ordered to the soul's own sanctification, is an integral part of the process of development of the spiritual life. It cannot therefore be called extraordinary, nor is it to be feared. It is, rather, greatly to be desired, as many writers recognize.[104]

Something should also be said of rapture and the flight of the spirit, which constitute other phases of mystical union even more sublime and fruitful.[105] This is a most blessed mystical state in which the soul is wholly on fire with divine love and is enriched with wonderful lights by which the purification of its faults and its consolidation in virtue are completed.

If these wonderful phenomena are genuine, as St. Teresa says, they ought to bring great light, illumination or revelations, caused through certain locutions or visions, which are precisely what produces so much good in the mystical soul; a sign that these graces, too—however marked or special they may be or appear to be at times—are not in themselves extraordinary in that sublime and blessed state, although they may be so in other lower stages.

Thus it is that all the great masters of the spiritual life agree in admitting and declaring how frequent such favors usually are and what abundant fruits of blessing they produce in well-disposed souls. In particular, St. Teresa, in spite of so many fears that many bad advisers were continually putting into her mind regarding these favors, never tires of pondering over the great profit they brought her and how, however much she tried, she could never feel regret at having received them[106]—rightly so, for the reasonable fear of being taken in by false currency is not a motive for blindly throwing away genuine coin.[107]

All agree in recognizing that in this high stage of union, and much more so in the state of espousals or of true spiritual marriage, great revelations, the manifestation of the deepest divine secrets, are now very common, as if the Lord, as St. John of the Cross says (*Spiritual Canticle*, note to cant. 23) could not keep anything hidden from such perfect lovers.[108] This is fully in conformity with the laws of all good friendship; and thus, in effect, the Savior promised when He said He was to manifest Himself to all those who truly loved Him and that those to whom He revealed His intimate secrets He treated as friends (John 14:21; 15:15).

To such, then, without their having any right to it more than that of sincere friendship, merely to please and favor them, and even quite apart from the good that may thereby ensue for the faithful at large, He ordinarily makes them great revelations.[109]

Consequently, however full of awe faithful souls may become, however possessed they may be with reverential fear, when the appointed hour comes and the longings of love press upon them increasingly, forgetting all the vain fears they may have had, they will not be able to help sighing for the sight of the Beloved and hearing His words of eternal life. All will unanimously cry out with St. Teresa and her daughters:

Let my eyes see thee
Sweet, good Jesus;
Let my eyes see thee,
Then may I die.

All will repeat with St. John of the Cross:

Reveal thy presence
And let the sight of thee and thy beauty slay me:
Look at the malady
Of love which is only cured
By a presence and a figure.

That is why all these visits of the divine Physician are really ordained to heal, strengthen, nourish, console, and sanctify the soul. He who has once experienced such great blessings, however much he may continue to recognize his unworthiness of them, will not be able to help wanting them and asking for them, hoping in the Lord's goodness that He will finally grant them again. And what is it that causes most suffering in the most painful loneliness and dereliction experienced by such souls but the fear that they will now not see that divine face again from which all their graces have come?

If these favors are, in addition, ordained to the good of other souls, this also can be the work, not of a grace properly to be called *gratis data*, but of one of the gifts of the Holy Spirit, always primarily ordained to the soul's own sanctification and that, in an eminent degree, redound to the great profit of one's neighbors. Such happens chiefly with the two highest gifts, those of understanding and wisdom, which cause the soul to penetrate into and taste by experience the marvels of God, to the extent of being able to communicate to others what they thus learn and feel. Although in this they participate somewhat in the condition of the graces *gratis datas*, yet it is always to the great profit of their own soul, true complement as it is of their own virtue and sanctity, that there is communicated to it in this way a very special light.[110] This cannot fail to be sufficiently ordinary and common in all souls already relatively perfect, since all should contribute, although each one in his own way, to the common edification.[111] This work ought not to be called exceptional or extraordinary, although frequently the special mode in which it is effected is so.

Those who have had the blessing of celebrating the mystical espousals are immediately entrusted in a special manner with watching over the interests of the Bridegroom and guarding His honor, and this requires certain very privileged lights and graces *ad hoc*, which cannot be common and ordinary in the lower stages but are so in this; where, for the better fostering of the good of the Church, it is fitting for such souls to have them, desire them, and ask for them from God in the greatest possible abundance, according to what the apostle says (1 Cor. 14:12): "Seek to abound unto the edifying of the church."

It greatly pleases our Lord to inebriate these, His dearly beloved, with the sweet wine of His love, and once He establishes charity in them, He causes them to go out of themselves and raises them in spirit to other spheres where He reveals His adorable mysteries to them. These revelations, says St. Bonaventure, are made to souls already well purified; before they were so, they could not have received them in this sublime manner, so clear, so intimate, so loving.[112] Hence it comes that these graces, which are wholly extraordinary in beginners and even in those who have made some progress, may be genuinely ordinary in the perfect.

What we have said of the state of espousals should, with greater reason and wider application, be said of the sublime state of *spiritual marriage*, in which those most happy souls are already wholly configured with Christ and made one thing with Him, and accordingly participate in His divine mission and in an abundance of graces and charisms with which to carry out their share in that mission. Thus, not only do they ordinarily have the seven gifts in their fullness, even in what is ordained to the good of others, but the gifts are accompanied by different graces that are truly *gratis datas.* Such graces perfect them and beautify their souls, at the same time facilitating their great influence for good on all other souls.[113]

Thus, many of the things that are most commonly, and, we might even say, wholly ordinary in that state, are clearly extraordinary in earlier stages.

When such is the case, there may be a certain danger in desiring them, because one is not wholly conformed to God's good pleasure, which may direct otherwise, or if they are desired with a less pure intention and not solely for the greater glory of God and the edification of the Church. But when God gives them, whether it be in an ordinary manner, because the present state of the soul requires them, or whether solely because they are fitting for the discharge of some special mission, then, if we try to use them in the most holy manner possible, there is no reason to fear them. We should bless God for them and give Him the most humble thanks for thus deigning to favor us with very special means of procuring His honor and glory and promoting the good of our neighbor. That is what God wants and requires: that we should be grateful for His gifts and use them in such a way that they bear fruit and that we should not cast them aside or despise them, or keep them hidden or idle. Hence it is that so many times He reproves souls, or their directors, for the little appreciation and the fear they have of them.[114]

This fear, more often than not, is usually completely unfounded: for the very people who thus fear supernatural gifts on account of the danger, as they say, of the vanity they might have in the use of them—although in themselves they always lead to humility—are never afraid of, but, on the contrary, earnestly desire other, purely natural gifts, the fruit of which, however great it may be, is of incomparably less value, and in which the danger of vanity and abuse is much greater.

If in human arts and sciences, all those who voluntarily set themselves to study them certainly aspire to possess them with all possible perfection and, very far from contenting themselves with the attainment of a low or mediocre standard, desire to go far beyond all that is commonplace and ordinary, and as far as they can to be outstanding—why in the true science of sciences, in the mystical science of the saints, which is worth more than all the honors and riches of the world and fills us with inestimable and eternal treasures, are we not to aspire with all our soul not to be mediocre but to be *outstanding* in the eyes of God, always growing from strength to strength, in order to be able to receive without any obstacle as many blessings as the divine Lawgiver may see fit to give us, and thus to grasp as clearly as possible the vision of God on the summit of His holy mountain, finally showing to our brethren some reflection of His wonders?

This is a clear fallacy against which the apostle sought to warn us when he said to us: "Follow after charity, be zealous for spiritual gifts; but rather that you may prophesy.... He that prophesieth ... edifieth the church" (1 Cor. 14:1-4).[115]

Here, then, is the point to which we ought to raise our desires and our high and great aspirations; these, very far from being vain and displeasing our Lord, are always most fruitful and pleasing to Him beyond measure. Therefore, not only does He show Himself very willing to satisfy them—saying to us (Ps. 80:11): "Open thy mouth wide, and I will fill it"—but He expressly charges us to try to attain perfection and excellency in spiritual things, aspiring to nothing less than to be perfect as the heavenly Father is perfect. We have the obligation, indeed, to "in all things grow up in him who is the head, even Christ" (Eph. 4:15), and very specially in "grace, and in the knowledge of our Lord and Saviour Jesus Christ" (2 Pet. 3:18). This is the true "knowledge of salvation" (Luke 1:77), which our Lord wants to communicate to all and which all need, the science of true distinction that is never eclipsed or obscured and makes all those who possess it great. It is a science that all could obtain if they loved it and tried to have it, for it goes out to meet those who desire it and manifests itself to them. Hence, to be continually thinking of it and trying for it is the acme of prudence and common sense.[116]

In this matter we cannot nor ought we to content ourselves with being just anything, with occupying the smallest and most obscure corner of Heaven, while we always remain as children; for if we do not grow, we are in great danger of perishing through weakness.[117] We ought to be like children in malice but not in virtue: in this and in the spiritual senses, we have to aspire to be perfect.[118]

Here there is no danger or deception (Prov. 3:16, 17; 4:12), and for a little hard work, precious fruit (Sir. 6:20); quite the contrary of what usually happens with the wild ambitions and aspirations of man. The latter always expose us to the gravest dangers and deceptions; and however successful they may turn out to be, in the end they all come to frustration in death, where they will only serve for our greater torment, and, more often than not, they are doomed to failure from the beginning, for there is nobody to guarantee them. But here to all those who thirst for justice, the mystical waters that flow out unto eternal life are freely offered and the last hour is when they give greatest refreshment (Sir. 6:29); and all will infallibly attain in due time, that is, at the hour that God has appointed for them, not only to what is *ordinary* in each stage of perfection but also to many most precious things that are truly *extraordinary*, or considered as such, which things in the divine plan are nonetheless even now in readiness for the faithful accomplishment of the very special and ever-glorious mission that the Lord wants to entrust to each one of us, and that He will in fact entrust to us, endowing us with the respective graces, if we do not make ourselves unworthy of them but duly prepare ourselves to receive them.

How disastrous, then, is the delusion of those who have so many aspirations as regards human honors and dignities, which are so difficult to obtain, so soon come to an end, and present so many dangers and responsibilities—for which great perfection in virtue is required—and yet, as regards the latter, which is what truly ennobles and never perishes, whereas they are easily able to reach the highest degree, they are content with the lowest, merely with what they call commonplace and ordinary.[119]

And the worst is that, accustomed to regard as "extraordinary" that which is not completely customary in ordinary people, this weakness of theirs leads them to be satisfied with what is virtue in appearance only, or is pure formality; or, not to force and do violence to themselves in the conquest of the kingdom of God, or enter along the narrow path that Jesus Christ pointed out to us, trying each day to make progress and rise higher, all they do is to recede and fall back. They expose themselves to dangerous undertakings and to falling from abyss to abyss, being already on the slope of that fatal "broad way," spacious, the "high road," along which go the many who are satisfied with little. Thus, they are left without anything and are going straight to their perdition. Lord, open their eyes! Show them your paths! "Who is wise, and he shall understand these things? prudent, and he shall know these things? for the ways of the Lord are right, and the just shall walk in them" (Hos. 14:10).

II. Excellence of the Contemplative Life in Comparison with the Active, and of the Mixed or Apostolic Life over Both

This will be clear if we merely reflect that the true excellence of the Christian life is measured by [the soul's] degree of charity, and charity cannot come to its perfection except with the contemplative life. When it is already truly perfect, since true love cannot be idle, it necessarily tends to express itself in that burning zeal and prodigious activity that, in the midst of their most sublime and almost continuous contemplation, the great mystics show.[120]

For this reason it is said in Ezekiel (1:8): "And they had the hands of a man under their wings." "The hands are under the wings," remarks Fr. Juan de los Ángeles (*In Cant.*, 2, 8), "in order that, when the flight of contemplation is over, the contemplative may exercise himself in some work of virtue."

Charity, indeed, to be stirred to life and to grow, needs to be revived with the fire of holy meditation (Ps. 38:4). It never reaches the perfection required until it is established in the mystical "cellar" of contemplation through the sublime gift of wisdom,[121] which makes us enjoy and appreciate divine things,[122] know them from experience, and judge with certitude, and according to God, of human affairs.[123]

Hence the essential perfection and true efficacy of the works of zeal of the active life come from the latter's being more or less informed and stimulated by the contemplative life:[124] without some share in this last it scarcely merits the name of Christian life; for it would be almost purely natural without the spirit of faith and of true hope, and therefore there would result a life wholly sterile, feeble, and at every step in danger of perishing.[125] For this reason St. Thomas says that "to be in the state of salvation it is necessary to share in some measure in divine contemplation."[126]

And if the external work of the active life is already a proof of love and merits love's reward, this in itself is accidental; the true, essential reward depends chiefly on the degree of charity that is fostered and even manifests itself much better in the interior work of contemplation than in the external one of action. For this reason the contemplative life is in itself more excellent than the active life.[127]

However, this very external exercise of devotion, moderated and informed by a certain interior life, helps greatly and prepares us to advance in contemplation. Thus, the true active Christian life, stimulating the soul and establishing it in virtue, far from being an obstacle, as some suppose, is a preparation for the contemplative life.[128] To this, in this way, may attain even those who through their fiery nature would appear most refractory.[129]

Once that, by means of divine contemplation, the soul has arrived at the stage where it is perfected in Christ, it will now be able, this being the case, to work with perfection in everything and to communicate to its neighbors, in the exercise of the active life, the lights and graces that to this end it has received from God — not what it had of its own store, which was ignorance and wretchedness. Thus it is that, however hidden its life, it will be able, as the Doctors say, to do more good now in a single day than previously in months and years of much activity.[130]

Consequently, the perfect and fruitful active life presupposes contemplation as its support and counterpoise and as the source of all its true efficacy.[131] Unless the former is well rooted in it, it is either reduced to mere appearances, which make much show without any lasting fruit, or at most it is an imperfect and impoverished life, whose fruit is very scarce, and more than anything serves as a preparation for the contemplative life. In the latter it will then be able to find the fruitfulness and stability that it lacks, since the perfection and heroism of virtue have to come from the gifts of the Holy Spirit, which only acquire their full development in that intimate converse with God that comes by means of prayer and contemplation.

Hence it is that souls who have little love for the interior life, however much zeal they may appear to show and however much activity they may display, as this is all full of imperfections and human views and is not wholly from God nor "according to knowledge," seldom produce fruit worthy of mention. All is smoke and noise, whereas true and fruitful activity is very silent, patient, and modest. The true fruits of blessing and of life presuppose much fervor and recollection and much vigilance in the guard of the heart, avoiding the noise and bustle of the world.[132]

No one, indeed, can give what he has not got, nor influence others, except to the extent of his own dispositions. The imperfect soul, careless or with little fervor, not yet sufficiently possessed with the zeal of God nor enriched with an abundance of divine treasures to communicate, and not taking care to have recourse to the feet of the Lord with continual prayer, in order to seek what it so much lacks, can only give from the impoverished fruits of its wretched store. With these, instead of strengthening and enriching others, it will end by being impoverished and weakened itself.[133]

But once a soul has succeeded, by means of self-denial and the interior life, in stripping itself of its own view of things and its own wretchedness and putting on Jesus Christ, then it will continually be able to give from the inexhaustible treasures of the divine Heart, with which it will always be in holy communication, thus receiving most abundant graces in showers from Christ's fullness and shedding them upon others, without illusion or deceit.[134]

Thus, what is then being given to souls is no longer something of the giver's own, nor that soul itself with all its vanity and wretchedness. It gives them the divine treasures in all their purity and makes them share more and more in God Himself, always preaching Jesus Christ and seeking His divine glory without ever going after worldly things. Hence, in a single day, such a soul will be able to distribute more graces and blessings from Heaven than other less perfect souls in many days and months of great labor, and than the imperfect throughout their whole life.[135] "He that abideth in me, and I in him," saith the Lord (John 15:5), "the same beareth much fruit: for without me you can do nothing." In whatever state and condition it may live, however hidden it may be and however useless a soul wholly united with God may appear, it will not be able to help always influencing its neighbors for good at least with its prayers and sacrifices.[136] It will always be giving forth the good odor of Christ, with which it will heal and gain for Him very many hearts.

The truly just and perfect interior and spiritual man, set as he is by the "river of water of life, clear as crystal, proceeding from the throne of God and of the Lamb," not only does not fail to give in each spiritual harvest, that is, on every opportune occasion, the appropriate fruit of the Holy Spirit, but even his very leaves, that is, all his exterior bearing and his manner of procedure, are "healing of the nations" (Rev. 22:1-2). How different from the man who lives carelessly and contents himself with a certain external formalism.[137]

No one can be called a "perfect Christian" unless he is conformed in all things to his divine Master (Luke 6:40). Christ withdrew to the desert before entering upon public life and then spent whole nights in prayer, and His days healing the sick and preaching.

The perfect soul, aflame as it now is in the fire of divine love, cannot keep this fire hidden in its breast and remain silent and idle. It necessarily tends to show and communicate it to others. Thus, it will not be able to content itself with its own fire but, even without thinking of or realizing it, will at the same time give light and warmth to many.[138] As the fervor of charity gradually increases, it will produce great living flames of love that not only give light to minds but kindle hearts and set them ablaze. His ardors are now lamps of "fire and flames": they give out *the flames of Yahweh*, as the Hebrew text puts it (Song of Sol. 8:6). Who, then, will be able to resist them? There are not sufficient waters to quench that fire of charity, nor can rivers cover over and hide it.[139] A single soul would thus be sufficient to set the whole world ablaze, if the world were not so refractory to this divine fire that the Savior came to set upon the earth with so much desire for it to be enkindled (Luke 12:49).

There has never been a soul well advanced in union with God who, in imitation of the most Blessed Virgin, did not draw many others after it, to lead and present them to the King of Glory (Ps. 44:15-16). The very perfect bring innumerable souls; and one alone of those who have attained to the sublime stage of *spiritual marriage*, and even to *espousals*, is enough to give intense pleasure to our Lord, appease His anger, and cause Him to change punishments into blessings, in this way coming to the salvation of great communities and great religious orders, of cities, provinces, and even whole kingdoms.[140]

On the other hand, he who is not sufficiently united with Christ, so that our Lord always remains before his eyes, will not succeed in producing true fruits of life, however much he may labor (John 15:4-5). He will have nothing to give or to trade with God with, nor will God bless what is not done in Him and for Him alone.[141] Thus in vain do we rise to work before being illumined with the divine light, and without having taken rest and gathered sufficient strength in prayer: "It is vain for you to rise before light" (Ps. 126:2).[142]

Consequently, prelates and preachers, as they have to feed the flock of God, which is always hungry or in need of good pasturage and at all hours of the words of eternal life, need to be well provided with heavenly riches, to communicate the divine treasures and not their own wretchedness, and to give in abundance without impoverishing themselves, giving Jesus as the Eternal Father gives Him to us, that is, retaining Him in His bosom, at the same time that He sends Him to us and communicates Him to us for our good. Intimately united with Jesus Christ, it will be Him whom they preach and whom they give for the good of souls; and in this way they will not preach or give themselves with great danger of losing souls and being lost themselves instead of gaining others. On the contrary, they will gain even more themselves.

Accordingly, as the Angelic Doctor teaches, they should be already perfect in both lives, active and contemplative, in order to be able worthily to discharge their most sublime ministry,[143] knowing how to sacrifice without danger to themselves, even the very pleasure of conversing with God, to go and serve Him in their neighbors.[144]

Then indeed they will produce most abundant fruits of life and will be truly "the light of the world and salt of the earth," when they are so enriched with the wealth of Heaven that they can give from it without losing anything. Then they will be at the height of perfection that is required for the apostolic life, which surpasses contemplative life itself, as does the latter the life that is purely active, for it is a greater thing to burn and give light, than to content oneself merely with burning; and it is a greater thing to have sufficient for oneself and for others than for oneself alone. This full abundance the apostle should have, to be able, without loss to himself, to be *all for all*.[145]

By being truly apostolic men, that is, interior, spiritual, contemplative, full of light and divine fervor, and thus knowing not only by study but also by their own experience the life of grace, that is, how to become true directors and pastors after the divine Heart, who will feed souls with knowledge and the doctrine of salvation.[146]

Thus the very grave evils that St. John of the Cross[147] and with him all true servants of God and the masters of the spiritual life deplore so much as coming from bad direction and the great dearth of learned and experienced directors will be avoided.[148] For "where there is no knowledge of the soul there is no good."[149]

On the other hand, if the generality of the ministers of God are what they should be and are always devoted to study and prayer in order to learn how to discharge their sacred functions in a holy manner, they will succeed in drinking until they are inebriated from the stream of divine delights, whence they will come forth radiant with light and burning with love. Then the whole Christian people will come to be filled to the full with heavenly riches:

"And I will fill the soul of the priests with fatness; and my people shall be filled with my good things" (Jer. 31:14).

From this truly apostolic burning zeal, and from the fruitful and prodigious activity we see all contemplatives display, to the very great profit of souls—all contemplatives of whatever state, sex, and condition they may be—from St. Paul, St. Bernard, and St. Dominic down to the holy Curé of Ars and St. John Bosco, and from St. Catherine of Siena and St. Teresa, down to St. Madeleine Sophie Barat, the Bl. Anna Maria Taigi, Madre Sacramento, and others—for, as St. Teresa herself observes, there is none who does not bring many others after himself; from the very great good that these intimate friends of God everywhere produce, we can gather how blessed the world would be if the gift of contemplation abounded in it, as it will abound, relatively speaking, if we truly try to banish all the prejudices there are against it and the very many obstacles that are put in its way.

One of the principal obstacles is the erroneous and fatal idea so deeply rooted, that the reason why the mystics are so few is because few are called; as if the Lord did not invite us all to drink of the mystical waters and enter into His mystical rest, and as if it were not we who are guilty for despising such a loving invitation. The worst is that, to justify their own neglect, some do not fail to go so far as to defend—as if instead of being a lamentable fact, it were something fortunate and providential—the fact that in reality there should be few souls consecrated to that life, which they consider idle and sterile and liable to many illusions and aberrations, or mental disturbances and neurasthenia; and that, "if all were mystics, human life would be impossible."

Unfortunately, all will *never* come to be so, not even the majority, however much the prosecution of so great a good may be inculcated and rendered easy; for this demands a great deal of abnegation, fidelity, and generosity; and, in spite of all, what is most common is resistance to grace and that we do not even do that which we are most strictly obliged to do.

But if by a miracle of Providence this should at some future time come to pass, the harmony of human life and societies will never run better or more smoothly; for never will the true duties of each particular state of life be fulfilled with such sincerity and dignity. In proof of this and to remove the error, God has willed that in all states and all legitimate professions there should be true saints who might serve the others as a model. And we see that no one has known how to discharge their various duties with entire perfection, as the saints did, even though in so doing they seemed to be further away from the things of the spirit.[150]

If it is certain, indeed, that there were never bishops, priests, or religious so excellent as those who came to be saints, it is equally certain, if we examine the matter carefully, that we shall not find kings, politicians, or even warriors—not to mention humble artisans and honest laborers—who can compete [in their respective functions] with those who wear the halo of sanctity—with a David, a St. Henry, a St. Louis, or a St. Ferdinand.

Seeking first the kingdom of God and His justice, such souls will come to receive all the rest in addition, and at times even a hundredfold. "Godliness is profitable to all things, having promise of the life that now is, and of that which is to come" (1 Tim. 4:8). Thus "He who should come to be free from human wretchedness and weaknesses, will be a precious and sanctified vessel useful before the Lord and ready for every kind of good works" (cf. 2 Tim. 2:21). For with divine wisdom all good things come together;[151] and in the abundance of its possessors is the salvation of the earth.

If, at times, to test people more, the Lord permits them to seem useless, very often, as St. Catherine of Genoa says, He gives them some compensating factor so that, although apparently idle, they will each do singly what not even twenty very hardworking people together would do.

Here, then, as Fr. Weiss remarks (*Apologia* X, Conf. 13, appendix), is what is most necessary today and the one thing that would bring an effective remedy to all the evils that afflict humanity: an abundance of spiritual souls, of holy souls, of contemplative and mystical souls in all states and conditions of life.

"Thou shalt send forth thy spirit, and they shall be created: and thou shalt renew the face of the earth" (Ps. 103:30). Amen.

Appendix 1

Referring to Chapter 1

Participation in the Mysteries of Christ

Every Christian, says the Ven. Olier, should share in a general way in all the mysteries of Jesus Christ, and in a special way in the following six: the Incarnation, Crucifixion, Death, Burial, Resurrection, and Ascension.

1. The mystery of the Incarnation brings about in us the grace of crushing all self-interest and self-love. Just as by the ineffably sacred mystery of the Incarnation the holy humanity of our Lord Jesus Christ was submerged in his own personality, so that he neither sought himself nor had any particular interest, nor worked for himself, for he had substituted the personality of the Son of God, who always sought the interest of his Father—so we ought to be dead, so to speak, to all designs of our own, to all personal interest, in order to have only the designs and interests of Jesus Christ. He is in us in order to live there also for his Father, saying to us as it were (cf. John 6:58), "As my Father sent me, cutting [off] from me every root of

self-seeking, withholding human personality from me, but uniting me to a Divine Person to make me live by him—thus when you eat me, you live by me and not of yourselves, for I fill your soul with my desires and my very life, which should consume and crush in you all that is your own, so that I may be the one who lives in you and desires it all and thus, stripped in yourselves, you will be clothed with me." This putting on of Jesus Christ is a second grace of the mystery of the Incarnation, for the latter produces in us that complete self-stripping which clothes us with our Lord through a total consecration of our being, just as he, when he became incarnate, consecrated all his members, sanctifying both ours and his, for the service and glory of his Father. And every day he continues this unceasing oblation, offering himself always, both in himself and in his members, on that altar on which every sacrifice is consummated. Jesus and the joint assembly of all his children form the victim. His Spirit is the fire and God the Father, adored in spirit and in truth, is the one to whom the sacrifice is offered.

2. The mystery of the Crucifixion gives us grace and strength to crucify all our members with the power of the divine Spirit. It is he who carries into effect the sentence pronounced against the flesh. The nails which he uses are the virtues which subdue self-love and carnal desires. This state presupposes, then, that the soul is still living to herself but struggling, and that the divine Spirit makes use of violence to mortify and crucify the body.

3. We share in the mystery of the Death of our Lord by Holy Communion, when we receive him in the state of victim and also receive the grace which he acquired

for us in this mystery. In the state of death, the innermost recesses of the heart do not move, however many disturbances or impressions come to it from without. The Christian is, then, so to speak, impervious to all, for he is dead in our Lord. "For you are dead ..." (Col. 3:3). Attacks may be felt and there may be great disturbance outwardly, but the inward self is at peace and is disturbed by nothing, since it is, as it were, dead and insensitive to the things of the world, because of that intimate divine life which absorbs into itself all that is mortal (2 Cor. 5:4).

4. Burial differs from death in that the dead man may still be seen by all, but the person who is buried disappears completely and comes to be forgotten and trodden underfoot.... The state of death merely indicates a condition of coherence, solidity and insensitiveness; but burial means putrefaction, the total destruction of ourselves and the producing of the germ of a new life. As, when the grain of wheat is buried a new plant springs to life from it, so when the old Adam in us is buried and destroyed, we are reborn to the life of the spirit, to rise again to that new divine life which the Holy Spirit produces there with all the effects and movements of sanctity which accompany it.... In the mystery of our Lord's burial we see his divine life being born again from within the tomb where the "wheat of the chosen" had been buried.

5. The mystery of the Resurrection gives us a grace of withdrawal from the things of this world and from all that is not God, and of a detachment from the present life which makes us long unceasingly for the homeland, like our Lord Jesus Christ, who, when he was risen, ardently

longing to be with his Father as he did, could scarcely live even with his disciples and did not allow Magdalen to approach him. The state of sanctity into which the risen soul enters presupposes detachment from everything in this present life.

6. The mystery of the Ascension implies a state of triumph and consummation in God in which anything that would seem to be wretchedness or human weakness is no longer apparent. Our Lord, when he was risen, had nothing of this; but he still retained certain signs of it, as when he stripped himself at times and in part, of his glory and made himself visible and palpable to his disciples. But after his Ascension, his glory could no longer brook any overshadowing, and the splendour of it was such that human eyes could not bear it. Thus he remains hidden in the bosom of his Eternal Father, and in union with him, sends us the Holy Spirit. Hence also it comes about that when a soul, by the grace that flows from this wonderful mystery, enters the sublime state of the divine Ascension, it receives from our Saviour a marvellous sharing in his Divinity, remaining so transparent with his very brightness, so inflamed with his love, so transformed into him and so deified that by its fervent aspirations and transports of charity, it too, after its own manner, sends the Holy Spirit to the hearts of the rest of the faithful, obtaining abundant graces for them. Such is the state of a soul already confirmed in virtue and perfectly conformed to Christ. (cf. M. Olier, *Catéchisme chrétien pour la vie intérieure*, pt. 1, lec. 20-25; St. Mary Magdalen of Pazzi, *Works*, pt. 1, c. 3-4 — in *Evolución mística*, pp. 512-513)

Mystical Death and the New Life

"The life of Jesus Christ," observes Fr. Grou (*Manuel pour les âmes intérieures*: "Sur la vie nouvelle en Jésus-Christ"),

> was a continual death, that is, a mystical death whose final act and consummation was natural death on the cross. Thus the new life which fervent souls must lead in Jesus Christ is nothing else but a continual dying to themselves. It is to die to the smallest sins and even to the slightest imperfections, to die to the world and to all outward things, to die to the senses and to the immoderate care of the body, to die to our character and natural defects, to die to our own will, to the esteem and love of ourselves and even to spiritual consolations, to die to support and security with respect to the state of our soul; in short, it is to die to all sense of ownership—or attachment—in matters concerning sanctity. It is through these different stages of death that the mystical life of Jesus Christ is established in us, and when the final death-blow has been given, then Jesus Christ raises us up again, communicating to us, even here below, the qualities of his life of glory in so far as it is possible in this world. Let us review briefly these different stages of dying to self.

> "Death to the smallest sins and slightest imperfections": the first resolution a soul that wants to be wholly God's must take is never knowingly and deliberately to commit the least fault ...; and not to refuse God anything it sees he is asking for, or to say: "This is a small thing, God will overlook this trifle in me." This resolution is essential and must be persevered in with unbroken fidelity. This

does not mean that faults will not escape the soul, first movements, faults of inadvertence, of frailty; but these, as they are neither foreseen nor deliberate, do not hinder us in the way of perfection.

"Death to the world and to all outward things." That is, the world must no longer be either loved or sought. We must concede to it only that which is absolutely essential and which God himself wills that we concede to it. We should groan in our hearts and feel pain at having to have even these indispensable dealings with it. The world, then, is no longer to be respected, nor are we to take account of its judgements, nor to fear its scorn, mockery and persecutions, nor to be ashamed, in its presence, of our duties or of putting the Gospel into practice, nor may we turn aside from such practice in any way, whatever the world may say....

"The death to the senses" requires that we be on our guard against softness, love of ease and sensuality; that we do not give to the body more than is necessary in the way of food, sleep and clothing; that we mortify it from time to time with privations and, in addition, if our health permits, if God inspires us to do so and our confessor approves, impose on it certain afflictive mortifications.

"Death to the character" implies its reform—a difficult matter this—so that what good there is in it is preserved and what is defective, corrected.... The means of achieving this is to look to the guard of the heart and restrain one's first movements, neither acting nor speaking according to our first impulse, but maintaining ourselves in peace and self-possession....

"Death to one's own will and own judgement" is a thing extensive in scope and difficult in practice. Before all, in ordinary matters one has to try to submit one's own taste and one's own will to reason, not allowing oneself to be carried away by caprices and fantasies, and deferring to the opinion of others when it is reasonable.... In our spiritual conduct, we should receive with simplicity what God gives us, stay as he places us, without desiring anything else.... We must practise obedience to our director and control the activity of our mind, always keeping ourselves in dependence upon God and refraining from reflecting upon ourselves.... In general, we must try to keep our mind and heart in a certain emptiness, so that God may put what he wills there, to his good pleasure....

"Death to the esteem and love of ourselves." As we can see, this death ought to be increasingly more penetrating, for the most deeply rooted thing we have is pride and self-love, which are the great enemies of God and of ourselves. God combats and persecutes them without quarter in a soul which has given itself to him. It has only to allow him to act and to second him when the opportunity arises.

"Death to spiritual consolations." When God withdraws these, because he wants, so to speak, to wean the soul, the latter finds pleasure in nothing. Everything is troublesome, wearies and tires it. It no longer feels the presence of God, and although it is at peace, it cannot realize this or even believe it has peace.... The soul must be generous and accept these privations, accustoming itself not to seek itself in anything, loving God with pure, disinterested love and servicing him for himself alone and to its own cost. At this time the service of God costs much to nature, which cries out and complains.... And we have to let it cry and be more faithful than ever.... We have to drag the victim to the sacrifice, without paying any attention to its repugnance.

"Death to spiritual support...." So long as the soul, in the midst of its temptations and trials, finds a certain support in the depths of conscience or in what its director says, it is not so difficult for it to bear the greatest trials. But when it finds itself, as it were, suspended in the void, and sees hell at its feet, when it has nothing to cling to for support, and is every moment nigh to falling—in a word, when it is convinced that God has abandoned it and that it is irrevocably lost, and when, instead of there being someone to undeceive it, everything concurs to confirm it in this belief, then its anguish is great indeed, and it needs heroic courage to persevere and submit to what God may will for it for all eternity.

"Death to all claims in respect of sanctity." As the soul has—in a certain manner—appropriated to itself the gifts of God, the virtues with which he has enriched it, and has taken a certain complacency in its purity, God strips it of everything, not in reality, but apparently, reducing it to complete nothingness, so that it can no longer see in itself either gifts, or virtues, or anything supernatural. It no longer knows what it is, or what it was, or what it will become. Its sins, its nothingness, its reprobation—that is what it sees in itself and what it believes itself worthy of. Such is the consummation of the mystical death. But resurrection and the state of glory are near at hand.

The Generous and Total Gift of Self and the Laws of Love

"Ah, Lord," exclaimed the Ven. Ana María de San José (*Autobiography*, n. 48),

> if we really leave ourselves in your hands and put all our faith, hope and love in you, our King, all good things come to us together, all success, all happiness, all achievements! How God rewards a resolute and confident determination that with generous heart resolves to seek the pearl of great price, that is, God himself! Afterwards, when with love, the soul leaves all for all to embrace the All through love, it never seems to it that it has done anything, or left or suffered anything. All is given it for nothing, gratuitously, for love teaches it the privilege of serving for love's sake. How the divine Master gives it delight! But how he mortifies it! In what a way does he withdraw it from its inclinations, at one time with delights so that it does not lose courage and faint by the way, and afterwards, when it is strengthened in virtue, with absences and loneliness! For he likes to be sought for love and that the soul should seek the glory of God and not its spiritual comfort—for we have already seen that other comforts are not admitted in the laws of love—for all one's comfort is to accommodate oneself to the divine and renounce all there is which is of Adam. With what artifice, then, does he who is the highest wisdom and prudence rule the soul, how does he console it, how does he suffer its irregularities and meannesses? He favours it in such a way that it appears that with the effects that remain from his mercies, all is

already won, that not only are there now no enemies, but that none will dare [to attack]. When the soul is in this state of joy, what it thought was vanquished rises up again and causes disturbance, conflict and fears; for as it pleases God so much that we should possess and esteem his gifts with humility, when by practice and grace the virtues have been acquired and our inclinations mortified, he will bring supernatural warfare and battles upon the soul. Since he is the very King of peace and has overcome nature with his grace, in order that the stone may be well and truly wrought [he tests it] not only with the conquest of vices, but with the custody of the fees of love, for which there are very strict rules. If the soul is naturally careless, love makes it cautious and careful in the midst of its heedlessness; and, since through love it is as simple as a dove, he also makes it cautious. Finally, since it is unadorned, candid and simple, he makes it careful of itself and prudent. Being always in the sleep of prayer, it watches over itself, for it is love that both lulls to sleep and causes remembrance.

Appendix 2

Referring to Chapter 2

How Excellent, Profitable, and Necessary Is the Exercise of Prayer: The Difficulties It Offers

"We understand by prayer," said Bl. John of Ávila (*Audi filia*, ch. 70),

a secret and interior conversation in which the soul communicates with God, thinking, asking, giving thanks, contemplating; and in general all that which in such secret conversation passes between the soul and God....

If men were not blind, it would be sufficient to tell them that God was giving audience, so that all those who wished to do so might go in and speak with him once in the month, or during the week, and that he would most willingly give them a hearing and remedy their evils and grant them favours. Thus between him and them there would be friendly converse as between a father and his children. If he were to give permission for them to speak to him each day, or even many times a day; if, also, for all night and all day, or for whatever time that they could be and wanted to be in converse with the Lord, he was pleased to hear them—who would be the man, unless he were a stone, who would not be delighted at such a long and profitable permission, and not try to make use of it all the time he possibly could, as a thing most precious for his honour, for he would be talking with his Lord, delight, for he would be enjoying this converse, and profit, for he would never go away from God's presence empty-handed? Why do not men delight in being with God, since his delights are to be with the children of men? "When I go into my house, I shall repose myself with her: for her conversation hath no bitterness, nor her company any tediousness, but joy and gladness" (Wisd. 8:16). Neither is there any lack in him so that he will refuse what is asked. Moreover, he is our Father, with whom we ought to enjoy talking, even if no advantage were to come to us from it. If you add to this the fact that not only does God give us leave to speak to him, but that he asks, counsels and sometimes commands us to do so, you will see how great is his goodness and how great his desire that we should converse with him, and how wrong it is of us not to want to do so when we are asked and also rewarded for it, whereas *we* ought to be begging for the favour and offering whatever might be asked of us. In this you will see how little awareness men have of spiritual necessities, which are our true needs, for he who has true realization of them prays in all sincerity and with much insistence asks for help.

"I value your love more," said Christ to His servant Sr. Mariana de Santo Domingo Riosoto (1743–1794), a Dominican nun of Seville (cf. *Life*, 1901, p. 132), "than they do mine. I go through their doors begging and pleading, and I give much if men give me their hearts. But though they see me wearied, lonely and perspiring from weakness they do not give them to me ... and to avoid being obliged to do so, they turn their thoughts away from me and leave me without an answer. They do not want my love, daughter; and thus I come to find consolation with you. Separate yourself from creatures and you will always have me with you."

"All the good of the soul," remarks the Ven. Mary of Agreda (*Escala para subir a la perfección*, § 6),

> is in practising prayer. Although this be so, there are very few who observe it. This was the complaint that my King and Lord made to me on one occasion.... He told me that those who sought to enter into converse with His Majesty were very few.... How is this, Lord? Perhaps this conversation is with some creature that causes us weariness. It is, perhaps, an affair in which we can lose something, since so few care for it? No, indeed. Rather from this communion and intercourse all good is to come to us. It is intercourse with the great King and powerful Lord of all, with him who forgives sinners, enlightens the ignorant, bestows favours upon his friends and rewards the just. He has both the power and the will to do so. He loves and enriches. Who is there, then, who will not come? How dim our sight must be that we do not see this and do not seek so great a good! Here we shall find rest in our labours, relief in sickness, balm for our wounds and wings so that our spirit may fly to its Creator. Oh, how many ills can come to us from not

going to this fountain, and how much good if we seek it with eagerness.

But, from the very fact that it is of such great value, it ought to cost us something; and God allows us to feel thousands of difficulties in it, for the most part caused through the ill-will of our enemy.

"As the devil," Ven. Mary of Agreda continues,

knows the good we acquire, and the advantage that he loses through our persevering in prayer, he puts all his efforts into hindering or preventing it. And in particular, he tries to bring about great slackness and cowardice in souls who are beginning it. He causes in them certain fears, in some that they will not succeed in attaining to it, that their nature is not suited to it; in others that they cannot control their faculties, that it is doing harm to their health. He raises mountains of difficulties.... All this confusion does the devil bring; and it all causes much affliction and great distress in the soul. At this time everything afflicts it, so much so, that the soul would rather go to any other toil, however great it be, even were it to rowing a boat, than to prayer.... Many are those who do not pass beyond this point. The devil is not conquered, it is the soul who is left vanquished....

Would that this harm could be remedied and all souls in the world encouraged not to leave this treasure, but to nourish themselves with the hope of finding it! What is necessary is great determination to overcome everything. Others have attained to this good and there is thus no reason that any soul should fail to obtain it. Were it only to reach such a happy state as that of being special friends of God, who would not resolve to yearn after this happiness? In this resolution and in much faithful effort all good consists.

"The difficulty," she adds (§ 19),

is not after having tasted the Lord's sweetness, but before tasting it, and even to taste so sweet a thing we had to make a beginning and to strive much. On account of the difficulties and temptations which arise—and they will be many and varied—we should not lose heart, but trust in God's faithfulness and hope in his mercy that he will be master, and will take it all upon himself. Let the soul draw near and resign itself to the divine will and with resolute determination begin and persevere, for it is certain and more than certain that God is favouring and teaching it.

What do I do to you in prayer? Do I not listen to you? Do I not give you delight? Do I not give you light? Do I not give you tenderness? Do I not forgive you?... Do I not stir your wills to fervour? Do I not delight your minds? Do I not give sweetness to your souls? Do I not purify your consciences?... Why, then, do you flee?... Why do you not stay in my presence? Yes, stay in my presence, for I am like the flower which gives out more fragrance, the more it is touched and handled. If you want to breathe my perfumes, stay in my presence, do not let go of my hand, and you will see how you will walk in the odour of these perfumes, as spouses do.... Pray, for if you are sinful, I will make you good; if lukewarm, I will make you fervent; if you are imperfect, you will find perfection. Pray and you will come to know what I am for you. (Bl. Francis Posada, O.P., *Carta del esposo*, no. XX)

"The spiritual life," says Father Faber,

is quite a cognizably distinct thing from the worldly life; and the difference comes from prayer. When grace lovingly drives a man to give himself up to prayer, he gets into the power of prayer, and prayer makes a new man of him; and so completely does he find that his life is prayer, that at last he prays always. His life itself becomes one unbroken prayer. Unbroken because ... it is an attitude of heart by which all his actions and sufferings become living prayers.

The life of prayer, therefore, which is the badge of the supernatural man, is the praying always.... To pray always is always to feel the sweet urgency of prayer and to hunger after it....

This influence of prayer comes out in a man's opinions and judgements of men, measures and things. It is heard in his language.... It is recognized in his dealings with others, and is the ruling principle of his occasional apparent want of sympathy with others.... To the eyes of the world such a man has all the strangeness and awkwardness of a foreigner, which in sober truth he is. (F. W. Faber, *Growth in Holiness*, ch. 15, London, 1855)

Appendix 3

Referring to Chapter 3

Important Counsels for Mental Prayer

Ven. Louis of Granada, in his *Compendio de la doctrina espiritual* (tr. 1: "Of Mental Prayer," ch. 27) gives, among other advice, the following:

1. "Whenever we set ourselves to consider some particular matter of those I have mentioned above, we ought not to be so attached to it that we consider it wrong to leave it for another, when we find more devotion, more pleasure or more profit in so doing.... This should not, however, be done for trivial reasons, but when its advantage is certain" (Bl. John of Ávila says almost the same in *Audi filia*, ch. 75).

2. A man should work to avoid too much speculation in this exercise ...; for that dissipates the mind rather than recollects it.... A man should come with the heart of an ignorant and humble little old woman, and with his will disposed and prepared to feel and find pleasure in the things of God, rather than with his mind eager and

anxious to scrutinize them, for that is the quality fitting for those who study in order to know.

Of all this varied advice, the chief thing is that he who prays should not be discouraged, nor desist from his exercise when he does not immediately feel the tenderness of devotion he desires. It is necessary to wait for the coming of the Lord with longanimity and perseverance; for it is in keeping with the glory of His Majesty, the lowliness of our condition and the exalted nature of the matter we are dealing with, that we should often be watching and waiting at the doors of his sacred palace. Then, when you have waited a little time in this way, if the Lord should come, give him thanks for his coming; and if it seem to you that he does not come, humble yourself before him and recognize that you do not deserve what you are not given. Content yourself with having made a sacrifice in this matter.... Believe me without hesitation, this is the most dangerous passage of our course at sea, and the place where those who are truly devout are tested, and if you come out of this well, all the rest will go prosperously for you.

In another place, namely, in the important treatise *De la oración* (ch. 9, § 1) he warns us that, even though it is ordinarily very fitting, especially for beginners, to have matter assigned for each meditation, yet in spite of this, if halfway through some other thought should present itself in which more sweetness and greater profit is found, one ought not to leave it merely in order to complete what one has begun. For there is no reason for rejecting the light that the Holy Spirit is beginning to give us in some good thought, in order to occupy ourselves in another, in which,

perh   will not give Himself to us. Besides this, as the prin-
ci   pose of these meditations is to acquire some devotion
          experience of divine things, it would be altogether unreason-
able that, when we have acquired this by some particular good
thought, we should go to seek in some other way that which we
have already acquired.

"Strive," he adds (ch. 9, § 2),

> to carry out this exercise, more with affections and feel-
> ings of the will, than with discoursing and speculation
> of the mind. For mind and will are, as it were, two bal-
> ances of our soul arranged in such a way that the rising
> of the one means the falling of the other....
>
> In this exercise we achieve success more by listening
> than by speaking; for, as the prophet said (Deut. 22),
> those who reach the feet of the Lord will receive of his
> teaching; as he who said (Ps. 84): *I will hear what the Lord
> God speaketh within me*, received it. For this, then, all one's
> endeavour should be to speak little and love much and
> to give freedom to the will that it may cleave to God with
> all its strength.

In addition, he continues (§ 3), "The devotion which we are
endeavouring to acquire is not a thing which has to be acquired
by force of arms, as some think."

Fr. La Puente (*Guía*, tr. 1, ch. 1, § 6), comparing prayer with
Jacob's ladder, says:

> Those who mount by these sovereign exercises to the
> very summit have to be angels in purity of life, stripping
> themselves of earthly affections.... You must not pre-
> sume to rise to the height of contemplation in a single

flight ... but first you have to practise quietude and repose in the other acts which dispose towards it.... You
must continue these exercises each day without stopping
or interrupting them. But [this] in such a way that you
never lose courage through seeing that you are very far
from resembling an angel and from reaching the summit
of the ladder; for prayer itself has the power to turn men
into angels and helps them to mount all these steps. And
even though you do not reach the summit, you will not
fail to derive much profit.

To this piece of advice he adds another, perhaps the most
important for fervent souls, namely:

Rules and regulations which are given should be interpreted
in such a manner that one chiefly bases oneself on the teaching of the Holy Spirit, paying more attention to practising
them than to knowing about them, without ever binding
oneself to the order in which they are set down. For even
though it is very important to know all this and in the beginning to observe it exactly, afterwards ... he who prays and
contemplates perfectly performs this work without remem-
bering the rules...; for to attend too much to this [i.e., the
rules] generally hinders the principal thing which is aimed
at.... Perfect prayer absorbs the mind so that it does not
make these reflections, nor remember any other thing but
God, in whose presence it is. For this reason among others,
the least learned are usually the most devout, because they
reason less and pray with sincerity without regard to the
manner in which their minds work. They taste the sweetness of this music of heaven all the more for being less occupied at the time in considering the rules of the art.

"The order which has been set down here," remarks Fray Juan de Jesús María again (*Escuela de oración*, tr. 2, q. 3: Lisbon, 1616), "is profitable so long as the soul does not feel itself drawn by the Lord in some other manner, but when it feels itself occupied at the first movement in petition (let us say) or in offering, it can well follow that impulse.... The soul should not be bound ... but be left free to attend primarily to the particular part to which affection most inclines it."

"It is not good," he adds (*Escuela de oración*, 9.4),

> to prepare many concepts or reasons, and then afterwards to repeat them artificially in one's prayer. What is needed is to be humble and simple, for in this way the soul is enlightened and comforted by the Lord with the reasons and thoughts with which he inspires it in the place of prayer. Similarly, one should not prepare the affection which one desires to obtain [from prayer] artificially, for if the meditation is good and rightly proportioned, the affection will be awakened by it.... It is not good to be too narrow, one should give the spirit freedom.

"[The soul] should understand for its part," says Fr. Tomás de Jesús (*Trabajos, avisos*, 9–12),

> that in all it does, it is only disposing and preparing itself for God to communicate himself to it and bring about in it with his gifts what he knows how to do in his power and wisdom.... Let it trust in God, who will operate his work in the soul in the manner that is most fitting.... Let it take care not to seek to be the judge of its own progress, nor to know or scrutinize the workings of God

in him. Our Lord many times does the works that we desire, without our realizing it, for this is good for us. On other occasions he lets us realize what he is doing at once, at other times, afterwards, he may desire that in this matter we should trust to his goodness, and that we on our part should always consider ourselves needy and imperfect and, being such, should not weary of calling upon him....

When [the soul] feels that the Lord is giving it tenderness of heart, and that its disposition is to linger over some one point, it should not pass from what is giving it devotion. As long as that spark lasts it should dwell on it lovingly, even though it spend the whole hour of the exercise upon it.... For, by fanning this spark, it can come to be live coals and grow into a flame of love, with which God works in the soul the desired change and the work that he intends to do. When it sees that that spark is dying away, it should return to the points of the exercise, but the soul is always left free that it may be inflamed with the love of our Lord in whatsoever way God may communicate his divine fire to it.

Many times it will happen to you that God will give you when you are not thinking of it what he refused you at the time of prayer, so that you may realize that all is due to his divine Majesty, and not to our work, and with this he enkindles our love and humiliates our pride....

By this means (the continual practice of the presence of God and fidelity to his inspirations) with perseverance in all things you may take it as certain that the Lord will open the door to you and scatter the cloud, and give you entrance into the house of the fragrant wine of his love and will establish charity in your soul, where, when he speaks, tongues will cease, and in peace and in the self-same you will sleep and take your rest.

"If you want to fortify and strengthen your heart in the way of God," said St. Bonaventure—and Louis of Granada repeats this (*Comp. de la doctrina espirit.*, tr. 1, "De la oración mental," ch. 1)—

> you must be a man of prayer.... If you want to uproot all the vices from your soul and plant virtues in their stead, you must be a man of prayer; for in prayer the grace and unction of the Holy Spirit who teaches all things, is received. Besides this, if you want to rise to the height of contemplation and enjoy the Bridegroom's sweet embrace, exercise yourself in prayer, for this is the way by which the soul rises to contemplation and enjoyment of heavenly things.
>
> For in every spiritual exercise, in all Christian warfare, nothing so reintegrates and guards the habit of the mind, the zeal for virtue, the eye of the heart, the desire of perfection, as the wrestling-ground of prayer. For prayer is an act of the mind directed by the light of wisdom and kindled by the warmth of the Holy Spirit, and when it is performed purely does not lack human counsel nor the adornment of words. In prayer the Paraclete teaches us what we ought to do when we pray, and how we ought to do it.... The working of *true* prayer is not within man's own power. It is for God alone to confer the gift of this, as of the other virtues. (St. Lawrence Justinian, *De casto connubio Verbi et animae*, ch. 22)

"Prayer," according to St. John Climacus (*Scale*, ch. 29),

is the union of man with God.... Strive as much as is in your power to raise your mind heavenwards and even at times to draw it away from adverting to the meaning of the very words you are saying, to suspend it in God, as far as is possible.... If you persevere continually and courageously in this exercise, he who will put an end and boundary to the sea of your thoughts will soon come to you....

The beginning of that prayer which is well made is that a man should drive away from himself at once and deny entrance to the wave upon wave of thoughts which arise.... The means to this is that our whole mind should be attentive to what we are saying or thinking; but the end to which it is designed is that we should be transported and carried away into God.

"... Always have firm courage and constancy in this exercise; thus you will have God as the master of your prayer, and he will teach you how you ought to pray.

"The soul then becomes aware," writes St. John of the Cross (*Living Flame*, can. 3, v. 3, 4), "that in this business God is the principal agent and the blind man's guide who has to guide us by the hand to a place to which we do not know the way. All our chief care must be to see that we put no obstacle in the path of him who is guiding us along the way that God has ordained for us in the perfection of love.... This impediment can come to us if we allow ourselves to be borne along and guided by some other blind person."

"When one feels oneself touched by grace," says Fr. Grou (*Maximes*, X),

however little, one cannot do better than to surrender, peacefully enjoying the feelings God gives us at that time; when the impression ceases, one should begin one's reading, etc., again. These passing touches are a small beginning of infused prayer, to which we ought to correspond with the greatest fidelity; they are momentary visits in which God communicates himself to us for a fleeting instant. Such visits, although brief, are of more profit to the soul than any thoughts or affections it might be able to produce itself. Why does one read, indeed, and why does one pray, if it is not to draw God to oneself? When he deigns to come, then, and through a certain secret impression lets us know that he is present, the soul already has what it desires. It should then content itself with this impression as long as it lasts. To do otherwise would be to fail in the respect due to God, to deprive ourselves of the fruit of his visits and to cause these to occur less frequently.

The principal effect of this recollection is to turn the soul inwards and to detach her from external objects.... This recollection is really the entering into the interior life, and the safest rule for seeing if a soul is really in the passive state.

St. Jane Chantal, for her part, used to give the following instructions for praying well:

1. We shall never enjoy familiarity with God if we do not resolve to follow him—with detachment and the faithful practice of all the virtues.... He who clings to interior sweetness and feelings does not know what it is to imitate Jesus Christ.... 2. What is most important is simplicity before God.... Happy are the souls who faithfully follow the divine impulse! The evil is that so often we

want to speculate and God does not want us to do anything more than love: let us abandon ourselves in all simplicity to his goodness, like a child in his mother's arms and at her breast.... 3. All the working of the human mind does is to harm us, guiding us along our own ways and not those of God. 4. When the affections are once moved, it is not good to multiply words; we should be still a little and enjoy this affection and let it sink into the heart.

The Most Salutary Influence of the Gifts of the Holy Spirit from the First Stages of Prayer

"Meditation and contemplation," remarks Fr. La Puente (*Guía*, tr. 3, ch. 3, no. 1),

> must be practical, and are ordained not only to knowing and loving, but to doing and carrying out the things God commands and counsels. For this we are helped with wonderful lights by means of the other four gifts (apart from the three which are chiefly operative in contemplation). The gift of counsel is a light with which the Holy Spirit reveals to us and inspires us as to what we have to do in his service, making us certain that it is he who is ordering it and that it is good for us to do it. Again, the gift of piety is a light similar to that of charity and by this the Holy Spirit gives us an affectionate delight in the things which belong to divine worship and in works of mercy in regard to our neighbour.... For this we are helped by the gift of fortitude with which the divine Spirit encourages us to undertake in his service

certain difficult things which exceed our ordinary strength, with great confidence that we shall succeed in them, and without fear of death itself.... Finally, with the gift of fear the Holy Spirit inspires us with the reverence we should have in his divine presence and what we should avoid if we are not to offend him.... These are the seven gifts with which the Holy Spirit enlightens our faith and vivifies our charity, by means of the lights and inspirations which he gives us through them. When you come to the exercises of the contemplative life, to pray, read, meditate or contemplate, you should always implore the Holy Spirit to kindle and trim these lamps, for without his light they are as it were extinguished. You should say to him with David (Ps. 17:29): "For thou lightest my lamp, O Lord: O my God, lighten my darkness." O divine Spirit, you who warm and burn like fire, set alight the gifts you have put in my faculties, so that with these gifts I may see and contemplate you, so that I may love and obey you and follow your directives in everything you may inspire me to through them.

Appendix 4

Referring to Chapter 4

The Director's Role

"The confessor," said the Ven. Marina de Escobar (*Life*, bk. 5, ch. 32, § 2),

should with great earnestness persuade the penitent who desires to make progress to practise the pursuit of continual prayer, and should set him down as far as possible at the gates of the divine mercy to ask for alms like another Lazarus. He ought to set him in the way of this practice along the ordinary road, as shown us by the saints, of prayer, meditation and giving of thanks ... and teach him to be continually mindful of God and his Presence. If, as he thus proceeds with this good, holy and profitable exercise, the Lord, who is master of all, should take him by the hand and set his soul in another way which is *not* so ordinary, the confessor ought not to turn him aside from it but ought to watch what the Lord is doing and guard his inheritance.

"To keep souls away from contemplation," the Ven. Madre Ángela María de la Concepción (*Riego espiritual*, ch. 28) used to say to her nuns, "would be to insist that they stop at the means and do not pass onto the end." "The general rule," she added (ch. 30),

> is that nobody should set herself to contemplation except when she cannot meditate; but if God should himself give her another occupation, she should accept it and not hinder the divine works with her own. For when God wants to possess a soul and work in it by grace, no impediment should be put in the way and the soul will put an impediment if it wants to make use to this end of its own diligence, since in so doing it does not receive God's lights purely. Neither will it be true humility to neglect to follow the inspiration of the Holy Spirit, whose love and gifts are given both to the perfect and to the imperfect—to the first to increase their perfection and to the second to draw them away from imperfection.... When the soul has enjoyed the spiritual good which God gives in meditation, his Majesty wants it to enjoy that of contemplation.... From this the soul does not receive any new profit neither does it receive pleasure.

Even the greatest contemplatives advise that at the beginning of one's prayer one should meditate, making a certain number of considerations calculated to bring one to the knowledge of the Creator's love, for contemplation also gives rise to meditation; but if by chance, having set themselves humbly to this end souls cannot meditate, they should resign themselves to the will of God, responding to his inspirations and call. They should trust in his goodness and he, seeing their love for him, will not let their labour go unrewarded. Let them ask and entreat, for they will be heard.

"Beginners," says Fr. Tomás de Jesús (*Trabajos de Jesús; Avisos*),

as they are new and have no experience, must necessarily be helped until they know how to proceed and do not need to be dependent on words or books; for to him who perseveres, Christ our Lord, *gives* words, motives, feelings, light, and interior affections, by which the heart is encouraged to run with confidence in the way of the Lord, the understanding is enlightened in the knowledge of Catholic truth and the will inflamed with love for what it believes and for the Lord who communicates himself and reveals himself to it interiorly, there teaching it more in a single moment than books and doctrine in a long space. But until this blessed hour arrives, or when the divine Sun of justice again covers over his rays, beginners need to make use of holy reading and Catholic teaching, with which the soul journeys without stopping or ceasing from the search for our Lord. For this reason the saints teach that those who do not know how to walk alone, until such time as God teaches them interiorly …, should always practise reading before prayer.

… He who has a master makes much profit in a short time, if he is receptive, as is seen in nuns who are well trained and established in the practice of spiritual things…. Where we see this method of training novices kept up … religious houses are filled with many men of spiritual valour and where there is not so much effort made in this direction, there are many who are good men but poor monks.

"In general," says Fr. Grou (*Manuel: Sur les réflexions dans l'oraison*, p. 320),

> so long as we are in the ordinary way and preserve the free use of the understanding, we should always proceed by reflection, applying ourselves to meditation although without tiring ourselves too much.... But there is a state in which reflections are dangerous and that is the obscure way of sheer faith. No one can put himself into this way of his own accord. It belongs to God alone to lead into it those souls on whom he has special designs.... The principal sign that one has been brought into it is to find that one no longer has one's former liberty in using one's faculties in prayer; also, when one can no longer apply oneself to a subject and draw reflections and affections from it but enjoys a certain delightful peace which is beyond all feeling and which holds one absorbed and forces one, if we may thus express it, to remain in repose and silence. When a prudent director has sufficiently tested this disposition in a soul,... there is no reason to doubt that it has been brought into the way of faith.

When mental prayer is at our door, meditation is rightly recognized to be superfluous and harmful. When, however, the former is wanting, the latter should be regarded as most useful and necessary. Meditation indeed leads to prayer, but mental prayer puts us in the presence of God and gives us possession of the Word, and the soul thus in possession of the Word gives forth a most pleasing sacrifice of praise.... And so for a long time it works at this business of meditating until through the frequency of mental prayer and fervour of love, it is joined to the Word. Inebriated now with the sweetness of his wisdom, it cannot be separated from his embraces. Then no law is to be applied to it nor is it to be instructed as to its mode of prayer. Love itself supplies the matter to be pondered over, gives the form of the prayer and infuses the perfection of it to a sufficient degree. (St. Lawrence Justinian, *De casto connubio*, ch. 22)

Everyone Should Follow His Own Way of Prayer

"If my servants considered," says the beautiful treatise *Espinas del alma*, speaking in the name of our Lord (colloquy 12),

> that there are not one (Ps. 15:11) but many ways by which I draw souls to myself; and if they considered that the heavenly Jerusalem has not one, but twelve gates (Rev. 21:12) ... that in my Father's house there are not one, but many mansions (John 14:2); and ... that the soil of men's hearts brings forth different fruits in different parts (Luke 8:15) and not one alone—they would not wear themselves out to no purpose trying to lead all souls by one way, to enter through one gate only, to have the same dwelling and to bring forth the same fruit.... I do not know why certain servants of mine weary themselves in striving that he to whom I gave only one talent should have two (Matt. 25:15).... The vocation that I give is stronger than theirs and thus, although they may call souls in one direction, it will serve them little if I call them in another—except to cause such souls to walk draggingly and painfully, for they want to be humble

and obedient and follow what they are taught and yet are not able to resist the force of my spirit, which shows them and leads them by another way. This is the reason why, after they have worn themselves out infusing fear into the soul, in the end it is love that works. Moreover, it is tantamount to insisting on fear when I am wounding the heart with love, and to calling the soul to meditate on my humanity when I am consuming and inflaming it with the fire of my divinity. Further, when I am giving the soul gladness and tenderness with the presence of my humanity, they clamour for the contemplation of my divinity. So that if my servants and ministers do not strive to understand the way by which I am leading a soul, and if afterwards they do not work in harmony with me, giving a teaching in conformity with mine, and not different from and contrary to it, they labour in vain; for in the end what I will and not what they will, will be done.

St. Jane Chantal said, speaking of St. Francis de Sales (*Oeuvres*, II, pp. 300–301) that "he was wonderful and altogether exceptional in directing souls in accordance with their respective vocations, without ever doing them violence. Thus he communicated to them a certain liberty through which he removed all their scruples and difficulties. His pleasure was to let the Spirit of God work in them with great liberty. He himself followed the divine attraction and guided them where he saw God was leading them, allowing them to proceed in accordance with the divine inspirations rather than by his own particular instincts."

Our Lord, the Ven. Falconi points out (*Camino*, bk. 1, ch. 14), is wont to give certain souls the gift of contemplation right from the beginning, so that they are utterly unable to apply themselves to meditation, however much violence they do themselves. And the more they persist in wanting to practice meditation, the more they find themselves dry, hard, and mentally tired. There is no reason why such souls as these should persist any longer in meditating. They should allow themselves to be led in the spirit and by the way to which God is calling them and should persevere therein; for God gives this gift ... to some in the beginning....

> I have said this because there are many persons ... very discouraged and on the point of giving up mental prayer; and not a few give it up out of sheer distress at finding that they cannot meditate.... Thus they think that God does not want them to practise mental prayer.... As on the one hand they see that they are imperfect and on the other that they can do nothing nor even make use of discursive prayer, they cannot be persuaded that the inability to meditate means that God is calling them to contemplation, for it seems to them too soon in their case. Thus they concentrate on the fact that they do nothing and have no prayer, since they do not meditate and all they do is to waste time. Usually they come across other persons who discourage and distress them, telling them that they are wasting their time so long as they do not meditate, and thus that they should do so even if the strain should prove unbearable, for the rest is not prayer: as if prayer were something that had to be done by the strength of one's arms and with violence. Thus, such people, who cannot meditate, have no reason to be troubled or to give up

prayer for that, but should persevere in remaining quietly with God surrendered to his will, even though otherwise they find themselves dryer and harder than a stone. In this way they have true prayer and are in a good state and with perseverance will see the fruits and effects of it in their souls.

"With this doctrine," he adds,

it will be understood that the common and ordinary way beginners have to follow, and their masters with them, is that they should be set to meditation … but, for all this it none the less remains true that our Lord calls some souls to contemplation from the beginning. It should also be understood that there is no need to tie souls, nor should they tie themselves, to go this particular way or that, but they should be left to go by the way which suits them best and in which they find most profit for their souls: that is, from which they come out with greater strength for conquest of self and of the devil, practising every virtue. This is the sure way, the one it pleases God that they should take and to which his Majesty calls them. Some apply themselves to meditate and not to contemplate, and in the matter of meditating, some use the Passion,… others meditate on their own wretchedness, others again think of the things of heaven. There are yet others who spend the whole time in making ejaculatory prayers and saying loving words to God, asking his mercy, giving him their hearts and making other acts and holy affections. Others know not what to say or what to ask, nor do they succeed in doing anything else in prayer but to desire to please and love God.… There are still others who cannot meditate on any account ... or succeed in making one single consideration. They only know how to remain alone and in silence, believing that they are with God and surrendered to his will. All these are very good methods of prayer, although so different and varied. For deriving profit from prayer does not depend on whether it is made in one way or another, but upon whether each soul uses the way which suits it best, from which it draws most profit and most persistent and fervent desires of pleasing God and imitating Christ. (Cf. Ven. Bartholomew of the Martyrs, O.P., *Compend. mystic. theologiae*, 2* pt., ch. 20; Louis of Granada, *Devoción*, ch. 5, § 17–18)

Prudent Counsels of St. Jane Chantal

The good and true *preparation* for making it [i.e., prayer] well is to mortify oneself and remain recollected at the side of our Lord during the day.... How greatly is it to be feared that the neglect to keep oneself attentive to God is nourished and covered by the pretext of not allowing one's recollection to be seen!... We ought, then, to seek God in the simplicity of our hearts with purity of intention and familiar conversation with his divine goodness, conversation which goes hand in hand with a great and holy reverence. For the activism of the human mind does not operate without working harm, leading us along our own ways and not by those of God....

The ordinary and most useful material is the life, death, passion and resurrection of our Lord, from which may be drawn the advantage of a holy imitation. After having put ourselves in the presence of God ... by a simple act of faith ... burying ourselves in his divine goodness as a little chick beneath his mother's wing, wholly recollected within ourselves so as to look at him within our hearts, ... in a word, as each one finds easiest, according to the attractions he experiences—being, I say, in the presence of God and after having humbled ourselves deeply and asked his divine help, we ought to begin very gently and simply to think over the first point, as soon as we can passing on to the affective colloquies on the matter proposed.

When the affections have been moved, there is no purpose in multiplying words, but one should rather stop a little, dwelling on our loving thoughts and engraving them gently on the heart, looking in a simple way at what our Lord did in that mystery, and from time to time saying a few words to him, according to the subject, either of love, of abandonment, of compunction and such-like things, as we feel moved. But such words must be said very softly and gently, and we should distill them with sweetness in his divine Heart, as if not wishing that anyone but he should hear them. When we see that a particular affection is passing away, we must endeavour to elicit another with some other simple consideration, or by means of the colloquies on the second and third points proposed, spending thus the rest of the time of prayer.

Those who are in a state of dryness can make all the acts of the prayer—for if it is without relish or feeling, it will not be without utility and profit, for the prayer of patience, submission and abandonment to God's good pleasure that they ought to practise in these circumstances will be no less pleasing to his divine Majesty, and indeed will even be more so than if they were bathed in sweetness. They ought to persevere, keeping themselves in God's presence with deep reverence and in an attitude of devotion, bearing their sufferings with love. For the truth is that when the dryness and inability to make acts are considerable, the poor soul, in such helplessness, cannot do anything else but suffer. But this pure suffering is a very pleasing prayer to God when it is accompanied by humility, submission and confidence, contenting oneself with his will alone and with the honour of remaining in his holy presence, whether as a slave before her Lord, a poor creature before God's sovereign wealth, helpless before the All-powerful, a disciple before her good Master, a bride at the side of her husband, or a daughter at the feet of her father, and other like affections, as the Holy Spirit inspires us, saying a few words to our Lord from time to time according to the state in which we find ourselves. I know that when they are rich with loving submission, such words are profitable and can always be said, even if it be without relish. It is also certain that we ought not to seek our own pleasure, but that of God who wills us to be in this state.

The prayer must always end with acts of abandonment, submission, love, confidence in God, with a firm resolution to amend ourselves with the help of his grace and faithfully to practise the desires and resolutions he has inspired us with. Acts should be added ... of thanksgiving, of offering and of petition.... For our prayer to be useful and that we may taste the sweetness of them, it is necessary to think and ponder over the mysteries of God with God himself.... If the soul corresponds by faithful practice of the virtues, which is the genuine fruit of true prayer, it will not remain at this stage.

I have to say simply a thing which up to the present I had refrained from making known for considerations of discretion, but which the need of souls obliges me to say here, with frankness. That is that, in proportion as I advance, I realize more and more clearly that our Lord is leading almost all the Daughters of the Visitation to the prayer of simple union and utter simplicity in the presence of God by a complete abandonment of themselves to his holy will and to the care of his divine Providence. Our blessed Father used to call it the prayer of simple surrender to God, which he said was very holy and salutary, and which contained everything which may be desired for the service of God. I know, however, that this is strongly contested by those whom God leads by discursive ways; and some of our sisters have been disturbed by this, being told that they were idle and wasting their time. But without wishing to be lacking in the respect due to such persons,[152] I assure you, my dearest Sisters, that you ought not to turn aside from your own way, on account of what they may say.... We ought to remain firm ... from the moment we are *attracted to this prayer*, for we must not enter upon it of ourselves, but await with humility and patience the hour our divine Saviour has appointed to introduce us into this happiness; for, finally, in order to go to God and find him, we have to allow ourselves to be led by his spirit.

Well now, there are different stages in this kind of prayer (which clearly now comes to be intense), as in all others. Some possess that unique simplicity and rest in a much higher degree than others, and receive great lights in it. But, in the end, all arrive where they are, almost without knowing it. And it appears that God uses this single direction to bring souls to the end of the day's march, and that in him they find and receive all the light and strength which are necessary to us in all things.

This attraction is so peculiarly our own that souls who are deprived of it seem to go away from their centre, lose their liberty of spirit, and become so oppressed and confused that they lose their peace and also lose considerable ground.... Go forward, then, Sisters, with humble security along this divine road, and put no method or industry in it, except to follow God's attraction very simply and faithfully....

Those who are led by this way are bound to great purity of heart, humility, submission and utter dependence on God. They ought to simplify their mental operations considerably in everything, cutting off all reflection about past or future. Instead of looking at what they are doing or what they will do, they ought to turn their eyes to God, as far as possible forgetting all things in order to keep this continual recollection and that alone, uniting their spirit to God's goodness in all that happens to them moment by moment, and that very simply.

Living in God: God Living and Reigning in Us

"There is a time," says de Caussade (*Abandonment to Divine Providence*, bk. 2, ch. 1, § 1),

in which the soul lives in God and a time in which God lives in the soul. And what is proper to one of these times is contrary to the other. When the soul lives in God (ascetical life) it provides itself carefully and very regularly with all the means at its disposal to arrive at union: it has all marked out and regulated.... But when God lives in the soul, the latter should abandon itself utterly to his Providence. It no longer has anything of its own and has nothing except what at each moment it is given by the principle which animates it. There are no longer any provisions for the way or any traced out path; it is as a child in the hands of him who is leading it.

Thus, when the soul has come into contact with the divine motion, he continues (§ 2), "it leaves all works, all practices, methods, books, ideas, spiritual persons, in order to be solitary under the direction of God and of this motion which now comes to be the sole principle of its perfection. It is in the hands of God, as all the saints have ever been. It recognizes that this divine action alone knows the way that is suitable for it, and that if it were to seek created means, they would not serve, except to turn it out of the way and hinder God's work in it."

"Our good Master," said St. Margaret Mary (*Oeuvres*, vol. 2, p. 141), "is a very wise Director, and when we surrender ourselves to his direction in everything, he makes us travel far in a short time almost without our noticing it, except for the continual hammering of his grace against our unmortified nature."

"Have no reserves, then," she adds (p. 261), "with him who wants to be within you as the seed of eternal life. There he wants to reign, to rule, to govern, to give impetus to all your operations and to be the object of all your affections."

"Since you are mine," said our Lord to the Ven. Isabel of Jesus (1611–1682, *Life*, I, 3, ch. 50), "I want you to live in me and for me and not to live in your own judgement or will … but that my Spirit may live in you."

Ligature of the Faculties

"As God guides such souls directly by his Spirit, taking their sanctification upon himself and giving them greater graces than others, he also sets himself to convince them more deeply," remarks Fr. Grou (*Maximes*, XXII),

> that they are nothing and can do nothing, and that he is the one who works all the good in them…. To produce this feeling of impotence and dependence in them, he takes possession of their faculties, not allowing them to make use of them freely in spiritual things. They thus come to feel themselves as it were bound and incapacitated so that they cannot occupy their memory, understanding and will on any particular object. He does not allow them any design or project and if they conceive one which has not come through his inspiration, he is pleased to frustrate and overthrow it. He deprives them of every practice and every method of their own choice. He forbids them all effort of their own and will not even tolerate their applying themselves as others do, to the acquisition of such or such virtue … reserving it to himself to govern and sanctify them in his own way, prescribing for them in due measure and season what they ought to do and avoid, and infusing the virtues into them himself without their being able to flatter themselves that they have made a contribution to this…. A condition exceedingly painful and humiliating for us, and one which mortifies our self-love to the utmost and obliges

us to the most exact fidelity, in which we shall not be able to maintain ourselves without great love and great courage under every trial…. He who thus sails at the mercy of the wind—differently from the man who is rowing—can do no less than recognize that to the wind he owes it all and that the only thing left for him to do is to unfurl the sails and allow himself to be borne along without resistance…. Thus in the passive state, one can appreciate all the value and efficacy of grace better.

"Our Lord," said the remarkable Salesian, Sr. Bernarda Ezpelosín (1850–1883; cf. *Life*, Madrid, 1906, pp. 160–161),

gave me to understand that he would sometimes grant me memory so that I might recall the benefits of God and my wretchedness; but that I should have neither understanding nor will to give thanks for the first and detest the second, and that this would cause me unspeakable pain. At other times he would allow the understanding to function, but without memory or will; and, finally he would leave me the will (on some occasions), but without memory or understanding, and this would be one of my greatest sufferings. He told me, lastly, that at one particular time, he would grant or withdraw the use of every faculty and it would always be to make me suffer more.

"Suddenly—after feeling great bursts of love," Sr. Filomena de Santa Coloma relates (*Life and Works*, pp. 167–168),

I find myself like someone who cannot have either desires or a will of his own in anything; and thus I reprove myself, on seeing that I have so soon abandoned my good desires of suffering great things for my Redeemer. But I cannot achieve anything until the one who took them away from me gives them back to me. . . . I have been made to understand that there is nothing to fear, because this paralysis of one's desires comes from the perfect union of the soul with God, so that there is no more than one single willing and not willing between the Lord and his unworthy slave.

"Such insensibilities," said St. Margaret Mary (*Oeuvres*, vol. 2, p. 402), "are to teach us that, in order to be capable of the love of God and his grace, one has to be insensitive to all created things and above all to the movements which self-love and one's own will would suggest."

"In order to attain to the total transformation of the creature into the Creator, it is necessary that the former be dead to its own living, feeling, knowing, power, and even to its own dying — living without living, dying without dying, suffering without suffering, and resigning itself without practising resignation. Not to disturb oneself for anything is to be happily dead" (Ven. Jean de St. Samson, *Maximes spirituelles*, 22).

"All one's work and natural movements," St. John of the Cross warns us (*Dark Night*, II, ch. 14), "rather hinder than help us to receive the spiritual riches of the union of love ... which God by his infusion and that alone puts into the soul passively, secretly and in silence. Thus it is necessary that all the faculties should cling to him and become passive to receive him, not introducing there their own unworthy work and base inclination."

"Then," he adds (ch. 16),

it is fitting that no operation should be left to it [i.e., the soul] nor any pleasure in the matter of spiritual things, because its powers and appetites are impure, low and wholly natural; and thus, although there is given to these powers a taste and desire for supernatural and divine things, they could not receive them except in a very low and natural manner, very much after their own fashion.... Whence, because these natural powers have no purity or strength, nor resources to receive and taste supernatural things according to their proper mode which is divine, but *only in theirs, which is human and base*, as we have said, it is fitting that they should also be in obscurity in regard to this divine (knowledge). Weaned, purged and annihilated in that first of all, they may lose that low and human mode of functioning and receiving and all these appetites of the soul thus may come to be prepared and tempered, so as to be able to receive, feel and taste what is divine and supernatural, after a lofty and sublime manner, a thing which cannot be if the old man does not die first. Whence it is that everything spiritual, if it does not come from above, coming down from the Father of lights upon human desire and free will, however much the love and powers of man be exercised upon God and however much they may appear to be enjoying God, they will not taste him in a divine and spiritual manner but in one which is human and natural.

The Simple Regard of Love

When a soul, Fr. Grou points out (*Manuel*, pp. 327–329),

has given itself completely to God that he may work in it whatever he wills in time and in eternity, he first simplifies it in its depths, introducing there a principle of infused and supernatural love which becomes the sole and single spring of its whole conduct ... this soul's one, single design. The soul remains as it were apart from itself, or at least always tending to strip itself of self and transport itself into the object loved.... He simplifies it in its intelligence, in such a way that it can no longer reflect or use discursive reason and the multitude of thoughts which surrounded it before disappear. All that remains to it is a single and confused light, which lights and directs it without allowing it to distinguish any particular object. Its prayer, which previously was full of considerations, affections and resolutions now becomes simple; it occupies the soul without the latter being concerned with anything in particular. It feels and enjoys, but it cannot say what it feels and enjoys. It is a confused and general feeling, which the soul cannot explain.... It does not know in what it is occupied; the only thing it knows is that it has engaged itself in prayer and is there as God would have it, at times in dryness, at other times in consolation ..., but always peaceful and united with him in the depths of its being. In this way it spends whole hours without weariness or disgust, although apparently empty of every thought and affection. This is because they have become simplified, terminating immediately in God, who is infinitely simple—it is little different outside prayer for whether it reads, converses, or is occupied in work and domestic duties, it feels that it is not so much in what it does, as in God for whom it does it. He is the deepest occupation of its spirit.... Thus it is as if the will, also being simplified, finds its centre and repose in that of God.

"My soul," Madre Ángela María de la Concepción says (*Life*, I, 4, ch. 10),

> desires nothing, not even holy considerations, except to remain in faith, knowing that God is there and recognizing what is there communicated to it of that divine Being and greatness, without wanting, seeking or admitting investigations or acquisitions on the part of the understanding, for if the mind comes with some thing, representation or concept, the soul says: "It is nothing of this, because what I understand is more." Thus it proposes to it nothing that can satisfy or separate it from that centre, where in another and higher way God communicates to it more sublime lights from his attributes and infinite greatness. As also with the light that it receives, it knows that the intellect cannot enter there. From this I understand that there comes to it the not attending to the mind's working, except when in quietude and attention, it is in conformity with the quietude of the will.

Signs That God Is Calling the Soul to Contemplation

The best signs for knowing that a soul is being led into the way of passive purgation, and that therefore its dryness does not come from tepidity or other causes, are, according to St. John of the Cross (*Dark Night*, I, ch. 9), the following: The first, he says,

> is, if whenever it does not find pleasure or consolation in the things of God, it does not find them either in any created thing. Because, as God places the soul in this dark night in order to dry up and purge its sensitive appetite, he allows it to find relish and enjoyment in nothing....

The second sign and condition by which it may believe that this is the divine purgation, is that ordinarily it
applies its memory to God with solicitude and troubled
care, thinking that it does not serve God, but that it is
losing ground.... In this it can be seen that this dryness
and lack of relish does not come from slackness and tepidity.... Wherefore, between dryness and tepidity there is a
great difference because what is [real] tepidity has much
remission and slackness in the will and in the mind, and
no solicitude for serving God. What is only purgative
dryness has with it ordinarily solicitude, with care and
pain.... But, although at the beginning the spirit does not
feel relish ... it does feel the strength and enthusiasm to
work, in the substance of its interior food, which food is
the beginning of dark and dry contemplation.... Usually,
together with this dryness and emptiness in the senses,
there is given to the soul inclination and desire to be
alone and quiet, without being able to think of anything
in particular and without having any wish to do so. Then,
if those to whom this happens knew how to quieten
themselves ... then, in that forgetfulness and idleness they
would feel that interior refreshment in a subtle way. This
is so delicate that usually if the soul has a desire or care to
feel it, it does not feel it.... In such a manner God puts
the soul in this state and leads it along so different a way,
that if it seeks to work with its faculties, it rather hinders
the work that God is doing in it.... For in this state of
contemplation, which is when the soul leaves discursive
prayer for the state of proficients, it is now God who is
working in the soul: so that it appears that he is binding
the interior powers, not leaving the soul any foothold in

the understanding, nor sap in the will, nor discourse in the memory....

The third sign ... is *not being able to meditate* or use discursive reason ... as the soul was wont to do, even though it would do more for its own part.

St. Jane Chantal, in the instructions she gave her daughters, went into greater detail and pointed out to them as many as seven "signs by which they will know," she said,

if their idleness and quiet in prayer is from God. The first will be, if, when they read their point, according to custom, they cannot make use of it, but, without using the slightest pressure feel their heart, mind and the inmost part of their soul gently drawn to this sacred repose. The second, if with all this sweetness they learn to obey God and their superiors without exception, to depend on divine Providence alone and to want only what God wants. The third is, if this repose detaches them from the love of creatures and of all created things and unites them to the Creator. The fourth, if it makes them more sincere and candid, so that they are open with their Superiors like a child. The fifth, if despite the sweetness they receive in this consoling repose, they find they are ready to suffer dryness and sterility whenever God may send it to them and to return to meditations and considerations when it shall please his Majesty. The sixth, if this impulse makes them more patient and desirous of suffering, without seeing any other relief and consolation than that of their divine Spouse. The seventh, if this idleness and loving sleep makes them despise the world and themselves more, to esteem only trials, the cross, humiliations.

"The surest sign," the Ven. Ángela María points out in her turn (*Life*, I, 4, ch. 10),

> is when the soul enjoys being alone with God in loving attention to him, without entertaining any particular consideration, but with interior peace and a quietening of the faculties; for then God communicates himself to the soul with spiritual light from his ineffable and divine essence, without distinction of attributes and persons, without any kind of image or picture or any other intellectual thing, but with a simple and pure light.... This sign is not usually recognized at the beginning: for one thing because this loving knowledge, as it is so spiritual in itself, is wont to be very subtle: and then, because the soul is used to consolations of a sensible kind in meditation, it does not recognize this new form at first; it is so sensitive to the soul that the latter, through not understanding what it is, is often unwilling to be governed by it. But let such souls not lose heart, for practice and custom will make them recognize and enjoy this prayer. Let them go on increasing in this loving knowledge of God; with it the soul will experience much peace and rest.

The Holy Idleness of Contemplation

"In mental prayer properly so called," Fr. Grou points out (*Maximes*, XIV),

> that is, in contemplation, the soul neither reflects nor forms affections and resolutions. However, neither the understanding nor the will is idle. If the contemplation

is clear, the mind sees the object God presents to it, although without reasoning; and if the contemplation is obscure, although it does not put before the soul any one object in particular, it brings the attention of the mind to remain in the presence of God, to humble itself before his supreme Majesty, to listen in silence to what he teaches without the sound or distinction of words (which is God's ordinary manner of teaching). This attention is a true act, although not perceived on account of its extreme simplicity. But it is none the less real for being direct and not reflective.

"One should understand," Fr. Osuna points out (*Tercer abecedario espiritual*, tr. 21, ch. 5), "that this not thinking of anything is more than a sleep, and that in no way is it possible to explain what it is, for God, to whom it is directed, is beyond explanation: I tell you rather that this thinking of nothing is to think of everything, for then we think without discoursing of him who is all through his marvellous pre-eminence. The least good that this thinking of nothing on the part of men of recollection brings, is a very simple and delicate attention to God alone."

"Among the many reasons which invite us to this way of quiet, silent prayer," said Fr. Blas López (*Adición al tr. V. de las virtudes*, by Ruysbroeck, ch. 39),

the following are particularly to be noted: The first, because although usually there is no reasoning process, there is petition, and during the short period or time that our Lord leaves the soul, there is full practice of virtue, not with particular acts, but with a general act and loving attention to God. For the soul who is silent in the presence of the

Lord in faith, does not cease to make petition, and appear-
ing as it does before him, its heart and desires are manifest
to his eyes, its desires being for God what voices are for
men. Thus David says in Ps. 37:10: "Lord, all my desire is
before thee, and my groaning is not hidden from thee."
God hears not only the voices, but also the desires of the
poor. In this way he who presents himself before the eyes of
God comes with faith, trusting and believing that all his
good is to come to him from there. In this way he speaks,
humbles himself and exercises himself, and in travelling
along and following the path of God, leaving his own way,
he finds all his good. The second, because it is a way which
gives a higher idea of God, as is due to his greatness. The
third, because by this way the soul spends longer time in
prayer; thence we conclude that the prayer of the saints was
in this manner; for discursive reasoning wearies, and yet
their prayer was continual. The fourth, because whatever
improvement a soul claims to attain by way of discursive
reason, we can see that the Lord is establishing it by this
means and way. Such people live greatly concerned for their
advancement, submissive to their superiors and elders,
mortifying their passions, accepting whatever befalls them
in the way of adversity and looking after their neighbours
very effectively. But this way of prayer is not for all, but only
for "those whom God puts into it and to whom he communicates it."

Spiritual Silence

"I have been with Jesus," St. Gemma Galgani used to say (cf. *Bi-
ographie* by Frs. Germano and Félix, C.P., Mignard, Paris, 1933,

ch. 19), "I have said nothing to him and he nothing to me. We were *both silent*. I looked at him and he looked at me. But, if you but knew, Father, how sweet a thing it is to be in the presence of God in that way.... One would like to stay there for ever. But then, suddenly ... the light vanishes, Jesus departs. But the heart does not grow cold so soon."

"At times," the Ven. Fr. Baltasar Alvarez points out (cf. *Life*, by La Puente, ch. 23),

> I am with our Lord resting in silence. This being silent in his presence and resting is a great treasure, for to the Lord all things speak and lie open before his eyes: my heart, my desires, my intentions, my trials, my inmost self, my knowledge, my power; and the eyes of his divine Majesty are such that they can take away my faults, kindle my desires and give me wings to fly, for he wills my good and his service more than I do.... If [the soul] does not reach what it desires, it obtains something else better, namely the conformity of its will with God's, for it lives in what he wants, not wanting to experience more than he might want to give; nor to go more quickly nor by other routes than those which he might wish to take.

This was also the theme that the Ven. Sr. María de la Santísima Trinidad sang of (1610-1653: cf. *Life* by Fr. Serratosa, 1912, ch. 33):

> If in silence God is heard
> He does not cease,
> He does not cease to teach:
> Nothing can equal silence.

Signs of Good and Bad Spirits

By *spirit* what is generally understood is an impulse, inclination, inspiration, or suggestion that carries us toward an object good or bad, true or false, but with a certain appearance of good. It is thus very important to distinguish the different spirits, for there are ways that seem to us good and their ends lead to death (Prov. 14:12). For this reason St. John bids us not to give credit to every spirit but to try them to see if they are of God (cf. 1 John 4:1). The way to try them is not as many do, by resisting or forcing resistance and grieving the Holy Spirit, a thing that we ought always to avoid with the greatest care (Acts 7:51; 1 Thess. 5:19; Eph. 4:30)—but by examining the conditions and effects of each impulse or "inspiration," with the object of rejecting all that is evil in it and retaining and cherishing the good.

According to St. Bernard (*Serm.* 33 *De diversis*), the spirits by which souls can feel themselves moved are six, namely: the divine, the angelic, the diabolical, the human, the carnal, the worldly. These can be reduced to three: the divine, the human, the diabolical. The first is always good; the third is always evil in its substance and in the results to which it tends, although many times it is accompanied by a great outward show of good; but the second can be good or evil according to circumstances or according to the influences it receives. It is thus usually the most difficult to distinguish and very frequently, because it finds itself to some small extent penetrated by the divine, it appears to be indistinguishable from it, whereas it is in reality quite distinct. Left to itself, although it appears very good, it is inconstant, superficial, and weak. It tends to what most flatters nature and self-love, seeking its own convenience in everything. Thus it is a great friend to comfort and presents and has a propensity to attachments; and even when at times it is harsh and rigorous with others, it is always wont to be compassionate and soft toward self, even in the midst of certain austerities that self-love may suggest.

The *divine*, as it is good in everything, is always true, clear, holy, pure, stable, sure, discreet, sincere, simple, humble, docile, fruitful, and so forth (Wisd. 7:22-23). In everything it shows itself in conformity with the faith, sound morals, and the mind of the Church; and even in the midst of the soul's greatest darkness, it makes it avoid deceptions and flee from dangers. If there are mistakes or stumblings, it is a sign of the introduction of some human or diabolical impulse. But there may very well be a true foundation, a genuine mark of the divine spirit, with which certain human errors of interpretation have come to be mixed. For this reason, in the case of interior illuminations, to avoid such risks of deception, one should look to the foundation and the fruit, as St. John of the Cross directs, and leave aside the branches of our tastes and conveniences. Thus also, to judge of these things accurately, one must look to what they bring with them and not to the abuses that may come about from them afterwards.

In addition to this, the divine spirit always proceeds with sweetness, discretion, modesty, and the greatest honesty, doing all things well and in due season. It is utterly removed from all duplicity, moves us to recognize the favors received, so that we give thanks for them and appreciate them, without appropriating them to ourselves or growing proud on their account, but rather considering them as something for which one is deeply indebted and for which one has to answer. It moves us to obey lawful authority promptly and to proceed in all things with sureness, firmness, and constancy, without losing time in trifles, drawing from all happenings the greatest spiritual profit.

The spirit of malignity is quite the contrary of this: deceitful, dark, astute, false, perverse, immodest, indiscreet, temerarious, mistrustful, obstinate, haughty, presumptuous, vain, undisciplined, and the enemy of obedience: it is from such things that it is best known and by which it cannot help showing its true colors, however much it may dissimulate (1 John 4:6). Under the appearance or pretext of good, it leads us up to great precipices, covering everything with darkness, so that they are not seen until we are right on the edge and then exaggerates tremendously the difficulties of returning to the right road. It moves us to do everything badly or at the wrong time, to shun mortification or to practice it so that we are praised for it, or else lose our health and become incapable of fulfilling the duties of our state of life. It tries to induce the soul to abandon its vocation and proper occupations for others with which it dazzles it. Causing it to fall into presumption, it induces it to forget its duties and leave its own profit on the pretext of helping its neighbors. By so doing, instead of helping them the soul scandalizes them with its bad example and at the same time rashly exposes itself to great dangers. In this way the spirit of evil continually causes it to dwell on great enterprises that are likely to attract attention and to forget present duties, losing time fruitlessly. It is inconstant and disordered, and just as quickly as it elicits great enthusiasms that first make it overconfident in itself and then fade out, so it casts the soul down and troubles it, persuading it to despair or laxity. But as it can transform itself very easily into "an angel of light" (2 Cor. 11:14), it is not easy to recognize it on many occasions, except by the sad results that, after a certain time, it is found to have left in the soul. By its fruits, said our Lord (Matt. 12:33), the tree is known; and thus the best sign that in a general way a soul is moved by the spirit of good is to see how, like a genuine tree of life, it produces its twelve precious fruits in their due season and how its very leaves—that is, its modesty and exterior bearing—edify and are salutary to the peoples (Rev. 22:2). When this happens, nobody should suspect evil of that soul, nor try to resist the spirit that moves it, thus hindering it from producing those manifest fruits of the Holy Spirit, against which, says the apostle, "there is no law" (Gal. 5:23).

On the contrary, it will be an unmistakable sign of the spirit of evil to find that ordinarily in a soul other fruits, very different from those twelve, are shown, or that the latter do not appear when most necessary, or frequently appear very much falsified or deteriorated. Thus, when we see that a soul fails to a marked degree in charity, or peace, or modesty, and so forth, or has indiscreet zeal, is impatient, envious, suspicious, ill-intentioned, or is fond of presents, applause, publicity, and so forth, such a soul, however sublime the prayer to which it may lay claim or which it may seem to have, is certainly deluded and may even come to be an impostor.

All God's communications bear the seal of holiness, honesty, and modesty. Thus, when a soul, on being favored by Him in a special way, comes to lose the use of the senses and to fall to the ground (a thing that rarely happens in public), it always remains in a modest posture and never sustains harm, quite the contrary of what usually happens when the loss of consciousness is natural or the work of the evil spirit. Similarly, divine visits always bring strength with deep humility and the soul's confusion. They begin with reverential fear and then leave the soul full of peace, strength, consolation, and holy joy. Diabolical visits, on the other hand, begin by fascinating with sensible pleasure and then leave only disturbance.

But although everything in God's communications is good, the human spirit can, either of its own accord or prompted by the spirit of malignity, misuse the lights and graces received and throw away, for the most part, their good fruit. Thus we see that, when the astute enemy cannot prevent the fruit altogether, he tries to render it useless or make it bitter with his poisonous breath. At times, in order to deceive us more completely, he tries to produce imitations and substitute other fruits, good in appearance, that he can produce and that then turn out to be very harmful and deadly. This happens with false zeal, which only causes disturbances and discord; with false peace, which makes compromises, with great offense to God; or with a special kind of patience, which is the fruit of cunning; feigned humility, which leads to depression and despair; continual anger with oneself and with everyone, whereas the humility taught by the good spirit is always sincere, cordial, and peace-loving, causing the soul rightly to consider itself as unworthy and vile—thus it willingly accepts contempt while at the same time it is happy and confident, for everything leads it to hope in God, although without presumption.

In general, "when it is the devil," says St. Teresa (*Life*, ch. 25, 7), "it seems that all good is hidden and leaves the soul, which then remains afflicted and disturbed and without any good effect; for although it appears to have desires, they are weak; the humility which it leaves is false, troubled and without sweetness. It seems to me that he who has experience of the good spirit will understand this."

It is more difficult, then, to distinguish the human spirit, which so many times is mingled with the divine and at others produces of its own accord certain fruits of natural goodness that at first sight can be confused with the supernatural fruits of the

Holy Spirit. But then we see how short a time they last and how little they are worth, however valuable they may appear; and although at times they are more or less supernaturalized under the influence of the spirit of good, they do not unite well and fit in well with the rest.

To prove that the fruits produced in the soul are really from God, they have to offer a certain divine fragrance, a certain maturity and sweetness into which passes the perfect harmony of all the virtues that should contribute to their production, or the special influence of some of the mystic gifts.

Thus we see that many acts of zeal—apparent fruits of charity—through being harsh, ill-tempered, or indiscreet and not according to knowledge, wisdom, spiritual prudence, although they appear good, show that they are suggested, or at least vitiated, by an evil spirit. In those that are of God, all is gentle and prudent, the most ardent charity being joined with peace, kindness, benignity, joy, and patience—and these qualities with a lively zeal, which will admit no compromise to the detriment of the divine glory. The fruits in which the influence, above all the *habitual* influence of the spirit of good, can be clearly distinguished are always more or less intimately linked and even seasoned one with another, so that none is wont to fail when opportunity calls for it, much less give place to its contrary. Inasmuch, then, as peace is positively disturbed or there is a lack of charity, patience, modesty, and so forth, however good this work be in its foundations and even however sure we are of the good spirit by which a person is ordinarily animated, it is undeniable that, in *that particular case*, he allowed himself to be influenced in a greater or lesser degree by his own spirit, or perhaps by the spirit of the world or of malignity from which God guards us. For this reason it is not sufficient to see some obvious fault, or some fruit or other that is not of God, to be able to affirm—as many do imprudently—that such a person cannot have a good spirit; just as it is not sufficient when from time to time someone succeeds in producing some good fruit, to declare at once that he or she is "of a good spirit," as if this would show the person to be habitually so. One swallow does not make a summer, as they say.

But when a soul habitually produces fruits in every respect ripe and luscious, well-seasoned with the concourse of many infused virtues and the influence of some of the gifts, so that it finds itself in a condition to produce in each circumstance, in each month of the spiritual year, its corresponding fruit; when its flowers of virtue are really fragrant with that good odor of humility and meekness of Christ, which attracts and captivates hearts for Him, then there is no doubt that that soul is animated and moved *ordinarily* by a very good spirit.

The sure pledge of the divine is then, as we said in *Evolución mística* (p. 400), the "sincere desire to suffer hardships for God, perfect conformity with the crosses he sends us, constant self-denial, annihilation and forgetfulness of self, with total surrender into the divine hands. This is what shows that we are animated by the sentiments of Jesus Christ—and allows us to receive his light and to be set ablaze with his love."

"I will give you," our Lord Himself said to Bl. Angela of Foligno (*Visions*, ch. 29), "*a sign not subject to illusions* ..., a sign which nobody can contradict.... For my love you shall bear all tribulations. If anyone offend you by word or work, you will exclaim saying that you are not worthy of such a grace. This love that I give you for me is the same that I showed you when I suffered patience and humility for you even to the Cross. You will know that I am in you, if every contrary word and action stir you not merely to patience, but to gratitude and desire."

"I felt the unction," the saint adds,

I felt it and with a sweetness so unutterable that I longed to die, but to die in the midst of all possible tortures.... I should have loved the whole world to favour me with every kind of injury and all the torments it has at its disposal. How sweet it would have been to me to pray for these who had done me that favour!... My soul understood the littleness of suffering in comparison with the good things promised for eternal life.... The same sign is the way of salvation, the love of God and of the suffering desired for his name's sake.

Referring to Chapter 8

Persecutions, Contempt, and Tribulations That It Is Necessary to Suffer in Order to Be Able to Enter into the Mystical Kingdom (Acts 14:21; 2 Tim. 3:12)

One danger there is in this solitude, remarks Fr. Osuna almost humorously (*Tercer abecedario*, tr. 20, ch. 6), consists of the "many scorpions" who

> bite in secret, murmuring against you. Judging you to be a hypocrite, they think it behoves them to beware of you as of a man who is deceitful. They do not think you practise recollection except to judge their dissipation inwardly.... The world will not keep back from you one iota of its blame. It will all be saved up for you until a good opportunity occurs, when it will be said that since you claim to be recollected, it cannot be allowed that you should do this or that. It attributes all your deeds to presumption. It says that recollection is pure fantasy and pretence which makes you despise others. When you

draw near to God they will say you are slumbering. Your peaceful tranquillity will be called laziness, and they will say that you purposely make yourself a fool, as if they did not understand that you do so more for ease than for prayer. You will be remarked on as to what you eat and what you wear, as if all this came from the resources of your parents; and when in this way they cannot find a vulnerable spot to attack, they will cast a slur on your lineage or on your age and call to mind the sins of your youth, and between jest and earnest they will mock you with words of hatred.... And if by chance you show anger, they will accuse you of losing patience, not regarding the fact that they have lost justice. They say that you do not imitate Jesus Christ in suffering, and they imitate the devil, whose function it is to tempt.... What the dissolute take most trouble about is in blaming the words of those who practise recollection and pulling them to pieces, to garble and condemn them, or you—as a man of no brains or possessed of the devil. What they do not understand, they consider wrong.... Do not fear the persecutions of men, even the worst possible persecutions; for in this whirlwind, like another Elias, you will be able to rise to the heaven of contemplation.

Thus, seeing itself despised, mocked, censured, and even hated and persecuted by its own people and those who ought most to encourage, console, and defend it, the faithful soul, in the midst of its trials, darkness, and desolation, will take courage saying with the prophet (Mic. 7:6-10):

A man's enemies are they of his own household. But I will look towards the Lord, I will wait for God my

Saviour: my God will hear me. Rejoice not, thou, my enemy, over me, because I am fallen: I shall arise, when I sit in darkness, the Lord is my light. I will bear the wrath of the Lord, because I have sinned against him; until he judge my cause and execute judgment for me: he will bring me forth into the light, I shall behold his justice. And my enemy shall behold, and she shall be covered with shame who saith to me: "Where is the Lord thy God?"

"If it make any delay, wait for it [the vision]: for it shall surely come, and it shall not be slack. Behold, he that is unbelieving, his soul shall not be right in himself: but the just shall live in his faith" (Hab. 2:3-4).

The Lord provides all these trials for the greater good of His faithful servants. "Do not be dismayed," He said to Sr. Mariana de Santo Domingo (cf. *Life*, pp. 231-234),

because creatures turn against you, for they deny and shun me, although I am their Creator.... You are my daughter, and for that reason they ill-treat you ... for they do not love those who hold converse with me.... Avoid seeking the company and consolation of creatures, for I am setting bitterness before you and allow you to find no pleasure in creatures in order that you may seek your consolation in me.... You know quite well that I must be your "alone with the alone," and that all you deprive yourself of in creatures, you will find in me.... There is nothing that draws me more to a soul than to see that creatures persecute and shun it.... How will he who cares for you and loves you have the heart to see you suffering anxiety in your search for me, and despised by creatures? If at any time I leave the soul who is in that case, my absences are not long, for I cannot leave one who desires nothing but my company and love, to which I invite her so fully, in solitude for long.

"Deny yourself everything once and for all," he added to her (*Life*),

and set your own honour beneath your feet. Receive all things, favourable as well as adverse, from my hand, and fix it firmly in your mind that nothing of what may happen to you is by chance, but that I allow it for your greater good.... Not because you feel trials will you then lose strength, thinking you are irremediably lost, for you cost me much and I chose you for myself. Have confidence in me, come with your faults, do not fear for I am a Father more patient than all the sons of men. Remember me when you are in affliction; I will console and teach you: go to my minister, for I have given him to you for that....

Although you see yourself deserted and in affliction and imagine that I am no longer with you, do not believe it; for the more you are in that case, the nearer I am to you. Do not desire that consolation should come to you but that my will may be done in all things. Although all your life should be like that, never fail to receive me, however troubled you may find yourself; for that is what your adversary is seeking. Daughter, if when one feels ill and weak, he withdraws himself from what was to give him health ... I remained [on earth] for man's sustenance and to give him life.

Advantages, Sufferings, and Mysteries of the Passive Purgations

"God's purging of a soul," said the Ven. Isabel of Jesus (1611–1682; cf. *Life*, I, 6, ch. 4),

> is a most sovereign mercy, because … we shall never learn to mortify ourselves properly, nor are our vices and evil inclinations torn up from the root with ordinary mortification. For this reason God takes matters in hand and arranges everything, even the natural humours, for there is no one who can resist him. Thus when mortification is passive and supernatural, value it, and make the most use of it you can, if it is mortification of the passions. If the sufferings and purgations are in the spirit itself, it is all to purify the soul and bear it to heaven clean and pure.

She adds that when her guardian angel was speaking to her of the interior purifications that cleanse the soul more thoroughly, he said to her:

> God usually takes away [the power of] discursive prayer in such a way that even if the soul should wish to do so, it cannot pray nor can it use what it had before, and it finds itself in a state of incredible dullness and ineptitude. However much it would like to throw this off, it is unable to do so, because the Lord is no longer helping it to this, for he wants it to be more deeply recollected. As the soul does not understand God's purposes, it thinks it is lost and is going back, and this causes it a grief which cannot be expressed; for it suffers a dislocation of the bones, together with interior distress, which causes

it great discomfort. It cannot have peace unless it is recollected in the deepest part of itself and, taught by very necessity, finds the remedy in listening to God and abandoning the natural work it was wont to do, allowing itself to be governed in silence and hope. At other times God hands it over to interior suffering and the devil does everything to drain it of patience. The rubbish you hear him say should not disturb you, for it is not you who says it or thinks it, but the devil himself. Do not answer those persistent thoughts, for you will not accomplish anything by so doing. Bear your purgatory to make amends for your soul's carelessness in the past, and have hope in the mercy of God that all this will end in tranquillity and sovereign peace. Through this the Lord wants you to value the peace which is to come to you afterwards, and that you should know your misery clearly, through experience, and as it were through the light of your own eyes, and that whichever way you look at it, of yourself you are nothing. All you suffer is entirely in the interior senses, and the soul is in a dark contemplation. If this gave you peace you would miss seeing it and fail to aim at it.

Crises of Suffering and Fears by Night

"In the time of the aridities of this night of the senses," observes St. John of the Cross (*Night*, I, ch. 10),

in which God makes the change ... drawing the soul away from the life of the senses to that of the spirit, that is, from meditation to contemplation ... spiritual persons suffer great pain, not so much through aridity, as through the fear they have of becoming lost along this road. Then they become weary and try to rivet their faculties, with some degree of pleasure, to some object of discursive reason. In this, drawing no profit in the one, they make no progress in the other; because, through using their mind, they lose the spirit of tranquillity and peace they had. Thus they are like a man who leaves what he has done to do it over again. At this time, if there is no one who understands them, they do go back, leaving the right path and wavering, or at the least they hinder [themselves] from going forward, however much diligence they put into going along the former way of meditation and discursive prayer.... They have now no obligation to do this, for God is leading them by another way, which is that of contemplation, very different indeed from the former.... Those who find themselves in this case ought to console themselves, persevering with patience, and not making a trouble of it, trust in God who does not abandon those who seek him with a simple and right heart, nor will he fail to give them what is necessary for this way.

Immediately the soul feels itself drawn to abandonment and interior suffering and to the uttermost stripping of everything of the senses, it should seek no relief in this cross, but to make itself more God's, and should stay stripped and abandoned as long as it shall please the divine Spouse.... The result of this darkness of prayer in faith is that the soul knows that God cannot be known, for he is infinitely beyond our knowledge, and that the knowing him is acknowledging that he cannot be known. The lights which at other times served to guide the soul to

God and unite it with his Majesty, now in this prayer are
all of no avail, because its darkness means that the soul
is lost and submerged in the abysses of God's sovereign
being, and is given clearly to understand that the higher
prayer is in the privation of created things. (Ven. Ángela
María de la Concepción, *Riego espiritual*, ch. 37)

Infused Recollection and Its Effects

"Recollection," wrote Vallgornera (*Théol. myst.*, q. 4, d. 2, a. 15),

is nothing other than the approach by which the soul, with
all its powers, is admitted to interior things and removed
from external ones.... The Lord therefore, through his
holy inspiration, is wont to call the contemplative soul
who is given to external things or praying vocally, or considering something useful for the moment, and to raise
both mind and heart and thoughts to interior things, the
soul itself doing almost nothing, and to set it down before
that table of light and love, at which it is abundantly refreshed. Then it is drawn as it were not reluctantly but
willingly ...; it leaves external things and so to speak naturally closes its bodily eyes and turns its sight and hearing
and the rest of its senses to internal things. Through the
practice of the virtues and assiduous converse with God, it
has now become, as it were, a heaven of God, in which he
himself dwells in delight.

This recollection, according to St. Teresa, is caused by the
sweet piping of the Good Shepherd, who draws the powers of
the soul to Himself. For this reason, St. Thomas, when he is

explaining the words "the sheep hear his voice" (John 10:3), says: "Christ is the Shepherd of the soul, and as a good shepherd, with the piping of his inspiration, he gathers up all the faculties of the soul together and leads them to his presence."

"It seemed to me," the Ven. Mary of Agreda remarked in reference to this (*Escala*, § 23),

> the Lord had entered my soul and made himself master of it. There as superior, he commanded everything and when he was served, through his goodness he called all the people of this house[153] and collected them together in the presence of their Majesty and Lord. I say that he called them, for I could not acquire such recollection of my own initiative. What my soul experienced here in the presence of his Majesty cannot be expressed.... So far as I remember ... I know not how my soul was called nor how the Lord came within it in such a form that it never forgot that guest, whom it had so close within its very self.[154] The mind knew this to be so and understood more than I know how to express....
>
> The effects which this caused in my soul were to humble me greatly. I was given great desires to serve the Lord, and was unconsciously brought to great peace and quiet. I forgot earthly things. It seemed to me that there within the soul was a furnace of fire in which everything was purified.... Sometimes the Lord brings about the entering into this recollection by giving some warning through his presence and grace in the soul. At other times he brings it about through the soul's preparation and eagerness for the good which comes to it in this recollection. Here the faculties do not cease working or operating, although they

do not do so uninterruptedly, and sometimes the soul hears the Lord speaking to the heart. . . .

A *useful piece of advice*. Sometimes the Lord calls us by means of some inspiration to recollect our inmost heart, and we respond. Let not that happen to us as it happened to the careless spouse, namely, not to notice that it is the voice of the Lord calling us and not to open to him, our attention being fixed on some obstacle which matters little or nothing, liking going forth un-shod (*Cant.* 5, 3). . . . Great would be the fault if God should call and . . . a trifle were occupying our attention. In our own interest we should respond. Is there any greater consolation or anything more glorious than this recollection? For if God is there . . . glory is there, too. There is no doubt that it is a pity that creatures endowed with reason should lack so great a good. O God, what a sad error is this! Dear God, what riches those who do not practise this lack.

The Prayer of Quiet and Its Fruits

"The prayer of quiet," says Mary of Agreda again (*Escala*, § 25),

is nothing other than a flash or glimpse of bliss, a vestige of the life beyond, and that is what it appears, for the soul begins to enter into and enjoy a most sweet quiet and the faculties are no longer so active. The Lord himself is the cause of this sweet quiet . . .; for what is there except his very presence that could cause this sweetness in the soul? This is so to the extent that the faculties are operative and in movement, but the two, memory and understanding, remain quiet before the presence and mind of God, and in this quiet the will is occupied with love.

The benefits of this manner of prayer and the good it brings to the soul are unutterable. In his goodness the Lord granted me the prayer of recollection and that of quiet ever since, on becoming a religious, I began to practise mental prayer and give myself wholly to it. The mercies the Lord communicated to me were great; the favours and joys I was sometimes not able to hide.... The effect this prayer always made on me was this ... never did I put myself into it and in the presence of my Lord, without his reproving me if I had imperfections. How very special are the Lord's reproofs. How much they teach us and how mysterious is what they teach. Merely by receiving them and the joy of putting into practice what they teach, it seems that His Majesty could be served.

"He gave me a manner of prayer," said the Ven. Mariana de San José (1568-1638), foundress of the Augustinian Recollects (cf. *Life* by Muñoz, 1645, bk. 1, ch. 11),

which it seems to me was very much higher. Previously I did something on my own initiative, but in that which I now speak of, I could do nothing. For when I put myself in the presence of Christ our Lord, I found him at my side. There he inspired me to gratitude and love for the goodness of God our Lord, so that I was unable to go away and remained several hours without becoming weary.

This mode of prayer showed me that the way was so spacious that when the soul shares in this good, it finds itself enlarged and in great consolation. The devil told me

this was wasting time without profit; but as the soul had
already found how precious this good was, although it was
not wholly without misgiving, it could not escape from
the hands of our Lord, who held it by force. Despite all
this, as I was so ignorant in these things, I put up a certain
resistance, not knowing the good that I was thus losing.

"It is in this infused and quiet prayer," writes the Ven.
Ángela María de la Concepción (*Riego espiritual*, ch. 38),

> that the soul, full of love at the great good that is given
> to it, learns to work at the mortification of its passions
> and appetites, for here there is pleasure in exercising the
> virtues. Here it learns how to suffer for God and love
> him. Here it learns to know his will and is so much a
> captive that it fears to enjoy its liberty again. Here it is
> able indeed to thank our Lord for the outward and in-
> ward crosses which it suffers for his love. Here, finally, it
> learns to want nothing but God, without the will's seek-
> ing to grasp anything, for it is ready not to enjoy any-
> thing of what has been mentioned if God does not will
> that it should, and this in order not to become unfaith-
> ful and so be deserted by our Lord for another soul more
> faithful to him. For this the soul could wish to be always
> withdrawn within itself, and that the Lord should make
> it his retreat, for with the light he gives it, it knows that
> although there is no room for him in the world he is
> delighted and pleased that the soul should make itself
> the throne of his sovereignty and majesty. The graces
> and favours which the soul receives in this state are so
> great that when it has tasted them once or twice, they
> will already leave its faculties so rich that the mind will

enjoy the certainty of the things of faith, and the will will have an intense love of the virtues, for these two powers of the soul remain so enlightened and so eager for the love of God and to put up with the dross of this world, that in a short time they gain more in this way than over a long period of meditation....

The greatest difficulty, and this is a real martyrdom, is thinking that in that quiet one does nothing, although it seems to the soul that to be in it is a very safe way. But as its state is hidden from it, and nothing can be seen or known by the human mind, it suffers great darkness, and the fear it suffers lest that loving union with its Beloved should fail it, is bitter martyrdom, notwithstanding the fact that it is given to understand that, in order to preserve this union, it is necessary that it empty itself of all that is not God, dying to all the old life to rise again to this new life of the spirit of the Lord, in which His Majesty works without its knowing that he does so, granting it only a dim sight, which guides it to God and is sufficient for it.

Love's Sweet Inebriation and Divine Fullness

"The Lord," relates Sr. Mariana de Santo Domingo (*Life*, p. 289),

communicated to me so much sweetness and bliss, that it inebriated me. I became aware that his divine Majesty was saying to me: "Beloved, this is how I delight those who mortify themselves and leave all for me. I shall fill you and it will be with longing for me, for this is the highest and most sublime table, and when you eat from it more ... you will find as dessert insatiable hunger and longings, which I shall not take away from you for ... this is a better and most tasty morsel.... Taste, daughter, taste with joy how sweet I am to those who love me.

How in the Mystical Sleep the Soul Sleeps and the Heart Keeps Watch

"I neither feel nor know anything," wrote Sr. Bernarda Ezpelosín in June 1881 (*Life*, p. 188),

> I only *feel* that I love God, that I love him very much and that he loves me more, much more. I know nothing else, here I lose myself and do nothing more.... It occurred to me that I was wasting time, that I was doing nothing, that my senses and powers were *asleep* and perhaps paralysed by my sins, but all that happened to me did not disturb me, neither, when I am like that, do I experience dryness from this very special state, to which it seems a supernatural force is drawing and subjecting me. I lose myself, I go down into the abyss. The less I understand, the more I experience, and when I experience more, it seems at the same time that I cease to feel more. When I see myself doing nothing and as it were asleep and dead, then, like a supernatural light—as is all that then happens to me—it seems as if I understand or am told that then, not only am I *not* doing nothing, but that in that way I do much.

"When, then, you find yourself in this simple and pure trust before our Lord—like a child in its mother's arms," says St. Francis de Sales (*Love of God*, I, 6, ch. 8), "—remain there without moving yourself in any way to make conscious acts, either of the under-standing or of the will, for this simple trusting love and this loving sleep of your spirit in the arms of the Saviour, includes *par excellence* all you are going about seeking for your pleasure."

"And if to this simple manner of being in the presence of God," he then remarks (ch. 11), "it were his will to add some passing feeling that we are all his and he all ours, O great God, what a desirable and precious grace is this."

"Imagine to yourself," said St. Gemma Galgani (*Biography*, p. 25, ch. 19), "a child who lets itself fall asleep on its mother's lap. There it remains, forgetful of everything, itself included. It thinks of nothing, but rests and sleeps, without knowing how or why: that is what my soul is like at that time. But it is a very sweet sleep."[155]

"That which is external suffers a kind of sleep and all care to inquire and know is cast away. The soul clings to love alone and to its most chaste embraces. In this stage the Lord himself, who offers wine for intoxicating bliss and sends sleep for quiet and joy, inebriates the soul with the wine of love, with the drink of charity, and thence causes it to forget all things, that it may sleep and rest on the heart of the Bridegroom" (Álvarez de Paz, I, 5, p. 3, ch. 7).

> O truly blessed sleep, then, in which the soul recuperates strength for labour and which the Lord himself diligently maintains in it. For he says to the young ones, that is, to those more imperfect souls who do not yet know this sleep by experience: "I adjure you, etc."
>
> The soul thus rich with spiritual riches, is roused from sleep so that it seems to it that it has risen to a new life.... In the mystical sleep the soul is allowed to presume that it needs nothing. Nevertheless, when that

has passed away, it remains fervent, devout, disposed to virtue. (López Ezquerra, *Lucerna mística*, tr. 5, n. 230, 241)

The Mysterious Way in Which God Shows Himself, Speaks to, and Teaches the Soul That Is United with Him, and How It Perceives Him by Means of "the Spiritual Senses": Wonderful Effect of These Divine Communications

I could not fail to understand that he (Christ) was by my side, and I *saw* him clearly, and *felt* him. There one clearly sees that Jesus Christ, the Son of the Virgin, is here. In this other way of prayer (quiet, presence of God) certain influences of the Godhead are represented. Together with these, it can be *seen* that the most sacred Humanity is also present, and wants to show us favours....

Thus God also teaches the soul in another manner and speaks to it without words.... It is a language so much of heaven that here it may be difficult to understand it. The Lord sets what he wills the soul to understand in the very centre of it, and this he does without image or form of words.... This manner of God's working should be carefully noted, for there the soul understands what God wants together with great and mysterious truths.... God makes the mind apply itself, although it costs it labour, to understanding what is said. There it appears that the soul has other ears with which to hear and that it is made to listen and does not become distracted.... The soul immediately finds itself enlightened and the mystery of the Most Holy Trinity and other very sublime matters are now so clear that there is no theologian with whom it would not dare to dispute about the truth of these great things. It remains so overwhelmed that one of these favours is sufficient to change a soul in everything and to make it love nothing but him whom it sees and who, without any labour on its part, renders it capable of such great good, communicating secrets to it, and dealing with it with so much friendship and love that it cannot possibly be written. (St. Teresa, *Life*, ch. 27)

"How wonderfully you teach the soul to be able to talk with you on these occasions (of union)," Sr. Catalina de Jésus María would exclaim (*Autobiography*, pt. 2, ch. 74). "How gently you speak to her without the sound of a voice. How well God and the soul speak together without the noise or weariness of words. Master, how hard it is for me to have to converse with creatures again. If you had not ordained it thus, I should not see or converse with them again."

"By these visions (of the divine immensity, etc.)," said the Ven. Marina de Escobar (*Life*, bk. 3, ch. 2, § 2), "the soul is so changed that it seems to have another, new, being and another new spiritual life very different from the ordinary one."

"When the operations of discursive reason cease, and God raises the soul and brings it into the knowledge of himself," said St. Alphonsus Rodríguez (*Unión*, ch. 1),

the more he gives it of this knowledge, the more is it inflamed with his love. This practice is most sublime and perfect, because God takes a hand in it, teaching the soul through himself and communicating himself to it in a sublime manner.... As the soul does not understand this, nor is it possible that it should, this knowledge that God gives it of himself causes such a great admiration and love of God, that it holds the soul entirely in a trance, as it were.... From this very great admiration and love of the will come raptures, particularly when God communicates his Goodness to the soul; and in that Goodness and infinite being of God many other great matters and sublime secrets of God are communicated to it, all simultaneously, without one thing hindering the other, as if the whole were not more than one thing alone. And if what God thus reveals to the soul concerns the perfections of God, as this Lord is the God of infinite being, each single one of these perfections is God of infinite being.

"With this communication that the Lord has with the soul inwardly and it with him," he adds (ch. 6),

it is transformed into him, a thing caused by the love of both. Thus the soul does not look at Jesus its beloved from without, but from within itself, through having him and feeling him through the whole body, enjoying him and all that he communicates of himself to it, particularly of his sorrows and sufferings. For as he is in it, he clothes it with this livery of himself—just as the sun which is covered by a cloud, communicates to it its great splendour and beauty. The soul no longer runs hither and thither, for it now has what it seeks with it, namely Jesus, its beloved. Thus both are joined in one, loving each other in mutual joy, the soul with him and he with it, transforming it into himself, Christ and the soul each giving the other all he has and all he is, like good lovers. Who will be able to say what passes in this contemplation between Christ and the soul alone, or the great things which he reveals to it of himself by clear knowledge without sound of words, and the great joy that it receives with the presence of its Beloved? Only he who experiences this knows it, without being able to express it, only to taste it by experience.

"As when in a sponge," said St. Teresa (*Revelation* 3), "the water is absorbed and drunk up, thus it seemed to me that my soul was being filled with that Divinity, and in a certain way enjoyed and held within itself the three divine Persons. I also heard: Do not labour to have me enclosed in you but to enclose yourself in me."

Diversity of the Divine Communications and of the Effects They Produce – Playfulness of God with the Soul: Absences and Desolations

As the ways His Majesty has of communicating himself in these [states of] prayer are so many and so different, not all can be declared or noted, for the activities of divine love have no end. Sometimes his presence and communication are felt by the deep annihilation which the soul experiences in itself. At other times he manifests his presence as if withdrawn into himself, and as the soul is attentive to this presence, it is reverent and serves its sovereign Master faithfully. On other occasions he deprives it of the use of its faculties, so that it can do nothing, but the Lord fills it full of himself. He leaves it very eager to seek him and to do only what his most holy will permits. At other times he inspires it with a spirit of sacrifice, with great detachment from everything, and it finds itself so full of God, that not only does its higher part enjoy the sweetness, but this sweetness overflows on to the other senses and all have joy. Finally, on other occasions the love of our Lord takes it captive to such an extent, that with the pleasure and sweetness it experiences, all the rest seems to it painful and insipid. In these states of prayer God is so lavish with the soul, that it seems as if it has not to take care of itself but to allow itself to be served and loved, and that even in its doubts, the Lord will raise it up and guide it, helping it on every occasion and in every need.... Sometimes [the union] gives so much joy to the soul that it seems to it it is enjoying heaven upon earth. At other times this union is one of justice and severity; for the Lord leaves it no more than the higher part of the will, which is united to God in justice, and in a way that, although severe and hard, is purity for the soul. It suffers and humbly endures an interior and exterior cross, on which the Lord lays it, uniting himself to it, with the signs and indications of severity—even if for the soul it is sweet, through the very ready conformity it has in this state with the good pleasure of God. This moves His Majesty always to favour it in the ways mentioned, for the Lord finds it so faithful that whether he unites himself to it in sweetness, or whether as severe and reproving, in either mode he finds it full of reverence for his will. Thus he favours it lovingly, now laying different crosses upon it, now purifying its loyalty more by his withdrawals, now urging it to perfect itself, now reproving its carelessness, and then, finally, he assists it in the needs of its inward spirit, enlightening the understanding and inflaming the will. (Ven. Ángela María de la Concepción, *Riego espiritual*, ch. 39)

"Do you know, dearest daughter," said the Eternal Father to
St. Catherine of Siena (*Dialogues*, ch. 144),

> of what means I avail myself to draw the soul from its
> imperfection? Sometimes I try it with the affliction of
> many and various thoughts, with dryness of spirit and it
> will seem to it that I have abandoned it, and that it is like
> someone who has no feeling in himself, except that in
> his will he does not want to offend me.... Perhaps it will
> seem to it that it is in hell; and without doing anything
> for its part, it will see that it has remained in great quiet,
> and will begin to enjoy the earnest-money of life eter-
> nal.... When it was exercised in prayer, I did not re-
> spond to it by sending it light, lest being still imperfect,
> it should think that it came from itself.

"In the pains and afflictions which I allow my servants to
suffer," he added (ch. 145),

> their patience is tested and the fire of their charity in-
> creases with the compassion they have for him who is
> hurting them.... Sometimes I make use of a pleasant
> illusion to preserve them in humility. I dull their senses
> so that it will seem that neither in the will nor in the
> senses do they experience any adversity, like one who is
> sleeping, not dead.... I say that it seems that their
> senses are asleep, for when they suffer and bear great
> burdens, they go along as if they were carrying nothing.
> Afterwards a thing which is almost nothing, of which
> the same soul would before have made a jest, makes so
> much impression upon them, that they are surprised at
> themselves and dismayed by it. My Providence permits

this so that the soul may be established in humility and increase in virtue and not forgiving itself, with hatred of this fault and offence, may punish its cowardly dispositions. With this chastisement it is lulled to sleep more perfectly.

"Very soon I find myself," wrote the Ven. Sr. Bárbara de Santo Domingo, O.P., in September 1871 (cf. *Life*, 1889, p. 248),

in a very great desolation, as if in a calm which holds the soul so to speak as in a trance. What mighty power is that of God, which causes the soul to suffer and rejoice at the same time!... This seems a contradiction, but it is how I experience it, for I rejoice in suffering.... Although I am in this state of dryness, I do not fail to experience great warmth of fervour in my heart and soul, so great that it sometimes seems that I have a volcano of fire in my heart.... Each time the love of my God is increased in an extraordinary way ... let it suffice to say that at one and the same time I feel myself penetrated by both suffering and love.

"When it is his holy will," she continues,

he sets me at the point of death, as he has set me now. All is caused through an abandonment of the soul by God, and it seems there is no God for me. What a great means of suffering it is for me when I find myself without my God. What anguish for my heart when I seek here and there, and however much I seek, sigh and lament, I continue to find myself without him whom my soul loves so much. Then it seems as if they are putting a slab of stone upon my heart and this oppresses it in the extreme. I cannot find ease anywhere. How true it is that it is only God who fills and refreshes the heart and soul.

"I suffer a withdrawal of God and so great a dereliction," another holy Dominican nun of the same convent of the Mother of God at Seville, Sr. Mariana de Santo Domingo, said a century earlier (*Life*, p. 299),

> that it leaves me as it were beside myself. Temptations are strong and continual. The persecution of enemies becomes unbearable to me ... the blows which they have given me cannot be counted. The doubts, fears and confusion which find room within me I cannot myself explain. Among all this the longing for God is very great. Thus, the love of God is accompanied by fear lest I have lost him and is a martyrdom which goes through my heart.... The Lord comes to meet me along the way and when I want to draw near he disappears. This is what makes me full of care and greatly distressed, and I then make loving ejaculations: but all this he feigns not to understand. In every way I am abandoned and resigned in God's hands and from him I hope for all things and I do not believe that my hope will be in vain.

"It pleases God much," remarks St. Alphonsus Rodríguez, speaking of the "playfulness of God with the soul" (*Works*, vol. 2, pp. 244-245),

> to see it weep and in tribulation and to have recourse to him. He, like a good mother who loves her child so much, takes the soul in his arms and embraces and consoles it in a sublime manner, speaking to it sweetly and familiarly and communicating to it his most sweet

love, while he gives it the freshest milk of his great sweetness and consolation. The most sublime matters of love that pass between God and the soul, no human tongue can rightly declare. For there the soul finds itself in God's lap. He plays with it gently, sometimes speaking to it with words of love sweeter in their own way than honey, as the mother speaks with her tiny babe. At other times he kisses it, just as the mother does, at others again, he embraces it, all in pure spirit. . . . The *lap* of God is the infinite uncreated being of God, and he, in himself, accommodates himself to the soul in such a way, that it seems to it that he holds it as in a lap, and there plays with it as the mother does with her child. The understanding and experience of this lap of God, is given by God himself to him who does not yet know it nor has experienced it. Such a man will thus see the goodness of this great Lord whose joy it is to treat with souls and give them delight. From this divine play, the soul comes forth so much in love with God, and so keen for his service, that all the creatures of earth or hell could not suffice to separate it from God.

The Sweet Laments and Contradictory
Sentiments of the Soul as It Faints Away
for Love in Search of Its Beloved (Sr. María
de la Antigua: Desengaño de religiosas
[*Enlightenment of Religious*], I, 5, ch. 28)

Hear me ye seraphin,
Angels hearken to me,
Ye Heavens, give ear,
For if I complain I rest.

For my good I suffer an ill,
Of which I do not expect to be cured:
For my happiness consists
In that ill's greatest increase.

I suffer a sweet fever
With which I burn and am delighted
With a continual thirst
Not of water but of fire.

For the penetrating wound
With which my breast burns,
Only the hand who wounded me
Can give the remedy.

Various things happen to me
With which I burn and freeze:
I fear and hope at one point:
I laugh and weep at the same time.

I feel a delightful restlessness
Which I understand and do not understand:
Perchance I sleep, keeping vigil,
And perchance sleeping, I am awake.

Tell him, then seraphin,
My spouse and sweet Master,
That for his love I live,
And to die of it is my desire.

Tell him that for many days past
I have been afraid yet expectant
That his rays, his eyes divine
And beautiful, will o'ershadow me.

If I have angered him
Let him punish but frown not,
For, seeing him face to face
I want to die at his hands....

Tell him, then, that his absence
Reduces me to such a pass
That I find pleasure in nothing
And my own self I detest.

Lost I go in search of him,
But I count myself as having gained,
For I gain in losing myself
And through finding myself, I am lost.

Another soul, similarly suffering from the disease of love, exclaimed more recently (May 1916):

I am living in fire,
Fire I feel within me,
But I feel a cold and ice
Such as never I felt before.

I live set within the All,
I feel that All is within me:
At the same time I feel a nothingness
Such as never I felt before.

I feel myself within plenitude,
I feel that it is filling me;
Nevertheless I feel a void
Such as never I felt before.

I feel myself within God,
God I feel within myself,
And from him I feel far off
As never I felt before.

I feel myself within his sanctity,
His sanctity within me,
And I see myself more guilty
Than ever I felt before.

I feel darkness and light,
Pain and joy at once,
Peace and war, death and life,
Felicity and torment, and

When I seek the better to express
Either my joy or my pain,
The best I succeed in doing
Is to forget myself and be silent.

Holy Follies of Love

"O God," exclaimed St. Gemma Galgani (*Biography*, ch. 17),

the bonds of your love are so strong that I cannot escape.
Leave me, leave me free, for I shall love you in all things
and seek you always. Oh Jesus, what have you done, what
have you done to my heart, that it is always beside itself

with longing for you? Ah, I can do no more: I need to sing, I need to rejoice. Live uncreated Love. Live the Heart of my Jesus! Oh if all sinners would come to this Heart! Come, come, sinners, do not fear, for the sword of justice does not penetrate here. Ah Jesus, would that my voice might reach to the confines of the whole world, I would call all sinners and tell them all to enter into your Heart.

Longings for God, Agonies of Love, and Prayer of Desire

"Who knows," exclaimed St. Gemma on another occasion (*Biography*, ch. 19),

> if Jesus will allow himself to be seen again? But if Jesus does not look at me again, what does it matter to me? I shall not lose sight of him and if he no longer wants me with him, I shall follow after him all the same. He will be the continual object of my thought and he will come back to me. Flee, flee Lord: for I shall always run behind you, sure that neither Heaven nor earth nor hell will separate me from you any more. If it pleases you to martyr me by hiding your sweet presence from me, it will be equally acceptable to me, provided I know that you are pleased. If you are pleased, all should be so. Live, hidden Jesus!

"Oh my God and love of my soul!" exclaimed another great servant of God: "you have given me to desire what is impossible even for the blessed in heaven. It has happened to me to go to his Majesty with such great longings of love, with the love with which all the blessed love him, that when the soul sees it cannot reach him, it goes to pieces and is undone; and with me this shows outwardly with such agony that I seem to be on the point of death."

"Love is a tyrant all the more rigid and pitiless as it is sweet and sacred. Love, love spirits away all things. This is the sickness which afflicts me most and this is the accident of which the Lord has told me many times I am to die" (Ven. Angela María de la Concepción (1668–1746), a Cistercian nun in Valladolid, *Life* by Muñiz, § 31).

"There is another way of prayer," said the Ven. María (*Riego*, ch. 39),

> which we may call prayer of desire. It is a great longing in the will for God and for union with him, without any more exercise of acts than to love him as one has known him by faith in general and in a confused way. Neither the attending to other business nor distractions in the mind and imagination hinder the soul from this kind of prayer and contact with God.... It is a gentle prayer, without weariness, and can be persevered in for a long time.... There is also another which is similar to this, a longing and desire for the Cross of Christ our Lord, to imitate him in his sufferings, and this is a very safe prayer.... It is called the prayer of union with God, inasmuch as in it and with it the will feels no other love but that which the Lord has for himself, and it unites with that unique love with which this Lord loves his infinite goodness, in which the soul's love is, as it were, a tiny spark which is swallowed up and submerged in that infinite fire of divine love. Thus ... the soul, completely submerged, cannot rest in anything that is not God. It is

for that reason that this love of unity is so valiant and mighty for the suffering of the cross and mortification, so that it appears there is no difference in it between cross and love.…

This prayer is such a unique favour from the Lord that in it the will appears not to need the help of the understanding, for, without any vision to guide it, it finds itself wholly occupied with the intimate inspirations which divine love gives it from its divine Spouse, and this is the magnet of its movements. This sublime prayer has such power, that although the soul makes no particular resolution as to the practice of the virtues, it loves and embraces them with special love, putting them into practice. A great affection arises in the will for every kind of mortification and cross which is offered to it to suffer, for in practising the virtues it has been given to understand that it will not be able to preserve this prayer if it does not live crucified by love.

Divine Fires, Wonderful Inspirations, Sighs of Love

"All the fervour and ardour of my heart," said Ven. Ángela María de la Concepción of herself (*Vida*, I, 2, ch. 8),

spread through my body and I felt it become like an iron which is thrown into the fire.… In the same way, I already knew everything in God, where the fire of his charity was burning me and I desired to be wholly consumed there with that pain. It is a suffering which brings a taste of glory with it and the soul is greatly refreshed by it, for it feels God's inspirations and embraces, and has the certainty, more than if it should see him in the flesh before it, that it is in His Majesty. It is there given to it to know that that is a very great favour.... At the same time it likewise receives knowledge of its unworthiness—for otherwise it is not allowed to think of itself. This is the other penetrating shaft and incentive of love, that it sees itself loved by so mighty a Lord whereas it deserves nothing more than to be thrown into the deep abyss. There it knows all, at one and the same time: its own baseness and God's highest Goodness; both help it to intensify that general and simple act of love of God, which he himself in his Goodness has given it. It loves and it seems to it that it does not love. It suffers, but the suffering is of little account to it, since all its sufferings are but longings to love and suffer for the Beloved, with laments and so to speak sighs which arise in force from the heart, and in the case of each one, cast all his affections into God, and the soul after them. In this employment it cannot say nor utter anything more than "O mighty sea" in which it seems to be saying to itself all that there is to say, and there it remains as it were submerged.

Shafts of the Divine Anger

In the midst of the calamities of the past and the earthquakes that occurred in Quito in her time, the Ven. Sr. Catalina de Jesús María once saw (*Autobiography*, pt. 2, ch. 79) our Lord speak to her in great anger and at the same time throw at her a shaft of fire. Then after replying to Him, "What do you want to do, my only good, behold your slave," she began to exclaim, "I am burning, I am on fire."

"For," she adds, "at the prick that shaft made in my heart and soul, both soul and body caught fire and the heart as it burned sought to break open the breast not with sweet love, no, it was not like that, but with that fire which the anger of God discharged, causing in my soul an inexpressible reverential fear, although love was not lacking, for I did not want to see him angry. Anyone indeed to whom this has happened will well understand me; but I was yielding up my very life with this fire of anger."

Participation in the Divine Omnipotence

"As iron united to the fire," remarked Fr. La Puente (*Sentimentos y avisos*, § VI),

> shares in the power and activity of the fire, so the soul united with God shares in God's omnipotence.... There are three ways of entering into the powers of God: first, through speculative knowledge ..., and this is fitting for learned people. David, however, does not speak of this, he rather says (Ps. 70:15–16): "Because I have not known learning, I will enter into the powers of the Lord." Ignorant of the world, I entered into the communications of the Lord. If the learned do not become as it were simple and ignorant, they will not enter into the powers of God. There is another way of entering, through knowledge of God's omnipotence which is more than speculative and less than experimental, and this is a knowledge with living faith of the facility with which the omnipotence of God can enter within me and make of my powers what it pleases.... In this disposition the soul is open and pliable for whatever God may want, and desires him

to come and change it and unite it with himself. There is still a third way, which is that of experimental knowledge ..., when a soul, feeling this union with the divine omnipotence, experiences a magnanimity for doing in God things which are heroic; as also for suffering the hardest trials.... Such a one shares in the divine omnipotence in all its powers. His prayer is omnipotent for obtaining from God what he asks of him, his obedience is omnipotent for executing whatever God commands, his patience omnipotent for suffering whatever trials God sends him.... Oh, that it might please your Omnipotence, most almighty Lord, that there should be many such omnipotent souls in your Church.... If you desire to enter into the powers of God, the way is to suffer humiliations.

The Divine Working in the Soul United with God

"In union, which is already a supernatural state," remarks St. John of the Cross (*Ascent*, III, ch. 1),

the memory wholly fails, as do the other faculties in their natural operations, and they pass from their natural end to that of God, which is supernatural. Thus, the memory being transformed in God, neither forms nor potencies of things can be impressed upon it; by reason of which the operations of the memory and of the other powers in this state are all divine. For, since God now possesses the faculties as their Sovereign Lord, by the transformation of them into himself, he himself is the one who moves and commands them in a divine manner, according to his

Spirit and will. Then it is in such a way that the operations are not distinct but that those the soul produces are of God. They are divine operations, in so much as he who unites himself with God becomes one Spirit with him (1 Cor. 6:17). Hence it is that the operations of the soul are united with the Divine Spirit, and are divine. Hence it is, too, that the works of such souls alone are acceptable and reasonable, and not unacceptable to God; for the Spirit of God makes them know what they have to know and leave aside what it is fitting to leave aside, remember what should be remembered, with forms and without forms, and forget what is to be forgotten. He makes them love what they have to love and not love what is not in God. Thus all the first movements of the powers of such souls are divine; and it is not to be wondered at that the movements and operations of these powers are divine, for they are transformed into the divine being.

"I hold," says St. Teresa (*Life*, ch. 20),

that a soul which arrives at this state (of ecstatic union, with raptures and flights of the spirit), no longer speaks or does anything of itself, but this sovereign King takes care of all it has to do. Oh God help me, how clearly can be seen here the explanation of the verse "Who will give me wings ..." and how it can be understood that it was right, and they all long to ask for dove's wings. It is to be clearly understood, it is the flight which the spirit is given for lifting itself up above everything created and above itself first of all.

Appendix 6

Referring to Chapter 9

How God Proves and Tries but at the Same Time Consoles and Delights the Soul

"I am afflicted the whole day long," exclaimed the Ven. Sr. Filomena de Santa Coloma in November 1867 (*Life and Writings*, pp. 238-239).

When I am awake in the night, it is to be the victim of pain; and it seems as if the sun, which comes out in the morning giving all creatures joy and making them new ... serves me as a darker night, for my soul is shaken and troubled by anguish and fear of death. I fear and tremble and am, so to speak, submerged in gloomy darkness. All the darkness allows me to see is the Lord's anger discharged against me. I find myself in great distress without any consolation, surrounded and assaulted by my enemies, who plot my ruin. My body is full of pain, but of greater moment is what my soul suffers.... I cry to heaven, I cry again and again, my voice grows hoarse and my eyes, flooded with tears, again and again have to look down on the ground to see the twelve gates closed. I force myself to cling to the sweet memory that within those twelve gates of heaven is my Beloved. I call him and call him again by his own name, but this most beautiful Beloved of mine does not allow me to hear his loving voice—much less does he show me his affectionate countenance. It seems to me that the more I call him, the more he is displeased.... I believe that if I loved God as I ought, at this very instant I should die of not dying, for although my existence here below is preserved, I lead a dying life and die without life; for although my poor soul longs so much for intimate union with God, it sees itself as it were abhorred and despised by him and, after calling him by sweet and affectionate names, falls into greater distress. What shall I do then, Father, in such a deplorable situation? Despair? Not that at all costs; I love, I believe and I calmly hope that he who so many times revived my courage in the midst of the struggle will remember me.... If I were to give account of the great calm I feel in my inmost soul, it would seem like a contradiction of all I have set down.... The consolations of the Lord abound in the midst of my greatest afflictions. My inmost soul remains unchanged and full of confidence in the promises the Lord has made us.

"When I find myself involved in these terrible combats," said the Ven. Sr. Bárbara de Santo Domingo in October 1871 (*Life*, p. 258),

I have recourse to God, but it seems that for me there is no longer any God and that if he does allow himself to be felt in any way, he is displeased. I look into myself to see wherein I have offended him, and I see myself in such a state that if I allowed myself to be carried away by what I see, I could not have even the slightest hope. But in the midst of all, without my understanding how it is so, the power of God is sustaining me ... so that I do not faint.

"The dereliction," she added in May 1872,

has increased to an extraordinary degree. I have been as it were in a dark lake full of every imaginable affliction ...; mortal anguish covers my heart, weariness has taken possession of me in such a way that it seems as if it does not want to leave me the power of action for anything good; I cannot even utter the sweet name of Jesus. Terrible temptations come down on me like torrential rain. It seems as if I am abandoned by the merciful hand of the good God and that I cry out for divine help in vain; but this, as you know, does not penetrate into the inmost centre of the soul.

"However," she adds, "I suffer martyrdom in an extraordinary way."

"What great darkness has surrounded me," she exclaimed again in September, "I seemed as if I were in a terribly dark place, and at times things came to such a pass that it seemed as if I had not even faith. I was in the greatest state of dereliction; but in the midst of it all, my soul rejoiced in its suffering.... And the more I seemed to be deserted by God and the more I suffered with all I have said, increasingly did my heart and soul burn with ardent desires of suffering much for God, and the more did I feel myself on fire with his holy love."

"I am," she says again a few days later, "in a fire of suffering: God gives me to drink even to the dregs of this most bitter chalice;

at the same time he has hidden within himself, and communicates, a sweetness which has to be experienced to be believed."

"O Lord," exclaimed Sr. Catalina de Jesús, María y José (*Autobiography*, pt. 1, ch. 8, p. 45),

> allow me to speak to you as to a most loving Father who tolerates everything in the daughter who loves him. With what pleasure you captivate the imagination in the beginning until you have the soul well in your hands. Later, whatever its will, the force of attraction which that which it has already experienced in you exercises upon it, will not allow it to separate itself from so good a Lord, however many trials he sends it. Many a time have I come to tell you, half in boldness and half affectionately: "How is it, Lord, that beforehand you make me think it is so easy? How can you say that your yoke is sweet, when as I experience it, my shoulders are weighed down?" I have said this many times—but you ... as the Father of love, as soon as you saw that in my weakness I could do no more, came forward to strengthen me with your presence, with which you blotted out all impression of the burden and left me longing for that very weight, sad that I had found it an affliction, for its absence now seemed strange. Thus, Lord, you burden the soul and thus do you console it.

"When I find myself, so to speak, beside myself," said St. Rose of Lima (cf. *Life* by Fr. J. A. C. Calella, ch. 34),

> in that wild whirlwind of darkness and shadows, it happens that suddenly I find myself restored to the light of noonday and to my former union with God, as if I were reposing in the arms of my beloved Bridegroom, with as

much security as if I had never fallen from that most blissful state. I feel within me great longings of love, like a full-flowing river, which breaks the barriers or dykes by which its currents are usually confined and rushes forward with its swirling waters so that the gates which before held it in check and blocked its passage are easily swept away. Then I breathe in the gentle breeze of the divine favours and the delightful fragrance of their perfumes is spread over the field of my soul. The latter finds itself submerged in the immense sea of the divine goodness and in an ineffable transformation is intimately united with the Beloved and becomes one thing with him....

Among these favours it seemed to me that I had thrown out very deep roots into God and that I was fixed in him, sure of his friendship and confirmed in grace. I also experienced a certain inexplicable and very rare gift, in virtue of which it seems to me that he makes me impeccable, so that I can say with full confidence with the Apostle: "Who can separate me from the love of Christ? I *am certain* that neither death nor life ... neither anguish nor hunger, will be able to separate me from my beloved Jesus."

"When the Son of God," writes St. Lawrence Justinian (*De casto connubio*, ch. 25),

finds a soul that, by a privilege of his grace and of his immense love, has been raised to the condition and dignity of spouse, he visits it again and again and speaks to it with full familiarity, seeming to multiply himself to console and bless it, as if he could not bear its absence. If he withdraws himself at times, it is in order to return quickly with greater tenderness and outpouring of himself. Do you not see him knocking eagerly at the door of the heart which belongs to him, awakening it from its mysterious sleep? (*Cant.* 2).

"Often in this state," wrote Richard of St. Victor (*De quatuor gradibus viol. caritatis*), "the Lord visits [the soul]. He often fills it with interior happiness and inebriates it with the sweetness of his spirit. Often he comes down from heaven and visits a soul sitting in darkness and in the shadow of death. Often the glory of the Lord fills the tabernacle of the covenant."

"Often when I came into choir tired, the Lord told me to rest in his arms and thus my soul found itself in them with delights and favours which I cannot express. At other times he showed me the opening in his Side and gave me to understand that he wanted to put me within his Heart and that the love I had for him compelled him to this" (Ven. Sr. Angela María de la Concepción, *Life*, no. 38).

The Most Painful State of the Soul When Persecuted by Its Enemies and, as It Were, Far Removed from and Abandoned by Its Most Sweet Master, Unable to Find Consolation or Support in Anything and at Times Incapacitated and, So to Speak, Insensitive to Everything

After relating (cf. *Life*, bk. 2, ch. 1) the torments and afflictions that the demons caused her, St. Veronica Juliani added:

All these sufferings were nothing in comparison with what I felt in my inmost soul, destitute and abandoned in the blackest darkness, and so far removed from God that I could not even breathe or send out a sigh to him.... Oh, unbearable suffering of the soul, to see itself deprived of all help and so far off from the Highest Good! It sighs, and is not heard. It calls its Bridegroom, but he does not come. The more it seeks him the more he eludes it. It entreats him and he will not listen.... My soul was in such great suffering that I think the death agony could not be greater.

What most afflicts the soul is its utter helplessness and the very insensitivity to which it believes itself reduced.

"I feel," the Ven. Mariana de San José said in 1608 (*Life*, bk. 3, ch. 6),

a great abandonment on the part of our Lord and a lack of any feeling of virtue. I am surrounded by the most subtle temptations, and my understanding has not the strength to make any kind of considered examination nor is it possible to find phrases in which to express this state and what is happening to me.... Wherever I turn the eyes of my soul, I find someone who hurts and wounds it. Wholly surrendered to this life of suffering, it is, so to speak, paralysed or like a new-born babe, who only feels and weeps without being able to say why, for ... it cannot even distinguish good from evil. It seems nonsense to say that the understanding is so dull that it cannot do this; for it is not really so, but it happens as I have said. To think that the soul can help itself is impossible, nor can it do anything more than a little lamb which allows itself to be bound and led to the slaughter without a cry of protest, for it has been deprived even of the possibility of complaint, so that it cannot even do that. It seems as if it has been handed over to a great crowd of enemies who torment it, but it neither fears nor hopes, nor does it know in what darkness it is held.... It follows its usual path, like a blind man who goes where they guide him—but it does not know who it is that guides it.... This seems such blind suffering that the soul cannot avail itself of anything more than what I have said, of letting itself surrender, bathing itself in the very tribulation in which it finds itself submerged.

"Here the soul," said the Ven. Ángela María de la Concepción (*Life*, bk. 2, ch. 15),

finds neither foothold nor support, for the things of this world tire and weary it. It desires without knowing what it desires, because it neither longs with eagerness for the things of heaven, nor knows to what to turn its will, for it finds itself clinging to God without wanting anything either above or below. His Majesty does not enlighten it, for it is his pleasure that it should desire, but not see the desire fulfilled. Thus he leaves it in a kind of trance, so that even if this gives it strength to resist evil and desire only good, it goes along as it were blindly, desiring to know how it may succeed in giving pleasure. This kind of suffering in this trance-like state without support or foothold in anything, is like being crucified between heaven and earth, which is a form of martyrdom. The less this suffering is perceived, the sharper it is for the soul. It purifies it in a subtle way, for if it indeed suffers and feels, it does so after the manner of children who have not the use of reason. Something hurts them, but they know not what, nor how to express it, and they suffer the more from it. This is one of the great benefits which God gives to the soul in this life—in this state it rejoices and accepts without perceiving what is happening, but immediately it returns to itself, and what has happened remains imprinted upon it.

Awe Produced by the Divine Holiness and Justice—Participation in the Sufferings and Joys of Christ

"This divine holiness," said St. Margaret Mary (*Autobiography*, at the end),

> was imprinted and weighed so deeply upon me that it made me incapable of prayer and of feeling the interior pain which I suffered. I felt such despair and such great suffering at appearing before my God that if the very power that was making me suffer had not sustained me, I should have wanted a thousand times over to throw myself into the abyss, destroy myself, annihilate myself, if it were in my hands. In spite of this, I could not withdraw myself from this divine presence that haunted me on every side as if I were a criminal ready to receive condemnation, but I had such submission to God's divine will that I was always ready to receive all the pains and sufferings which he thought well to send me, with the same pleasure with which I should receive the sweetness of his love.

In December 1805, the Lord deigned to reveal to His faithful servant Sr. Maria Josefa Kumi (1763-1817), a Dominican nun and stigmatic of the convent of Wesen (Switzerland), the many sufferings He had reserved for her in expiation of the sins of the world. "You will suffer," He said to her (cf. *Vie*, ch. 6, 1906), "such bitterness and sadness that you will come to believe you are suffering the pains of hell, for I shall hide myself completely, withdrawing from your soul all that is mine."

"Your sufferings," He added another time (*Vie*, ch. 9), "will come to such a point that all you have suffered up till now will seem to you as nothing. You will even feel the tortures of remorse for certain crimes, and thus will accuse yourself of those supposed sins as if you had really committed them. When that time comes, follow the judgement of your confessor and hide nothing from him, for he will have light and grace to guide you."

"Some days," said Sr. Bárbara de Santo Domingo, in October 1872 (*Life*, p. 382),

> I have much suffering in my spirit, but it increases in particular on Wednesdays in the afternoon, and I spend all Thursday and Friday in such great pains that sometimes, if God were not to strengthen me, it seems to me impossible that I could suffer them.... This good, kind God, who on occasion communicates himself to me so generously, filling my soul with heavenly consolation, so that it seems that all his delight is to come to this vile creature of his, as if she were the only one in the world—this God hides himself so much from my soul ... that it seems as if there is no God for me.... I think much of the dereliction that God experienced on the Cross and in the Garden of Olives, and when I think of this it seems as if the anguish and other interior sufferings increase in me. But all this creates my soul anew, for I find my greatest delight in suffering both physical and mental. It would seem that if things are as I have said, I

ought not to have any of the loving visits of God, but it is not so; for as this Lord is so good and kind, he does not treat us altogether with severity, but with the bitter, gives the sweet.

"It is impossible to understand," she added after a few days, "how a creature can enjoy suffering in the way I enjoy it, and that the greater are the trials, the greater the pleasure and joy I have in them. This is very certain. I find more pleasure and joy when God fills me with affliction than when he refreshes me with sweet consolations.... When I have little to suffer, I am like the fish out of water and cannot live."

Deification of the Soul Submerged and Lost in God: Participation in His Divine Immensity

"And so when the mind," says Denys the Carthusian (*In Exod.*, art. 42),

> burning with the fervour of all-consuming charity is thus joined to God through speculative contemplation and luminous, burning, unitive wisdom, it is said to enter the cloud and, after the example of Moses, to be separated from all things. For it is united to God, so to speak, directly, as to the incomprehensible and even to the absolutely unknown; yet to behold him thus is to contemplate, in the utmost clarity and sweetness, and the highest kind of contemplation possible in this life. Then, therefore, all is unfolded in that infinite light, is firmly centred upon uncreated Truth, and is joined to the super-essential Godhead and the super-blessed Trinity so radiantly, lovingly and closely, that the mind is

aware of nothing else, nor does it attend to its own action, but flows down from itself and back into its own source, and so is borne away into the riches of glory. It is consumed in the fire of immense uncreated love, plumbs the depths of the abyss of the Godhead, and is absorbed, so that it seems in a certain manner to throw off created being and to put on uncreated and ideal being—not that the substance is changed or its own essence is taken away, but because the mode of being and the quality of living is deified, that is, it is assimilated to God and his super-blessed beatitude supernaturally and absolutely gratuitously. Thus what the Apostle says is abundantly fulfilled: "He who cleaves to God is one spirit with him."

"Lord and Father of love," exclaimed Sr. Catalina de Jesús María (*Autobiography*, pt. 2, ch. 76),

you caused my soul to be rapt from this world, and, it seems to me, to be caught up to the highest heaven. I saw my soul so extended, I do not know if I should say that it seemed to me immense.... I saw in spirit all the empyrean orb and the other heavens, with all the centre of the earth, and its abysses, and that your immense Majesty filled it all, extending even to what cannot be expressed or imagined, even where there is no longer any world or thing created. It seemed to me that my soul was or extended itself to all this greatness, that it saw itself full of all this immensity of God and also within all that divine immensity, so that it seemed to me that my soul was also an immensity which, akin to God's immensity, looked at and understood it all. It seemed to me that my soul was not one thing and God other, but that God and my soul were so much one, that division was impossible. Even to this height had my soul grown. The latter, although it thus saw itself wholly deified, in possession of a great peace as if it were one of the blessed in heaven (I cannot express it in any other way), besides that measureless love, did not fail to recognize you, Lord, with reverence and great lowliness of heart. It would never want to lose that peace with our loving God. At the same time, I found myself like a great lady who was treading the whole world underfoot, with dominion over all that did not please God.... In this union I began to understand how very many immeasurably good things are distributed with full hands to all the chosen and to all men, wherefore no one can complain, except of his own ingratitude. Of all these good things and great favours ... I knew that our Lord Jesus Christ was the distributor.... Then I heard the voice of the Lord saying: "These good things came to men through me, since I became man for them, which is the greatest of these benefits with that of having remained in the world in the Sacrament to be with them."

Another time she declared (pt. 3, ch. 18) how the Holy Spirit came to her in a special manner and made her share in that divine immensity. "He came towards me," she said,

stripped of every image, giving me to understand that he was coming to his own dwelling. My soul opened its gates to their Master, for it knew that it could not resist him.... Introducing himself within, he remained, not as guest, but as absolute master of the house. And then, in

that unexpected coming, it seemed to me that this divine
Spirit engrafted himself into my soul, so that it remained
one single thing with him, and a thing so broad of ex-
panse that it seemed to me the soul stretched itself to the
measure of his immensity. And as the immensity of God
has not to limit itself to the confines of the soul ... it
seems to me that within this Divine Spirit the soul becomes immense ... not because this comes to the soul
through its own working, but through the Immensity
which united itself to it.

The Substantial Touches of God – Their
Wonderful Effects: Deep Knowledge

"Only the soul who reaches union with God," said St. John of
the Cross (*Ascent*, II, ch. 24),

can have this deep and loving knowledge (about the divine attributes), for this knowledge itself is actual union.
For having this knowledge consists in a certain touch
which is made by the soul on the Divinity and thus it is
God himself who is felt and tasted in it, and although he
does not manifest himself clearly, as he does in glory, it
is such an exalted and deep touch of knowledge and
love, that it penetrates the substance of the soul.... Such
knowledge is a foretaste of the divine essence and of
eternal life.... There is a certain knowledge and certain
touches like these which God makes in the substance of
the soul which enrich it in such a way that not only is
one of them sufficient to remove immediately all the
imperfections which it had not been able to get rid of

throughout the whole of life, but it leaves it full of the riches and virtues of God. These touches are so pleasant and of such intimate delight for the soul, that with a single one of them one would consider oneself well rewarded for all the trials one had suffered in this life, even were they innumerable. The soul remains so full of energy and with so much eagerness to suffer many things for God, that to see that it does not suffer much is a special grief to it....

These favours are not given to the selfish and acquisitive. They are given with very special love of God which he has for such a soul, and the soul also offers itself to him with great detachment. This is what our Lord meant in St. John (14:21) when he said: "He who loves me will be loved by my Father and I shall love him and shall manifest myself to him." In this are included the knowledge and touches we have been speaking of that God manifests to the soul which reaches him and truly loves him.

The Kiss and Embrace of God: Great Mysteries Are Here Enshrined

"By *kiss*," remarks Fr. Antonio del Espíritu Santo (tr. 1, d. 1, s. 6, no. 4),

> is signified a certain very deep sweetness in the soul infused by God in the communication of the divine Spirit.... By *embrace*, however, is meant a certain touch, which contains something of the delights of eternal life. Espousals and matrimony, however, are spoken of when God, who dwells in the soul's essence, comes down in an

ineffable manner into the purified soul and manifests himself, raising up the mind to a certain divine light, so that it recognizes him as existing and present to itself, and by an affective touch on the will, so that it most ardently loves God who is intimately joined to the soul, and kisses and embraces it. In a mutual embrace of love the soul is joined to God and, being altogether transformed and absorbed into him, enjoys him most sweetly and delightfully. Now this divine indwelling is not given to the mind of the blessed in the manner described. For them it is effected through the intuitive vision of God, but only through the real presence of God and union with him, not with the will alone, as some would have it, but also with the intellect.... When marriage takes place in the centre of the soul, there God manifests himself immediately and directly.

"In a union of this kind," he adds (no. 11), "God is perceived by internal touch and embrace, and in a certain manner is felt by the soul, and communicates to it immense treasures of divine grace. All of this the soul sees clearly" (cf. St. John of the Cross, *Spiritual Canticle*, ch. 22).

"Having surrendered myself to Jesus," wrote a certain soul (F., April 13, 1909),

I was raised by him to the heart of the most Holy Trinity and I felt how inseparable from the Father and the Son is the Spirit of love who proceeds from them. I felt the ineffable sweetness of the embrace of the Father and the Son, and it was given to me to understand how every act of love derives from this principle of all love. Every act of charity is a communication of and derivation from this principle and I felt that since I had God within me, in me the Father and the Son loved each other and produced the Holy Spirit. I also understood that Communion produces grace in us, since it is God's embrace of his creature, a reflection of that which Father and Son give each other.

"I have felt," she added (April 14),

Father and Son loving each other in me and producing the Holy Spirit; and I understood that sanctity is the liberty left to this Love of Father and Son, and that if sin is so appalling, it is because it hinders this Love from producing itself in the soul. It is an obstacle to God's action. I understand that only in the Heart of Jesus has there been the fullness of that love, and in order that this fullness might be accomplished in humanity, it was necessary that the Word should become incarnate.... I understood how the Eucharist brings to us the Divinity united to the Humanity, and it seemed to me that the principal reason for the institution of the Eucharist was the need God has to love himself in his creatures and always to increase in them that presence of the Father and the Son loving each other continually.... Jesus becomes my food and incorporates me in himself to perfect and complete in me each time more deeply what takes place in him.

The Abyss of the Dark Night

The following is a recent description of the dark night by a soul who found itself suddenly submerged in it, after experiencing the ineffable embrace of the three Divine Persons:

"I felt myself," this person said,

much more in God. It seemed to me that he was nourishing me, that he was the air I breathed, the life I lived, that he was more my soul than my soul itself was.... The day of the most Holy Trinity (1915), the favour was renewed, but in an even more intimate way. Afterwards ... what has happened? I do not know, but it seems as if I have lost it all—all, without anything more remaining to me than a sensation of nothingness and death which paralyses me.... It seems as if I have fallen into a very deep and dark well, where I neither see nor hear, nor know anything.... It seems as if I have lost God, faith, hope, love, as if I had never felt them. I feel like an insane person who can neither suffer nor desire.... I cannot work either through fear or hope, for I feel as if after all there is nothing more than nothingness.

In the depths of this dark chasm
In which I live dying, but do not die,
If I feel myself without God and do not love him,
What awaits me? What do I wait for? To succumb....

Believing without faith and without hope,
Vainly forcing myself to trust,
I ask myself: Without life, how do I live?
Without air, how can I breathe?

If at least I suffered, I should live,
But I lack both life and suffering.
I am left with nothing more than nothing,
I have lost all, even feeling....

In the sad darkness in which I find myself,
In this bitter and lonely solitude,
Ah! Let me repeat at least one cry:
May thy will, Lord, be done in me.

(July 25, 1915)

State of Another Soul, Incapacitated and Reduced to a Single Feeling of Suffering Love (1915)

Will a chord suffice for me?
One note alone?…
A harp was mine,
Sonorous and beautiful.

How joyfully it sang
At each hour!…
But one day when I plucked the strings,
Divine hands…

Broke one by one
Its slender strings.
Ah, broke its strings
And broken they lie!…

How shall they now give notes
Varied and beautiful?
An "ay" or other moan
Perhaps they give forth.

Ah no, the broken strings,
The strings are silent.
The muted harp
Does not sing now.

Its strings no longer tremble,
The harp is weeping!...
How could it sing,
Finding itself absent

From the Divine Lover,
Unable to find him?
In vain in holy fear
I long to strike a chord.

The chord fails to tremble,
I cannot sing.
I gaze at heaven in vain,
I cannot see him.

Today, his desire
No longer invites me to sing.
One chord alone remains,
That of suffering:

If it is plucked, it responds,
A lone note, Love....
For the Lover who one day
Alas, robbed me.

One chord, one chord alone
Left trembling,
Which sings ... only at the touch
Of a loving God.

Neither fear nor hope
Remains vibrant....
Nothing is now left to me
To which I can cling.

The strings of my harp
Alas! have been broken,
For the hand that has wounded me
Broke them!

To give beautiful sounds
To the broken harp,
Will one string suffice,
One note alone?

For one string is left to me,
That of pain.
One note alone sings
Love, Love!

Transformation in Suffering

This ineffable transformation of the soul into God through pain
is the complement of that effected through pure love and causes
the latter to prove its full worth. As St. John of the Cross remarks
(*Night*, I, ch. 12), it is through sufferings and afflictions that one
reaches the highest touches of divine love. This is how in the year
1892, a certain soul (M. C. S.), who knew this by experience, expressed it. Giving account to her director of "how our Lord communicated himself to her when he made her share his sufferings,"
she said:

> When the Lord in his goodness and love raises the soul
> and ... brings it into the mysteries of the love of Jesus,
> and Jesus communicates to it his own sufferings, his
> agony, all the torments of his Passion, and allows the
> divine blood to pour down in torrents over that soul

from his most holy heart, as he does with me, it seems as if the blood of Jesus is mingled with my own blood, giving extraordinary strength and vigour to my body....

Just as through the transformation of love he unites the soul to himself in the most intimate and precious manner, so he also intimately unites it to himself through the transformation of suffering. As the soul in this state is wholly surrendered to the divine will, God by one of those divine and loving touches which he makes on the soul, renews in it the transformation of love or pain, as it pleases the divine Goodness, and makes it share either in his sufferings or in his consolation and ineffable sweetness. Just as when ... the Three Divine Persons transform it into themselves through love, the soul has joy and is overwhelmed in an ocean of delight and glory, in the same way Jesus Christ, as bridegroom of my soul, in one of those divine touches of pain, transforms it into himself through suffering, in such a way and in such a spiritual manner that it cannot be expressed, so that I feel myself saturated through and through with the suffering love of Jesus, and I feel in my spirit and my whole being a new life and the purity and sanctity of Christ, just as if his most holy Humanity had communicated a divine power to my body as well as to my spirit. It seems to me that my body is not mine, but that, just as my soul is transformed in God and made one thing with him, so also my body shares in a certain manner in this blessed state ... already tasting here below as it were a tiny drop of glory....

In the prayer of love, as in the prayer of suffering, all God's working in his goodness and love is in my soul, and the body has joy and suffers in a certain measure through an overflow.... This makes me remember the resurrection of the flesh and is a proof that our bodies are to rise again some day.

As the soul, as I have said before, in the transformation of love enjoys the ineffable sweetness and consolations of glory, so in the transformation of pain, it seems to be and is submerged in a sea of sufferings and divine bitterness, but most sweet and delightful sufferings. It would seem that this cannot be true, but by experience I know that it is so. The soul united to God through love and transformed into him through love has joy and suffers at the same time, for love raises the soul to the Holy Mountain, to the summit of Calvary, and through love alone it comes to enclose itself wholly within the Cross of Jesus, is fused into Jesus and becomes one with Jesus. Love makes this sweet and delightful.

The value, as I understand it, of this divine suffering and the graces the soul receives through it and obtains from God for other souls, depriving itself of the merit of suffering in favour of them, are so great that there are no words with which to express their worth. For as the soul is transformed into Christ and suffers with Christ, it merits as Christ does, for our divine Lord makes over to the soul his own merits in suffering. How great is the goodness and mercy of God!

"In this transportation of pain," wrote the same person in June 1891, "in which my soul, and my body too, suffer all the torments and pains of the Passion, love gives strength to bear them and infuses into them something of heavenly delight, which inebriates my soul at the same time that the sufferings cause it pain.

"My soul feels like Jesus, suffers like Jesus, in Jesus, within Jesus.... I do not know how to express this most divine suffering. It seems as if I am the person of Jesus and that my flesh is that of Jesus ... and my bones the bones of Jesus."

Ineffable Divine Communications in the Blessed State of Spiritual Marriage

This is how the person already quoted (M. C. S.) described them in 1891. "There is no pen, nor tongue," she wrote,

> capable of expressing what my soul receives from God in this most intimate union and highest prayer, nor the power and security that it has in this blessed state and in this most sublime contemplation; nor the treasures of grace with which it has been enriched by its Divine Bridegroom and by the most blessed Trinity, the Father communicating his power to it, the Son his wisdom and the Holy Spirit his love. Before the spiritual marriage of Jesus with my soul, during that lovely time of the mystical espousals, the Lord ... stripped it of everything earthly, prepared it and adorned it with the most precious jewels ..., and afterwards he united it to himself and transformed it into himself, so that the soul became one single thing with him. The soul in this most exalted state, being already the spouse of Jesus, received each day from our Lord fresh gifts and greater graces, and the most Blessed Trinity associated it with Itself, making it share in all its concerns and revealing to it the highest

secrets of heaven. The torrent of divine light that my soul receives from God is so abundant that it floods it in every part. The knowledge it has of supernatural and divine things is so deep that it penetrates God's designs upon souls, upon the future of the Church, upon the centuries . . . , penetrating the hearts of men.

"Before . . . God worked in my soul, *without my soul*. Now God works in it, *with it*. For through his divine grace, the soul merited that God should give it a share in all his concerns . . . , and he now no longer says to it as formerly, "I will work this marvel in you. Rejoice in me and refresh yourself in my goodness," and other things that God says to the soul which he wishes to prepare to become his spouse, things which cannot be expressed. Now, as the soul is transformed into God, divinized, and understands and loves in the divine manner, God speaks to it differently, saying: "Let *us* work this wonder. Let *us* do this marvel. Let *us* rejoice in this everlasting glory." He shows it his hidden secrets and opens to it all the treasures of his love and utters for it, when he speaks to it as Bridegroom, such mysterious words that the human tongue cannot relate them. They are more than words . . . like a mysterious and most sweet whisper of love, which the soul can only perceive within the very heart of God, for it is then made one single thing with him. What the soul receives from God in this most sublime prayer and contemplation, what it understands in it, what it enjoys and how much it loves, is so sublime and so divine that it cannot be told. . . .

These aspirations of God to the soul, of God in the soul, of the soul in God and of God and the soul, in which the soul gives God back to God himself, are the greatest proof of this most intimate union of my soul with God [cf. St. John of the Cross, *Spiritual Canticle*, stanzas 37–39]....

In this most sublime prayer ... my soul receives an abundant and clear light to see the Godhead, though it is not intuitive. Thanks to this divine light, it sees in itself all the tiny specks of the imperfections into which it falls. It sees them notwithstanding the fact that it finds itself in so sublime a prayer, wherein it enjoys God in the manner in which the blessed in heaven enjoy him. Only with a light so special can it see them....

The more a soul is illuminated by God to plumb the depths of and penetrate supernatural and divine things, the greater is the knowledge it has that there remains very much more for it to understand.... I have no words to express ... how intense is this light, thanks to which my soul sees both things divine and the tiny specks of the imperfections into which it falls, and it knows itself.

This light is like a brilliant torch which burns in my soul and lights it constantly. If my soul moves down from this sublime stage of love to another lower stage, this most intense light is changed into faith, but into such a lively faith of what the soul has seen in itself, that this faith sustains it in the deep knowledge it has had of itself, and forms a counterpoise to the happiness which it experiences from the divine favours. Thus the soul which sees itself so much loved of God in this way does not become proud, but remains faithful to its God and Lord who shows himself so loving and kind with it, though it does not deserve it. His divine eyes deign to rest on this vile and wretched creature who for its sin deserved only hell.... This faith is a burning faith, which, at the same time that it humbles the soul, raises it up to hope everything from God. To express it better—this light does not change into faith.... There is nothing more than the stepping down one stage.... Rather than resolve itself into faith, it serves to vivify faith. This light, joined with that of faith, united with it, remains permanently in my soul, enlightening it, setting it ablaze, for it is a light that not only gives light, but also consumes. With this light my soul sees the most blessed Virgin and the saints as they are, and with the higher light it sees them in God, when the vision is more sublime and more perfect.

Similarly words fail me to express what passes in my soul in this most sublime prayer, in which it remains in one single act of love for I know not how many hours, for time has no meaning for my soul. All the time it is in prayer is a single instant of supreme happiness for it. I cannot say anything except that my soul is there and that it is not doing nothing, as it is in another, lower prayer ... when it is rapt in ecstasy without doing anything more than receive what God gives it. That is when God works in the soul without the soul itself.... I would say that in the time that this act of love lasts, the soul is not doing nothing, but I cannot say what it does. All I can say is that my soul in that act of love is.... To say that then it is rapt in God, in ecstasy, contemplating his infinite perfections and inebriated with love and joy, is little.... In this most sublime prayer it is.... All I can say is that it understands in a divine manner, loves in a divine manner; that is, it understands like God and loves what God loves. Not only does it understand God's operations in it, but how God works in the soul with the soul. It has a deep knowledge of the operations of God in souls, in the universe, in all things. Not only is the soul in ecstasy contemplating such marvels, but as the Lord has associated it to himself and has given it a share in all his concerns and wants it to work with him, my soul does what God does. For this reason he now says to it—"Let *us* do this wonder." …

God says such divine things to my soul that they cannot be expressed. I cannot speak of things so exalted, nor have I words to express how sublime is this prayer, for which God prepares the soul as for the Beatific Vision. In this act of most pure love, my soul sees God in the light of God and loves him with the burning love of the cherubim who are the spirits most ardent in the love of God [sic]. … With this light my soul sees or understands God's operations in it and in souls. It penetrates the divine secrets and the greatest mysteries of heaven. … As it sees God in God's own light, it understands and loves in the divine manner, and does what God does. It does not see divine things one by one … but … sees all things that God wills it to see at a single glance. It takes in everything at the same time, like God. …

I cannot express what my soul understands or what passes in it in this most sublime prayer in which it sees God in his own light and through a luminous veil or through a transparent and very fine cloud. Still less can I express the wonderful and marvellous way the Lord has of showing himself to my soul when, now wholly transformed into God, it feels itself transformed anew, in a new manner, for all that the soul receives from God always seems new. It feels itself transformed in a more perfect manner, with an increase of love, with greater strength, and sees God, not through a luminous veil … as … before, but my soul rises still higher. The Lord raises it to such a height in this wonderful transformation, that it sees God through a shining cloud of fire, and one so resplendent and bright that instead of this hindering the soul from seeing God, it enables it to see him more clearly, although it does not see him as he is in himself. … This prayer is so exalted that it is impossible to speak of it. … This vision … the most sublime after the Beatific Vision, God does not usually give, so far as my soul understands, except very rarely. … If my soul with seeing God, through the medium of a scintillating cloud of fire, on one single occasion, has to admire, enjoy and love without losing a single instant, while life lasts … what will it be there in our heavenly home? … Dear God, blessed for ever.

Endnotes

1   St. John Climacus: *Spiritual Ladder*, ch. 29.

2   Wisd. 7:11.

3   Cf. *Evolución mística*, p. 608 (references here given are to the Spanish edition of this major work by Fr. Arintero. An American translation appeared in 1950—*The Mystical Evolution in the Development and Vitality of the Church*, by Fr. Jordan Aumann, O.P. [Herder, St. Louis, MO.]); Weiss, *Apolog.* IX, Lecture IV.

4   Gal. 3:27.

5   Rom. 6:4; Col. 2:12; 3:3.

6   "Every one shall be perfect, if he be as his master" (Luke 6:40).

7   1 Pet. 1:13–15; 2:21–5; Gal. 2:19–20; 2 Tim. 2:11.

8   Rom. 6:5; 9:24.

9   Rom. 12:4–5; 1 Cor. 12:12–37.

10 Rom. 8:5, 14, 16; 1 Cor. 6:19; Gal. 5:25; Phil. 2:2; Eph. 4:22–24.

11 Eph. 8:15, 16; Gal. 4:5.

12 Eph. 1:13; 2 Cor. 1:21–22; 3:18.

13 Rom. 6:23; 1 John 2:20; 5:11; cf. ibid., 3:15.

14 John 4:14; 7:37–39.

15 Rom. 6:6.

16 *Credo ... in Spiritum sanctum, Dominum et vivificantem.*

17 1 Cor. 6:19–20.

18 Rom. 8:14, 21; Gal. 4:5–7; 5:18; 2 Cor. 3:17.

19 Ps. 72:28.

20 I Cor. 6:17.

21 John 6:45; Isa. 54:13.

22 Acts 7:51; Eph. 4:30; 1 Thess. 5:19.

23 Cf. Ps. 84:9.

24 St. John of the Cross: *Living Flame of Love*, cant. 4, v. 2.

25 Prayer, said St. Teresa (*Life*, ch. 8) is "to treat as a friend ... alone, with one whom we know loves us." "What is prayer, St. Alphonsus inquires in turn

(*Declaration on the Our Father*, ch. 2), but the soul being occupied with God, loving him and contemplating his perfections?"

But "perfect contemplation," said Fr. La Puente (*Guide*, tr. 3, ch. 4), "consists in forming proportionately within our spirit, which includes the understanding and the will, a living image of the glory of God himself; that is, of his divinity and of his infinite excellencies and perfections."

The one who perfects our formation, and imprints this living image upon us, is the Holy Spirit, imprinting Himself upon us as the living seal of Christ and thus bringing us to share in the divine glory and to know it through experience; so that whereas in meditation, as Fr. José de Jesús María Quiroga observes, "we proceed to the knowledge of spiritual and divine things through abstraction from created things ..., in this divine contemplation we proceed to the knowledge of God and his divine perfections through *participation* in them, for our understanding receives supernatural knowledge of divine things in their spiritual nature and their purity, by means of the single light of faith and the illumination of the gift of Wisdom."

And indeed: "The formal ground by which we know these causes," says John of St. Thomas (In I-II, q. 70, disp. 18, a. 4, no. 6), "is a *certain interior experience of God*, and of divine things, in the very savouring of them: either through feeling and delight, or it may be described, where these spiritual things are concerned, as an interior touch of the will. For out of this union the soul becomes as it were connatural with divine things, and through her very savouring of them, distinguishes them from created things and those of sense."

"Since, therefore, the gift of wisdom is not just any sort of wisdom but the *spirit of wisdom*, that is, it is in feeling and spirit, and since it is by the very giving of this gift that we experience in ourselves what is the good and well-pleasing and perfect will of God, judging from divine things themselves, it is necessary that the formal ground by which the gift of wisdom attains the highest, that is, the divine cause, is the very knowledge which it has experimentally of God, in so far as he is united with us, deeply rooted within our hearts, and gives himself to us: this, indeed, is to know according to the spirit and not only by the light of our own minds, or by discursive reason demonstrating the essence of a thing. To know according to the spirit arises from the very experience of union" (ibid., no. 9—cf. *S. theol.* 2-2, q. 45, a. 2).

26 "In Christ all are crucified, all dead, all buried, all indeed are risen again" (St. Leo, *Sermon* 64, 7).

"Whatever was wrought in the cross of Christ, in his burial, in his resurrection on the third day, in his ascension into heaven, and in his sitting at the right hand of the Father, that was wrought that to these things ... the Christian life which is here lived might be configured" (St. Augustine, *Enchiridion*, 14).

"We cannot be pleasing to our heavenly Father," says Dom Guéranger, "except in so far as he sees in us Jesus Christ, his Son. This divine Saviour, full of goodness, deigns to come to each one of us; and if we are willing to allow him to work, he will gradually transform us into himself in such a way that we shall no longer live by our own life, but by his. Such is the end of all Christianity: to divinize man by Jesus Christ who thus communicates himself to man. Such is the sublime mission entrusted to the Church who, with St. Paul (Gal. 4:19) says to the faithful: 'My little children, of whom I am in labour again, until Christ be formed in you.'"

27 "No one abandoning lowly things," warns St. Gregory (*Moral.* 1.22, ch. 19), "suddenly rises to the heights, for, so far as the merit of perfection is concerned, while the mind is daily drawn upwards, it is beyond question that one attains to perfection, as it were, by ascending certain steps."

28 (Luke 18:1; 21:36; 1 Thess. 5:17; Phil. 3:20.) "It is no light argument in favour of recognizing the power of prayer," Fray Juan de los Angeles points out (*In Cant.* i, 5), "to observe that the two chief glories and manifestations of Christ which were revealed in his baptism and transfiguration occurred when he was at prayer, for in truth, if a man is to reform his habits and become transformed and changed into a new man, there are no practices and no way like prayer. It is there that the mind receives light and there that the vesture and adornment of the soul is renewed and made whiter than snow.... Daily experience has shown us that, at whatever pace prayer moves forward, so does the spiritual life, like the sea and the moon ... and thus it is certainly the case that according to the waxing or waning of prayer so is the increase or diminution of devotion and of the spirit.

"For there is no light of virtue, no heavenly and divine good, apart from this virtue of prayer, or which that virtue does not contain, or obtain from God.... Wherefore as each man excels in holiness, so he will excel greatly in love of and assiduity at prayer" (Fray Luis de León, *In Cant.*, ch. 4).

29 See the beautiful treatise *Espinas del alma*, colloquy 7, in the Works of St. John of the Cross (Sp. edition), vol. 3, p. 259; and cf. La Figuera, *Suma espiritual.*

30 1 John 1:3. Cf. St. Teresa, *Life*, ch. 8; à Kempis, *Imit.*, bk. 2, ch. 1. "Prayer," said St. Lawrence Justinian (*Lignum vitae*, tr. 13; *de Orat.*, ch. 7), "is the affection of man cleaving to God and a certain familiar and pious conversation." "It is the loving turning of the mind to God, uplifted by faith, hope and charity" (ibid., ch. 1).

31 Cf. La Puente, *Guía espiritual*, tr. 3, ch. 3, no. 1; Nouet, *Introduction à la vie d'oraison*, vol. 1, entretien 7.

32 "When a strong man fears where there is cause for fear, this is virtue; if he did not fear, it would be vice. If, however, strengthened by the help of God,

he should be afraid in nothing, this would be virtue beyond the human mode, and such virtue is called divine. Acts of this kind, then, are perfect.... Therefore ... they are either acts of the Gifts, or acts of the virtues in so far as they are perfected by the Gifts....

"For that man is meek who is not irritated. But this may be possible through virtue, namely, that you be not angry unless for a just cause; but if you should even have just cause and not be provoked [to anger], this is beyond the human mode. And therefore he says: 'Blessed are the meek ...'" (St. Thomas, *In Mt.* 5; cf. St. Thomas, *In III Sent.*, D. 34, q. 1, a. 1 and 3; 1-2, q. 68, a. 1; q. 69, a. 1, etc.).

33 From this will be seen how inaccurate is Rodríguez's statement (tr. 5, ch. 18) that contemplation is "a very special gift of God, which he does not give to all, but to whom he pleases; but plain, ordinary mental prayer, the Lord denies to nobody." Yet he adds, however (ch. 19), "I knew a Father ... a very great preacher, whose prayer for a long time consisted in saying to God with humility and simplicity: 'Lord, I am a beast and know not how to pray, do thou teach me'; and with this ... he came to have a very high prayer, namely, contemplation and not meditation."

"From imperfect vocal prayer," said the Eternal Father to St. Catherine of Siena (*Dialogue*, ch. 66), "by persevering in the exercise, the soul will come to perfect mental prayer (which is infused contemplation); but it will never be able to reach this point if it merely tries to add to the number of its vocal prayers and deserts mental prayer for them. There are souls so ignorant that when they set themselves to recite a certain number of prayers, although I then visit them in many different ways, they are unwilling to receive my visit lest they interrupt that which they have begun. This (unless such prayers are of obligation) is a manifest error. As soon then, as they are aware of my visit, they ought to suspend their devotions.... Perfect prayer is not acquired with many words, but with the affection of desire which rises up to me, with self-knowledge, and knowledge of my Goodness, and thus it will be vocal and mental prayer at the same time."

St. Lawrence Justinian (*De perfectionis gradibus*, ch. 12) affirms the very great usefulness of vocal prayer as the door or ordinary channel by which we begin to taste the sweetness of contemplation, that is, of infused prayer, made entirely in spirit. According to this writer, this already begins in some measure with affective prayer, however much one has to make use in it at times of various devices for remedying dryness and arousing the senses. His words are "Vocal prayer is very useful, for it is the door and gateway to the experience of mental prayer, the prayer which is wholly in the spirit (John 4).... This clearly is a mode that is wholly spiritual, formed from the heart's affection in the presence of God, not from our own industry, a mode which the Holy Spirit certainly infuses into the mind of him who practises it, as he leads the soul to ask for it. Whatever is asked for in this mode of prayer is easily obtained, for the Holy Spirit co-operates with the heart of the suppliant, teaching him and, beyond all question, moving him to ask—for the rest, when in the meantime (not, however, without the divine disposition) the mind of him who prays is dry and left to its own resources for it has now expended its devotion, he causes it to be lifted up and stirs it to pray to God, not always uniformly but in many different ways, as it feels itself drawn." Thus what is infused becomes blended with what is acquired, the passive with the active.

34 "It is an amazing thing," says St. Teresa (*Way of Perfection*, ch. 37), "how high in perfection is this prayer of the Gospel; like the Master who teaches it. I was astounded to find here in so few words the whole of contemplation and perfection contained, so that it appears we need no other book, but to study this, for here the Lord has shown us the highest method of contemplation in its entirety, from the beginnings of mental prayer to the most sublime and perfect contemplation." "In this way," she adds further on (ch. 42), "this marvellous prayer contains within itself the whole spiritual path from the beginning until we are wholly absorbed in God and given to drink abundantly from the fountain of living water."

35 "Meditation, particularly on the Passion," says St. Teresa (*Life*, ch. 13), "is the way of prayer by which all have to begin, proceed and end, and a very excellent and sure way, until the Lord raises them to supernatural things." [After "all," Fr. Arintero has inserted *los letrados*—"the learned," or "instructed persons." This does not occur in St. Teresa's text.—Tr.]

36 "Returning to those who use discursive prayer, I say that they should not let all the time slip away on this, because although it is very meritorious, they do not realize, for it is a prayer in which there is pleasure, that there ought to be ... a time in which one should refrain from work. Therefore it appears to them that the time is lost, but I consider this loss a gain. As I have said, they should imagine themselves in the presence of Christ, and without weariness of the mind, should be speaking with him and delighting in his presence, without tiring themselves by composing speeches to him, but presenting their necessities.... As I spent much time in this stage, I have pity on those who begin with books alone, for it is strange how differently one understands (from books) from what is afterwards learnt by experience" (St. Teresa, *Life*, ch. 13).

"This loving conversation," remarks St. Louis Bertrand (*De la oración*, ch. 8, no. 1), "the saints call the practice of aspiring to divine love. To this end, meditation and prayer and all other good exercises are ordered. Wherefore it is given as a general rule to all those who pray, that they should strive as far as possible to raise the mind to this divine conversation, that is, to speak and converse with God himself, especially in converse of love and exercises of aspiration."

"To pray well," said the Curé d'Ars (*Life*, by Monnin, vol. 5, ch. 4), "much speaking is unnecessary. Since we know that God is there, in the sacred tabernacle, let us open our hearts to him, let us delight in his holy presence. This is the best prayer."

"On going to prayer," says M. Olier (*Catéchisme chrétien*, pt. 2, conf. 10), "the only thing the soul has to do is to unite itself with Jesus Christ, who is the prayer and praise of the whole Church; so that if the soul is united to our Lord and gives heartfelt assent to all the praise which he gives his Eternal Father and to all the petitions that he makes, it does not lack profit; on the contrary, it makes much more progress than if it were to pray of its own initiative, wanting to persist in adoring, loving, praising and praying to God, of itself and by its own acts. Through this union, the soul becomes wider than the sea, for it expands like the soul and the Spirit of Jesus Christ, who prays throughout the whole Church."

37 James 1:17; cf. Louis of Granada, *De la devoción*, ch. 5, no. 17.

38 "Faith believes, hope and charity pray and by praying, they obtain" (St. Augustine, *De orando Deum*, Epist. 121, ch. 8).

39 "In the gifts of the Holy Spirit, the human mind does not behave as moving but as moved" (St. Thomas, 2–2, q. 52, a. 2, ad 1). In this way meditation itself might be regarded as an initial form of contemplation. "Meditation," says Vallgornera (*Théol. myst.*, q. 2, d. 6, a. 2), "is the first stage of the life of contemplation and ordinarily we cannot rise to contemplation without it."

40 "As the discursive prayer," remarks the Ven. Palafox (*Varón de deseos*, pt. 3, Sent. 5), "is practised to move the will, when the latter is aroused, it would appear to be superfluous, so that in this case it is not necessary to suggest motives for loving what is already loved. But (ordinarily) it is always good to begin one's prayer by setting before oneself motives or holy considerations, so that the soul may not delay to recollect itself and also so that it does not become over-confident." Although the most ordinary way is for God to lead souls to perfection beginning by discursive prayer, "some, nevertheless," notes Álvarez de la Paz (*De inquis. pads*, bk. 4, pt. 3, ch. 2), "he is wont to place in the state of affective prayer right from the beginning of their conversion and without meditation, and to burn away all that is impure and sinful in them with the fire of his love. Then, indeed, meditation is not to be insisted upon, but the soul should move quickly along the path of affective prayer.... We recognize that someone has been called to affective prayer if he is unable to meditate ... and, conversely, if he easily rises to affective love, if he finds peace of heart in it, ... and if he makes progress in every virtue. He to whom this applies is not to be bound to meditation, nor to thinking out points beforehand and preparing discourses, but to be taught gently according to his vocation and method of prayer."

41 "The souls in the Mansions we have passed through" — says St. Teresa, beginning to speak of the fourth mansion in which the soul is already entering
upon supernatural prayer — "almost continually use the mind in prayer, and
practise meditation, and their way is good because more has not been given
to them, although they should strive to occupy themselves for a time in
making acts and in the praise of God, in delighting in his goodness, that he
is who he is, and in desiring his honour and glory. Let them take great care,
when the Lord grants them this, not to leave it to finish their customary
meditation.... To make much progress in this way and rise to the Mansions
we desire, the thing to do is not to think much but to love much, and thus
what will most stir you to love, that do."

"Although all the time of prayer," says Fr. Massoulié, O.P. (*Traité de la
véritable oraison*, pt. 3, ch. 3), "be passed in the exercise of a single virtue,
for instance of divine love at the sight of a crucifix, it would be very perfect,
for the soul would possess what is the end of all prayer, namely, union with
God, which is effected by love."

"Just as when we reach harbour navigation ceases, and when the end is
reached the means cease, thus," says Molina (*De la oración*, tr. 2, ch. 6, no.
1), "when a man by means of the work of meditation arrives at the rest and
delight of contemplation, he should then leave discourses and considerations
and, content with a simple view of God and of his truths, should rest, looking at God, loving him, and worshipping or delighting in him, or exercising
himself in other affections.... At any time during prayer, if a man should
feel this inward recollection and [find his] will drawn and moved by some
affection, he ought not to let this pass through the desire of pursuing other
considerations or points which he had prepared, but should remain at that
as long as it lasts, even if it should last the whole time of the exercise. But
when that light and affection passes, and the soul feels that it is distracted or
dry, it should return to meditation and the ordinary course of its exercises."

"From the frequent occurrence of these aspirations which are contained
in affective prayer," says Álvarez de la Paz (vol. 3, bk. 4, pt. 3, ch. 1), the mind
rises occasionally to mystical theology, that is, to that untaught wisdom,
wiser than all human learning ... by which the mind enjoys God without
reasoning."

"Some souls," he adds, "our Lord calls to this prayer gently and in
stages, and they ought then to prepare their affections. But others he calls
not only manifestly but with violence and so patently that they know clearly
that they are being drawn to this prayer. Then it is not necessary to prepare
anything — for to do so rather renders the soul cold and less apt — but to
follow the lead of the divine Spirit and in one's aspirations to follow his
suggestions. Then the soul experiences the force of the saying: 'They who
are led by the Spirit of God, they are the sons of God.' For it is led on to

ineffable affections by a certain powerful hand of God. It also understands the saying: 'The Spirit of God asketh for us with unutterable groanings.' For it feels within itself the pedagogue or master who, as is fitting, forms it by means of various affections and makes it ask what is right for itself and for others. He who finds himself in this state should proceed confidently, should allow himself to be moved by God and follow his leading and inspiration, provided, however, that he consult his visible director."

42 "There is no doubt that this difficulty of being unable to work discursively in one's prayer," said St. Jane Chantal (*Pensées et lettres*, Paris, 1899, p. 50), "is the way to a prayer of greater simplicity; and however little the soul, when faced with this difficulty, feels disposed to stay reverently in God's presence, it should have confidence in that way along which God is certainly calling it. However much it may suffer from poverty and distractions, it should not leave this way, but stay calmly in God's presence without wilfully heeding the distractions. When it finds itself too much troubled, it should from time to time repeat words of submission and abandonment to God's will, of confidence and love, doing this gently and without straining.... However slightly God may draw us to this prayer of simplicity, taking away from us the power of using the mind discursively, we ought to follow the attraction, for otherwise we should obtain nothing but rather harm the head."

43 "Many deceive themselves," says St. Francis de Sales (*Directoire de religieuses*, ch. 45), "thinking that to pray well much method is necessary; and they worry themselves seeking a system which they think is indispensable.... I do not say that they should not make use of the methods taught by the saints. What I say is that the soul should not be completely tied to them, as happens to some who never think they have made their prayer well if they do not go through the considerations before the affections the Lord gives them, whereas these affections are the purpose of the considerations. Such people are like those who, finding themselves close to the place they are travelling to, turn back without entering it, because they have not got there by the way they were shown."

44 "When I go to prayer, said Marie Lataste (*Oeuvres*, vol. 3, let. 19), "I do not put before myself a point chosen beforehand, nor do I make use of a book. I could not reconcile anything of this kind with the attraction I feel each time and therefore, far from being useful to me, such choice or preparation would be harmful and troublesome to me. In prayer, then, I begin with the sole disposition of receiving the attraction which is given to me. Sometimes I feel myself moved to seek God straight away and I seek him humbly and with docility. But at other times this attraction is long in coming, and then I rest in God's arms, humbling and naughting myself in the presence of his immense Sanctity ... and remaining resigned even though he does not allow me to find him. But this is not really so—for, sooner or later, he comes and

says to my soul: 'Seek me.' And I seek and find him. For God, in fact, cannot resist our full and complete submission to his divine Will. God communicates and reveals himself to the soul in many ways."

"The great method of prayer," St. Jane Chantal herself remarked in this connection (*Oeuvres*, II, p. 260), is that there should be no method.... If when we go to prayer, we could turn ourselves into a pure capacity for receiving the spirit of God, this would replace all methods. Prayer should be accomplished by grace and not by artifice."

45 "When I pray," said St. Teresa of the Child Jesus (*Life*, ch. 10), "I simply say what I want to God, and he always understands me. For me, prayer is an *élan* of the heart, a simple glance raised to heaven, a cry of gratitude and love in the midst of trials as in the midst of joy. It is, in short, something sublime and supernatural which enlarges the soul and unites it with God. At times, when I find myself so dry that I am unable even to produce a good thought, I say an *Our Father* or a *Hail Mary* very slowly; for these prayers alone fill me with delight, feed my soul with things divine and are sufficient for it."

"To tell it all to our Lord," Maria Agnus Dei Hervé-Bazin wrote in April 1901 (*Une religieuse réparatrice*, 1912, p. 323), "without books, without methods, without any rule beyond that of a humble but intense love, that is the secret of countless graces."

"May our Lord teach you the secret of true prayer, in which every good is hidden ...; this prayer of the heart, intimate, penetrating, which gains all and transforms life" (ibid., p. 331).

And, indeed, our Lord enjoys treating us and being treated with an astonishing familiarity: "You do not know," our divine Lord said a little earlier to his servant Sr. Gertrude Mary (June 30, 1907), "the Heart of God, you do not know how to approach him; you do not know how to exclaim: Father! Few souls on earth treat God with this familiarity that he none the less desires his children should have." — "If you but knew the power over my heart of a soul who gently yields to this familiarity!... I can deny it nothing. And would that this disposition of my Heart were better known and this sweet familiarity better practised" (Sr. Gertrude Mary, May 24, 1907).

46 "If I could see what is happening within me," said Sr. Catherine of Jesus, Discalced Carmelite (cf. *Life*, 1631, pp. 52–53), "I should be divided, and that would not do, for I must be wholly occupied with suffering and love."

47 "The signs by which we may know," says the Ven. Falconi (*Camino derecho para el cielo*, bk. 1, ch. 5), "when it is time to give up meditation and pass to contemplation, are two, namely: the not being able to meditate and the finding no pleasure in doing so and the applying oneself to remain in silence in that general knowledge of God, without discoursing."

"The most certain sign of supernatural and infused contemplation," says *The Cloud of Unknowing* (ch. 1, n. 6), "is not to have it whenever we please, nor to cease from it when we will, but that it should come when God wills and fail when God pleases."

48 "I think," says Richard of St. Victor (*De contempl.*, bk. 4, ch. 6), "that what is most wanting here is compunction and not intellectual investigation … frequent laments rather than copious arguments…. 'Blessed,' says the Scripture, 'are the clean of heart, for they shall see God.' Let him who desires to see God, then, him who is in haste to rise to the contemplation of divine things, aim at cleanness of heart."

49 "The business which looks directly to the glory of God," said St. Margaret Mary (*Oeuvres*, vol. 2, p. 233), "is very different from that of the world, in which there is much to be done; for in that of God, very often one has to be content merely to follow his inspiration and then leave grace to do its work, following the movements of grace with all our power."

50 "This most sublime way of praying is called contemplation; it is reached by reasoning about the mystery; and ceasing [from all activity], the soul contemplates with great reverence and feeling what Christ our Lord communicates to it. The soul finds itself with its Beloved, both God and the soul being in silence, and it enjoys its God" (St. Alphonsus Rodríguez, *Unión y transformación*, ch. 7).

51 Cf. *Evolución mística*, pp. 640–641.

52 "As this water does not have to be brought through conduits like that previously mentioned," says St. Teresa (*Interior Castle*, IV, 2), "if the spring does not choose to produce it, it profits little for us to tire ourselves. I mean that although we make more meditation, although we strain ourselves more and more and arrive at tears, this water does not come by that way. It is only given to whom God wills and often when the soul is least thinking of it."

53 "Although this Mansion of self-knowledge is the first," remarks St. Teresa (*Interior Castle*, I, ch. 2), "it is very rich and of so much worth that if the reptiles are cleared out from it, one will not stop there but will go on further…. It is very fitting for those who are to enter the second Mansion that they should try to ignore business and affairs which are not necessary, each one doing so as his state permits. This is a thing of such importance for reaching the principal Mansion, that if souls do not begin to do this, I consider that impossible."

54 "The second Mansion," says the saint, "is for those who have already begun to practise mental prayer and who have understood how important it is for them not to remain in the first Mansion, but who have not yet sufficient determination, on many occasions, to leave it, for they do not leave the occasions

of sin, which is a great danger.... There is great hope that they may progress further.... Such people already understand the calls the Lord is sending them, for as they gradually get nearer to his own dwelling, he becomes their good neighbour. He is so good and merciful that, even when we are turned to worldly things ... when we fall into sin ... our Lord is so anxious for us to desire him and strive after his companionship that he continues to call us to come close to him. This voice is so sweet that the poor soul is distressed at not being able to do what he orders immediately.... Let such souls trust in the mercy of God and not in themselves and they will see how his Majesty carries them from one Mansion to the next, putting them where the wild beasts cannot touch or harass them, for he places the beasts in their power and laughs them to scorn. The soul enjoys many more things than it can desire, even in this life."

55 According to the author of *The Cloud of Unknowing*, ch. 8, there are five principal stages in mystical contemplation: the first of these is constituted by affirmative or "acquired" contemplation; the second, by the loving and general awareness of God; the third, by the prayer of recollection (in which he thinks there is still something acquired together with an infused element); the fourth, that of quiet, wholly infused; and the fifth by ecstatic, together with transforming union; which, therefore, he considers as "the highest stage of prayer there is."

According to Fr. Dosda (*L'union avec Dieu*, pt. 4, ch. 19), in mystical union there are only four stages: (1) incipient union, which comprises recollection and quiet; (2) simple union; (3) ecstatic union; and (4) transforming union or spiritual marriage.

56 "A feeling of the presence of God came upon me quite unexpectedly," said St. Teresa (*Life*, ch. 10), "so that I could not possibly doubt he was within me or that I was all enclosed in him" (Cf. Letter 2 to Fr. Rodrigo).

57 "My soul," said the Ven. Mary of the Incarnation (*Vie*, by Chapot, pt. 1, ch. 4), "did not cease to tend towards God in a constant and wholly spiritual manner. I found myself tormented with the desire of possessing him in a new way of which as yet I had no experience and which I could not define. I saw him in all creatures."

"There is another kind of union, obscure, arid and without pleasure, which might be called a certain knowledge of divine things linked with a certain painful love; this can even be said to be a union disposing to contemplation and it comes about through dereliction or passive purgation.... Another kind is a sweet union which comes about through contemplation, then infused, or through transformation" (Schram, *Theol. myst.*, no. 172, schol. t. I).

58 "If a soul," remarks Saudreau (*Les faits extraordinaires*, p. 22), "continually returns in its prayer during whole weeks and months to the same text of

Scripture, which is sufficient to keep it united with God … it can with certainty consider that it has received mystical lights."

59 "In contemplation," Álvarez de Paz remarks, "suspension of the mind follows this elevation. This suspension is nothing else than a certain very perfect attention to what is contemplated and an utter forgetfulness of all lower things."

60 "When a soul recollects itself by a special movement from God," says Fr. Luis de la Puente (*Avisos*, no. 10), "just as we may say that it enters into itself and there finds God, so also it enters into God. When this is experienced, it knows itself better than it can express. When a soul is in this state, it immediately becomes aware with whom it is speaking, it has no need of discourse, nor indeed is it capable of discourse. All is colloquies and affections, contemplating the majesty of God and one's own vileness. There it cries out, there it entreats, there it loves, there it rejoices, there it grows sad, there it detests itself, there it takes courage, there it finds fresh strength to obey, to suffer, to give pleasure to God through God. In this way what the saints say may perhaps be understood, that contemplation is the soul's tomb where it enters and buries itself, dies and is entombed, and again they say that it enters into itself and into God."

61 "In the prayer of quiet," observes St. Teresa (*Way of Perfection*, ch. 31), "the Lord begins to give us to understand that he has heard our request, and that he is now beginning to give us his kingdom here, so that in truth we may praise his name and strive that others may praise it. It is a supernatural thing and one which we are not able to obtain ourselves, however much diligence we employ; for it is the soul enclosing itself in peace, or the Lord putting it into his presence, as he did in the case of holy Simeon, for all the faculties become quietened and the soul understands in a way far beyond that of comprehension with the outward senses, that it is now joined with God, so that with but a little more, it will come to be made one and the same thing with him, through union."

"This enkindling of love," says St. John of the Cross (*Night*, II, ch. 12), "accompanying the union of these two powers, understanding and will, which are here joined together, is a source of great riches and delight for the soul. For it is a certain contact with the Godhead and already a beginning of the perfection of the union of love which it hopes for. It does not arrive at this touch of such high feeling and love of God, without having passed through many trials and a large share of its purgation."

62 "This repose, which is in a certain sense mysterious, is called 'Noonday Sleep,' a sleep, that is, which is usually brief, being nothing more than to rest a little and then return to the pastures, or to work; for quiet contemplation is usually brief…. Of this St. Bernard complained, saying (*Serm. 32 in Cant.*), 'Rare

hour, brief pause.' It comes every now and then and lasts only a short time. And it is necessary to ask God at one and the same time to reveal to us the place of pasture and the place of rest, so that, when the rest of contemplation fails, we may return to the food of meditation" (La Puente, *Guía*, tr. 3, ch. 6, no. 2).

63 "The effects of the prayer of quiet," says Vallgornera (q. 4, d. 2, a. 16, n. 12), "are internal peace which remains even when the quiet has passed, deep humility, ability and readiness for spiritual exercises, heavenly light in the mind and in the will a firmness towards good and all virtues, which the Lord himself grants much more abundantly than they can be acquired by one's own industry.... Whence it is a moral certitude about one's own salvation."

64 "Oh dear God," exclaims St. Teresa (*Life*, ch. 16), "how happy a soul is when it is in this state! It could wish that it were nothing but tongues to praise the Lord. It gives vent to a thousand utterances of holy folly, always striving to content him who holds it thus.... What I see seems a dream and I should like only to see those suffering from this sickness.... I beseech your Reverence let us all be mad, through love of him whom they called mad for our sakes. Since your Reverence says you care for me, I ask you to show it in disposing yourself so that God may show you this favour.... A fine liberty it is from one's captivity, to have to live and behave in conformity with the laws of the world."

"This interior joy," she adds (Relation 1), "St. Francis must have felt when the robbers who were going about the countryside shouting, ran across him and he told them he was a herald of the Great King; and the other saints who went off through the deserts to preach the praises of God, like St. Francis. I knew one, called Fray Pedro de Alcántara (for I think his life was like that), who did the same thing and those who sometimes listened to him thought he was mad. Oh, what a madness is that, if it were to give us God!"

65 "The prayer of quiet differs from the prayer of union," remarks Vallgornera (q. 4, d. 2, a. 16, n. 1), "because in the prayer of union the soul bears itself as it were passively, to its spiritual refreshment, neither does it labour in taking food. It finds food within itself, not knowing how this is so. But in the prayer of quiet, the soul labours a little, although so gently and quietly that it does not feel its labour. Further, in the prayer of union, all the powers of the soul are often suspended from their connatural operation."

66 "God fixes himself in the interior of that soul in such a way that when it turns in upon itself, in no way can it doubt that it is in God and God in it" (St. Teresa, *Interior Castle*, V, ch. 2).

67 "From this wound," says Godinez (*Teología mística*, bk. 6, ch. 12), "a very delightful swooning is caused at times. In this, love is engrafted in pain and

the fruits of this engrafting are tender sighs, compliments of love, fervent affections, celestial jubilation, peace, joy, quiet union and a mode of loving which I cannot explain."

"For God does not leave all souls," remarks the Ven. Mariana de San José (*In Cant.*, 2, 2) with these outward signs. To some I have known, His Majesty grants the favour that all remains within."

68 Thus, whereas in ecstasy the soul tends to fall senseless to the ground, in rapture it seems that it tends, so to speak, to rise into the air as if it had lost its weight.

69 Dr. Imbert (*La stigmatisation*, vol. 1, at end) says that among the 321 cases of stigmata that he was able to mention in his work, 293 belonged to different religious institutes and only 49 are men. "The Order of St. Dominic leads," he says, "with its 109 cases; then the Franciscans with 102; then come the Carmelites with 14, the Ursulines, also 14, the Visitandines 12 and the Order of St. Augustine 8. In addition there are 6 Cistercians, 4 Benedictines, 3 Jesuits, 3 Theatines, 2 Trinitarians, 2 Jeronymites, 2 Conceptionists; and, lastly, 13 each belonging to one of other different religious congregations."

70 Of this purgation of the senses, Vallgornera says (*Myst.* q. 2, d. 8, a. 1), "the formal cause is the withdrawal of sensible grace ..., out of which withdrawal various desolations come, to a certain extent painful, with continual aridities both in the affective and the cognitive senses.... The efficient or effective cause is the good and merciful God himself, although he may appear austere and exceedingly angry to the beginner.... The final cause of passive purgation in the sensitive soul is that this lower part, fittingly purified, may be conformed to the higher part, to which it is subordinate even when purified from its evil dispositions, so that each part being thus well disposed and at the same time consenting readily, may concur in intimate union with God."

"In prayer or meditation," he adds (ibid., a. 3, n. 448), "three good things are found, namely devotion, sweetness and consolation; and in the passive purgation are found the three opposite evils—weariness, aridity and desolation; and they are ills sent as a trial."

71 (Ps. 26:8; 76:3). "What I do not lose," said the Ven. Sr. Bárbara de Santo Domingo in September 1872, "is the memory of God ... but it serves me for greater pain, for as it appears that he is displeased with me, I suffer much from seeing that I cannot disarm his anger. In this darkness I can discover in the hidden depths of my soul a certain calm, a very interior peace, accompanied by a certain assurance of my salvation.... But this is so hidden that it can scarcely be discerned. It is for support, but not to alleviate one's suffering in the slightest degree."

72 "There were added," says Sr. Catalina de Jesús María, O.P. (*Autobiography*, pt. 3, ch. 2), "many sicknesses which at this time increased beyond all expectation.... The heart suffered so much from its great desolation that I felt that from it terrible sufferings were spread over the whole body ... and fever which never leaves me.... However short the distance I walk it tires me and stops my breathing, causing me terrible accidents.

"This in general ... for as to this matter of external ills, I am somewhat indolent in relating them. I speak of those of the soul as far as I can, for they cannot all be told, since it is scarcely possible to give a bare outline of them. Only the one who goes through them knows them, and only the one who experiences them understands them—they cannot be the subject of a narrative."

73 The Holy Spirit Himself teaches the soul how it should behave, saying: "Son, when thou comest to the service of God, stand in justice and in fear, and prepare thy soul for temptation. Humble thy heart, and endure: incline thy ear, and receive the words of understand: and make not haste in the time of clouds. Wait on God with patience: join thyself to God, and endure, that thy life may be increased in the latter end. Take all that shall be brought upon thee: and in thy sorrow endure, and in thy humiliation keep patience. For gold and silver are tried in the fire, but acceptable men in the furnace of humiliation" (Sir. 2:1-6).

"For thus saith the Lord to the house of Israel: Seek ye me, and you shall live.... Seek him ... that turneth darkness into morning, and that changeth day into night" (Amos 5:4, 8).

74 "Why dost thou endeavour to shew thy way good to seek my love.... How exceeding base art thou become, going the same ways over again" (Jer. 2:33, 36). For not forcing themselves to move forward and climb up to the top of the holy mountain, they go back and come down even to ... abyss after abyss.

75 "My people have been a lost flock, their shepherds have caused them to go astray, and have made them wander in the mountains: they have gone from mountain to hill, they have forgotten their resting place" (Jer. 50:6).

76 "He that shall overcome, shall thus be clothed in white garments, and I will not blot out his name out of the book of life" (Rev. 3:5).

77 Rev. 3:21; 2 Tim. 2:12; Eph. 2:6; Luke 22:28-30.

78 The Ven. Sr. Bárbara de Santo Domingo relates (October 1872—see *Life*, pp. 375-376) that one day when she had just communicated, our Lord showed Himself to her and said: "Come, daughter, I want you to be consumed with me and to be one thing in me." "Then," she continues, "I approached my God and felt him set me wholly on fire with his love. This divine fire consumed

me and united me so closely to God that in a short time ... I no longer was aware of myself but only of him; and ... I find myself so completely lost in God and as it were transformed into him that I can say with all truth that I do not know if I live: I think I am dead, for I no longer live except in God.... It is a much more intimate union than the one I had; for now I am wholly in God....

"The clear vision of God that my soul enjoys prevents me on certain occasions from seeing the light of day as others do, for I see it so dim that I should rather call it darkness than light. All is strange for me; I am like a person who comes from far-off lands, to whom everything seems strange.... As I see God uninterruptedly ... all the rest is martyrdom to me."

79 "These two Mansions" — that is, the sixth and seventh — St. Teresa points out (*Interior Castle*, VI, ch. 4) — "could well be joined together, for there is no closed door between the one and the other." Even if "there are things in the last which have not been manifested to those who have not reached it."

80 The *espousals*, in the strict sense of the term, are a promise made by our Lord to a soul that finds itself in the state of union, of eventually reaching the spiritual marriage.

81 This is how an admirable religious who lived in the Dominican convent at Quito in the eighteenth century summed up her experience. "You began" — she says to our Lord, after having heard from His divine lips that He had His kingdom in her very self, in her heart — "you began to fill me with delight and amid your caresses you gave me to understand that we should exchange wills. I agreed, and then in a special way you made the exchange, saying to me or giving me to understand: *Let my will be thine* (and when you said this I felt your will being infused into my soul), *and thine mine*; and when you uttered this other phrase I felt that I was giving it you with my whole soul and that it was infused within your divine Majesty" (Sr. Catalina de Jesús, María y José Herrera, *Autobiografía inédita*, pt. 2, ch. 40, p. 298).

82 See *Desenvolvimiento y vitalidad de la Iglesia*, I, pp. 166-167.

83 "This night," said St. Bonaventure (*Breviloquii*, pt. 5, ch. 6), "is a certain learned ignorance in which the spirit is raised and carried away to the clouds and the heights. No one knows and understands that nocturnal and delightful illumination except he who experiences it, and no one experiences it but he who receives it from grace and it is given to no one except to him who prepares himself for it."

Those souls, then, who have passed through it are quite right to cry out and bless it with St. John of the Cross and with his two great disciples, María de San Alberto and Cecilia del Nacimiento, who wrote respectively:

Oh night which guided me,
Oh night more lovely than the dawn:
Oh night which joined Bridegroom with bride,
Bride transformed into Bridegroom.

(St. John of the Cross)

Oh night of bliss,
Offering security with favour
To the soul in love.
Who falls asleep in it,
And thus the day seems night to it.

And thus it remained enjoying
The secret rays of the Beloved,
And already possessing
Without force or care
The house and its dwellers which has been given it.

(M. S. A.)

Oh night of crystal, that
Joined with that lovely light
In a divine union
The Bridegroom and the bride,
Making of both one single thing.

(C. N.)

84 "But how is it that this ray blinds, when it ought rather to give light? But this blindness is highest light and is in the highest point of the mind beyond the penetration of the human intellect" (St. Bonaventure, *In Hex.*, serm. 20, n. 11).

85 Of this night of the spirit Vallgornera says (*Myst.*, q. 3, d. 6, a. 1.), "Its formal cause is the most radiant light of contemplation which, penetrating the most secret depths of the heart and the centre of the soul, shows it all its defects, even its smallest and most hidden ones, bringing to mind the circumstances, chiefly with regard to the offending and offended person, and crucifies it in a wonderful way, clouding over the mind with darkness and reducing the will to extreme anguish by a certain dejection and despair.... The efficient cause is God, kind and merciful, who by purifying the souls of his elect prepares them for union with himself.... The final cause is intimate union with God, for which purgation of this kind worthily prepares and fitly disposes the soul."

86 "In a certain manner," said the servant of God, Sr. Filomena de Santa Coloma, a nun of the Order of Minims in Valls (1841-1868, cf. *Life and Writings*, by Sucona, 1897, p. 162), "the three divine Persons vie with each other to

beautify my soul with supernatural gifts and graces.... In the first place it seems as if the eternal Father clothes my poor little soul with great power and majesty, above all created things, giving me courage to undertake great things in his honour, assuring me of his help and removing from me all fear, making me the terror of hell.... The Son, who is highest Wisdom, seems to take pains to communicate to the soul something of his infinite wisdom, showing it the right paths which are to lead it to eternal life, at the same time filling it with heavenly and divine light – The Holy Spirit, fount of love, seems to communicate to me abundantly the fire of love in which he burns, forcing me to communicate some of it to my sisters, those whom he orders me to love with perfect and burning charity."

87 "The most holy Trinity is shown to it," says St. Teresa (*Interior Castle*, Mansion VII, ch. 1) "... and through a wonderful knowledge that is given to the soul, it understands with very great truth how all three Persons are one substance, one power, one knowledge, and one only God: so that what we hold by faith, here the soul grasps, we may say, by sight.... Here all three Persons communicate themselves to it and speak to it.... It sees in particular that they are in the interior of the soul.... It feels this divine company within itself."

"From the intellectual vision of the most holy Trinity," she remarks on another occasion (Relation 9), "there remains a progress in the soul, which passes to a point incomparably higher than any reached by many years of meditation, and without being able to understand how."

88 "This state requires," says Antony of the Holy Spirit (tr. 1, q. 1, s. 6, no. 12), "that God reveal clearly to the soul that it is in the state of grace and in the number of the elect. Thus St. Lawrence Justinian (*Tract. de casto connubio Verbi et animae*, ch. 25) and others; cf. Philip. a Trinit. (*Discursus proem. a. 8*)." – "Souls in this state," he adds (tr. 4, q. 4, s. 7), "are given certain privileges which were granted to our first parents in the state of innocence" (see *Evolución mística*, pp. 470–477).

89 I am despite myself now so much of God,
   Transformed into my Beloved,
   That my nothingness being annihilated
   We both give forth a fragrance.

(Mystical Ladder)

90 "I have never been so generous in communicating my grace," said our Lord to the Ven. Ana María de San José (*Life*, n. 36), "as in these times, for although I punish men, I love them in every way as their Father; at no time have I had on earth so many just souls, so many friends who serve and love me and surrender themselves to me. These I sanctify with the trials I send them and with those which I justly give to others for their sins. For my servants are

made perfect in the charity and mercy which they show to others, with the prayer and intercourse they have with me. Moved by the compassion they feel towards others, they relieve their necessities. Those who are mine and live carelessly and ungratefully, I bring back to me through the trials I send them and they become less sinful."

The same and perhaps much more could, we think, probably be said today. For the greater the evil, the greater should be the number, and even, according to St. Louis de Montfort, the merit, of those who secretly run counter to it and propitiate God's anger.

91 She was born in Villacastín (Segovia) on January 6, 1581, and died with a high reputation for sanctity on May 14, 1632. Her *Autobiography*, from which we take this account, was published in Salamanca in 1665 and reprinted there in 1862. [The Spanish of this account lacks literary style and is obscure in places.—Tr.]

92 Presumably from the prayer of quiet.—Tr.

93 When the way is shown, remarks St. Augustine, we are not told to remain, but to pass beyond.

94 Sp. text *legísimos*, presumably *lejísimos*.

95 John 14; 21; 15:17, 24. Roughly, as Dom Guéranger remarked (*L'année liturgique*, Friday after Pentecost), "contemplation is the state to which, in a certain measure, *every soul* who seeks God, is called. It does not consist in those phenomena which the Holy Spirit at times sees fit to make manifest in certain privileged persons, to prove the reality of the supernatural life. It simply consists in that most intimate relationship which is established between God and the soul which is faithful to him in what it does. For this soul, if it does not put obstacles in his way, he reserves certain favours, the first of which is the enlightening of the mind by means of a higher light due to the gift of intelligence ... by which such favours are discovered in the mysterious, ineffable harmonies, the existence of which was not even suspected before.... All seems new to it.... This gift is an immense help for the sanctification of the soul." "The second favour which God sets aside for it"—he then adds—"is the gift of wisdom, a gift even higher than that of intelligence."

"These things," as Fr. Simon, a Franciscan of Bourg-en-Bresse, said as far back as 1657 (*Saintes élévations*, pp. 34–35), "are only high and extraordinary according to an erroneous opinion or on account of the slothfulness and corruption of our evil nature; and as they do not demand high speculation but consist principally in love, it is very certain that they are for everyone and particularly for the most simple; for in reality all they require is a will that is good, true, sincere and fervent.... The not daring to aspire to such things through the dangers and illusions of Satan is, then, a fault and ignorance; for the dangers of the sea and pirates are not sufficient to deter men ... from the rich traffic of the Indies."

"To crown the evil," he adds (p. 38), "the majority of preachers, doctors, confessors and directors are completely ignorant of these divine things, at least as regards practice and experience ...; thus they despise, discredit and calumniate them and turn souls away from them."

"A great thing is the soul," exclaims St. Bonaventure (*Hex.* XXII); "in the soul the whole universe can be portrayed." "The soul has everything in itself, as the Church has in her many souls. For any contemplative soul you like has a certain perfection, so that it sees the visions of God" (*Hex.* XXIII).

96 St. Catherine de Ricci, during her long raptures, frequently went in procession with the nuns, carrying the crucifix and stopping at the different stations; but they used to see her come through the air, without touching the ground with her feet. Similarly, the ecstatic, Sr. Beatriz de la Concepción, a Discalced Franciscan nun in Salamanca, even served in the refectory: "She went through the air, her eyes turned up to heaven, and gave to each one what she needed"—as is related in her *Life*, n. 227.

97 Cf. *Evolución mística*, pt. 2, ch. 7, § 2. "Corporeal visions," said St. Bonaventure (*De profect. relig.*, bk. 2, ch. 76, n. 3), "neither make one holy nor show that one is so; otherwise Balaam would have been holy; and his ass, who saw the angel.... The intellectual vision is different and through this the eye enlightened by the light of truth contemplates in a pure manner truth in itself."

"The effects of intellectual visions," said Vallgornera (*Myst.* q. 3, d. 5, a. 3), "are very many and most precious—quietude of soul, enlightenment of mind, glorious joy, sweetness, purity, love of God, humility, the raising of the spirit to God."

Over and above these, there are others even more precious and valuable. "Often," remarked St. Alphonsus Rodríguez (*Unión*, ch. 16–17), "the spiritual servants of God are wont to experience such deep things of God, treating with him, and he communicating himself to them, that such great benefits cannot be uttered or expressed or enter into the hearts of men. He who experiences them understands them in a certain manner, although not as the blessed do who see God face to face. God communicates himself to him spiritually (as to his beloved) when he is alone with God, contemplating his divine majesty, goodness and glory. But he who will advance further in perfection ... will obtain from God greater light to know him, and greater love to love and find joy in him, and according to the measure of this, greater or less glory."

"These revelations I have mentioned and many others of this kind," said the Ven. Ana María de San José (*Life*, a. 34), "cannot be seen with the eyes of the body nor, many of them with those of the mind, but they are established in the deepest contemplation which in that case is a manifestation which shows God in himself, loved [after the manner] of the blessed, for all is manifested to them in God together with the intention he has in manifesting it."

"It happens," writes St. Teresa—and what she says confirms this (*Int. Cast.*, VI, ch. 10)—"that when the soul is in prayer ... there suddenly comes to it a transport in which the Lord gives it to understand great secrets which it seems to *see* in God himself.... It is not an imaginary vision, but one that is very intellectual, in which there is revealed to it how all things are seen in God and how he has them all in himself. *It is of great profit*; for, although it passes in a moment, it remains clearly imprinted on the mind and brings one into very great confusion.... It also happens very suddenly and in a way that cannot be expressed, that God shows a truth in himself in such a way as to seem to leave all the truths there are in creatures darkened and [the soul] is very clearly given to understand that he alone is truth and cannot lie."

98 According to Scaramelli (tr. 2*, ch. 14, n. 148), for any particular stage of contemplation, including ecstasies, raptures, locutions, and intellectual visions, the gifts of wisdom and understanding are sufficient, without there being any necessity to have recourse to graces *gratis datas*. Thus all this should be called "ordinary." And even though they be looked upon as the work of very special graces, it should not be understood that these are strictly *gratis datas*, but sanctifying graces in the highest degree.

"Others are commonly called *gratiae gratis datae*," said López Ezquerra (*Lucerna myst.*, tr. 4; ch. 1, n. 6). "These are directed not to the good of one's neighbour, but to the salvation of the soul of the receiver and in a broad way are said to be *gratiae gratis datae* because they are certainly benefits freely given by God ...; and of this kind are *visions, revelations, raptures, ecstasies, and things similar to these.*"

But even those graces that are really *gratis datas*, although ordained to the *common* good, can at times serve as a complement to one's own sanctification, their purpose being that this may reach its full splendor with the perfection that is desirable.

"The *gratiae gratis datae*," said Schram (*Teología mística*, vol. 1, pt. 2, ch. 4, § 244, schol.), "are not indeed precisely required for extraordinary (that is, infused) contemplation but they are for its complement and perfection, the virtues and gifts being in that case presupposed. It is lawful to grant that the *gratiae gratis datae* are not those through which man is joined to God, but they *foster more* and *confirm* the union effected per *gratiam gratum facientem*.... At least they elicit and prepare for greater union."

In this sense they may be very desirable. Such is the case with the gratuitous gift of knowledge, insofar as it is ordained to the perfection of the faith, as well as to its defense. Knowledge, however, that is ordained to the defense of the faith pertains to the *gratiam gratis datam*, of which it is said (1 Cor. 12:8) to others is given "the word of knowledge, according to the same spirit": and this is not on account of the necessity of the gift, "but of the perfection of faith" (St. Thomas, *In III Sent.*, d. 35, q. 2, a. 3, sol. 2).

99 "Besides these *habitus* or graces *gratis datas*," remarks St. John of the Cross (*Ascent*, II, ch. 24), "perfect persons or those who are already advanced in perfection, *very commonly* are wont to have light and knowledge about things present or absent, which they know through the light they receive in their spirit, now enlightened and purified.... Those who have the spirit purified with much facility can know even in a natural way and some more than others, what there is in the heart or in the interior spirit, and the inclinations and talents of persons, and this through external indications although they be very slight."

100 "Not every gift, although spiritual," says St. Bernard (Serm. 49 *in Cant.*), "do I say proceeds from the *wine cellar*, for there are other storage places the Spouse has, having different gifts and charisma stored up in them according to the riches of his glory.... Are there not these things stored up with me—he says (Deut. 32) and assigned to my treasures? Therefore through the diversity of the storage places there are divisions of graces and the spirit is manifested to each one to his profit. And to some indeed is given the word of wisdom, to others the word of knowledge, to others again prophecy, to others the grace of healing, to others divers tongues, to others the interpretation of speech, and other gifts like to these, to others; yet none of these will be able to say that he was introduced into the wine cellar on account of something of this kind. Out of other cells, or treasure houses indeed, these are taken."

101 "St. Teresa," remarked the holy Doctor (*Love of God*, bk. 7, ch. 3), "aptly says, that when union comes to this perfection that it keeps us captive and bound to God, it does not differ from rapture or trance of the spirit: but that it is only called union or trance when it is short, and when it is long ecstasy or rapture."

102 "From all the said five stages (illumination, inflammation, sweetness, desire, satiety) which love brings about in the heart," observes the holy abbot of Montserrat (*Ejercitatio*, ch. 30), "proceeds the sixth, which is called *rapture* of the mind ...; not that such a rapture requires that a man see visions, or anything corporeal: but it does require that a man should find himself *enlightened, inflamed, refreshed* and raised up by love to his Creator, in such a way that what he feels and sees cannot be expressed by any tongue, by reason of its sublimity, goodness, beauty, purity and mobility."

Endnotes

103 "Behold the beloved are inebriated," wrote Richard of St. Victor (*De contempl.*, bk. 4, ch. 16). "Now inebriation produces mental aberration and a certain infusion of heavenly *revelation*, and equally leads the beloved into cloudiness of mind. It was this inebriation the Prophet meant when he said (Ps. 35:9): *They will be inebriated from the richness of thy house*, and, *from the torrents of thy delight thou wilt give them to drink.*"

104 *Ecstasy* and *ecstatic union* are not synonymous, as Fr. Naval rightly points out (*Ascética y mística*, n. 252), for the former can exist without the latter: ecstatic union is a stage in contemplation; ecstasy is no more than a transitory and isolated happening or phenomenon. Supernatural or divine ecstasy is of two very distinct kinds: *prophetic ecstasy* and *ecstasy of union*. The first results from some isolated vision that man may receive without the stages of contemplation being involved; the second is mystical union.

Thus, however much certain kinds of ecstasy—such as those of St. Bernadette and many other souls who from their childhood and long before they attained to mystical union often remained abstracted from themselves, and received special revelations—ought to be considered as wholly extraordinary favors that it is not right to desire, they are in no way connected with the mystical ecstasies that are a complement of union itself, are ordained to one's own sanctification, and can be looked upon as ordinary and therefore desirable.

Although many authors affirm that it is not lawful to desire ecstasy, "we," declares Lehodey (*Ways of Prayer*, pt. 3, ch. 13), "see no reason why a soul which has reached the stage of quiet or of full union, may not desire a continual increase of infused light and love even when the withdrawal of the senses should prove to be the consequence: the intentions of the soul are upright, this hope gives it greater courage for virtue and it is not temerarious after the favours already received. The soul desires that everything should take place in secret: in what could it be deserving of blame?"

"Certain authors," Fr. Poulain remarks in turn (*Graces of Interior Prayer*, ch. 23, n. 26, note), "say that ecstasies ought not to be desired. But in this there is confusion which should be avoided. Such writers are speaking of ecstasy *in so far as it is external*, visible to all: otherwise they would contradict themselves as Canon Lejeune points out (*Introd. à la vie myst.*, ch. 1, n. 2)." José del Espíritu Santo makes this distinction clear, saying (vol. 3, disp. 17, n. 110, p. 293): "There are two things in rapture: the withdrawal of the senses and its cause. It is not the first of these which enriches the soul; for otherwise those who sleep would become enriched. But in regard to the *cause* of this state, spiritual persons do not want to be deprived of it; they rather desire it fully and with all their strength. *That they desire with all their strength.*"

105 "The door for entering into visions and revelations," said the Ven. Mary of Agreda (*Escala*, § 29), "is usually rapture. It is certain that the Lord does not

only give them for what is external, but their beginning is for some good purpose of spiritual profit."

"In this Mansion," St. Teresa remarks, referring to the sixth mansion (ch. 6), "raptures are many, and there is no way of avoiding them even in public, and then the persecutions and murmurs.... [The soul] does nothing but ... entreat His Majesty to lead it by another way (as it is counselled) ... but as it has found *such great profit* thereby that it cannot fail to see that it is leading it to heaven, it never ceases to desire it although it would like to do so, but leaves itself in his hands." "Oh when the soul once more comes to itself, what confusion it feels, and what very great desires it has of attending to God, in how many ways would it like to be made use of! If so many effects remain from past prayers as we have said, what will be the case with a favour so great as this? I should like to have a thousand lives to use them all for God and that as many things as there are on earth might be tongues to praise him" (ibid., ch. 4).

106 "I was never able to be sorry," she writes (*Life*, ch. 29), "for having seen these heavenly visions, and I would not exchange them even once for all the good things and delights of the world; I always considered it a great favour from the Lord and it seems to me a very great treasure; the Lord assured me of this many times. I found myself greatly increasing in love for him: I went to complain to him of all these troubles; I always came away from prayer consoled and with fresh strength."

"It should be noted," she then said (ch. 37), "that in each favour the Lord gave me, whether vision or revelation, my soul was left with some great gain; and in the case of some visions, with many. When I saw Christ the impression of his tremendous beauty remained with me and I have it still today." "In short," she adds (ch. 38), "it is a very great favour the Lord gives to the person to whom he gives similar visions, for it helps greatly; it also helps in bearing a heavy cross..... It is very usual, when I receive some particular favour from the Lord, for me first to have been reduced to nothing, so that I may see more clearly how devoid of meriting such things I am."

107 The Ven. Ángela María de la Concepción (*Riego espiritual*, ch. 47) very pertinently advises directors "not to be so obstinate when people relate some vision to them, in refusing to give credence to it so that they judge it all to be an illusion of weak women; nor so easy and soft in believing these things, that they declare them true, when they have had only one good instance and communication from such souls. Let them wait and watch the effects which are the indication of what is interior and of its genuineness—as, for instance, much love of God and one's neighbour, mortification, obedience and humility; and then it may be believed that the vision or other favours,

however great they may be, are from the Lord who can do all things and wills to work in souls."

"The soul," she adds (ch. 47), "cannot doubt, even should it want to do so, that this is true, for the favours of God bring with them a power which is greater than human and diabolic power and thus they banish beyond question all the fears and doubts which the soul might suffer. The visions of the enemy produce very contrary effects; so, either through God's permission … or because he cannot work in another way, the soul knows quite well that what is the enemy's work comes to it wholly from without; but the voice or vision of God seems to it to come from its own inmost depths; and the interior movement is always so, even though the voice be external."

108 "In the sublime state of *spiritual marriage*," remarks Vallgornera (*Théol. mist..*, q. 4, d. 2, a. 6, n. 1093), "the Bridegroom, Jesus Christ, reveals to the soul of his spouse wonders of the hidden things of heaven and the mysteries of his secrets: for the mutual love of those loving each other dearly, admits of no secret: for when the Bridegroom gives himself wholly to the bride, he opens all his inmost heart to her, lighting it up and laying open its deepest secrets; not only in our heavenly home … but even here when the bride, already perfectly adorned with the ornaments of virtue, has deserved to enjoy the company of and familiarity with, her Bridegroom."

109 "These souls, whom our Lord in his goodness loves so much, remarks the Ven. Marina de Escobar (*Life*, bk. 5, ch. 23, 5), "through this love he has for them, without there being any extraordinary or particular cause … deigns and wants, and it is his good pleasure, to communicate himself to them and visit them both himself and through his saints, just as a great prince might communicate with and reveal his secrets to certain … of his favourites … not now for that reason (of public utility), or for that end, but because he loves them so much that solely for the love he bears them, without any other reason, there is hardly a thing in his heart which he does not reveal to them."

"When the Lord comes to a soul," wrote St. Teresa (*Life*, ch. 21), "he communicates very great secrets to it. Here are the true revelations in ecstasy and the great favours and visions, and all is of profit to humiliate and strengthen the soul, and that it should value the things of this life less, and know more clearly the greatness of the reward which the Lord has prepared for those who serve him.… Since His Majesty pays so generously even in this life … what will it be in the other?"

According to the saint, certain of these favors, which are usually considered extraordinary, constitute a real stage [of prayer] higher than simple union. Thus, she adds (ch. 22): "He who shall come to have union and *not pass beyond—*I mean the *raptures and visions and other favours*, which God gives."

"Oh how sweet is this union to the soul that experiences it," said the Eternal Father to St. Catherine of Siena (*Dialogue*, ch. 89), "for in experiencing it, it sees my secrets, whence it comes about that it will often receive the spirit of prophecy to know things to come."

Thus, to such souls can be applied what the apostle says (Heb. 12:22-25): "You have come to Mount Sion, and to the city of the living God,... and to the company of many thousands of angels,... and to God the judge of all, and to the spirits of the just made perfect.... See that you refuse him not that speaketh."

110 "Through the gift of understanding," said St. Bonaventure (*De septem donis Spiritus Sancti*, pt. 2, s. 6, ch. 4), "the Holy Spirit causes us to penetrate all the veils which obscure for us the truths of Scripture necessary for our salvation, until we enter upon the pure illuminations and contemplation of the truth. The gift of understanding whenever it thus deeply penetrates all the veils of truth, also leads the mind to its interior teaching to such an extent that it there hears 'words which it is not granted to man to utter' (2 Cor. 12:4), for such things cannot even be properly expressed through a human mouth: for since they are intellectual words, having nothing corporeal about them, neither image nor similitude, therefore they cannot be uttered through a mouth of flesh. And therefore no one *knows* them except he who *accepts* them" (Rev. 2:17).

"Some men, however," writes St. Thomas (2-2, q. 45, a. 5), "receive the gift of wisdom in a higher degree: in the contemplation of divine things—in regard, namely, to certain higher mysteries—they both know them and can explain them to others, and in the direction of human affairs according to divine rules."

111 "The Holy Spirit is wont," remarks Fr. Tomás de Jesús (*De contempl. divin.*, bk. 3, ch. 9), "by means of the gift of understanding to make his way into the minds of contemplatives and to infuse the rays of his light so abundantly into them that they are able to penetrate truths hidden under the veil of sacred Scripture and, under the bark of the letter, it is common for them to grasp sublime and heavenly teaching. For generally, pure minds who direct themselves to the contemplation of the Scriptures, search for so many and such various and deep meanings almost for every word ... and they relate them all to the fostering of divine love."

112 "Now this revelation is made when the Holy Spirit, through the gift of understanding, raises our mind from earthly things, purges and inflames it. For earthly and animal affection impedes the understanding, and it cannot penetrate spiritual things: for 'the sensual man perceiveth not these things that are of the Spirit of God,' says the Apostle (1 Cor. 2:14). Therefore to such people revelations are not made. The Holy Spirit, withdrawing the mind, will, memory and the whole household of the spirit from lower things, impels it

to seek and possess the Lord" (St. Bonaventure, *De septem donis Spiritus Sancti*, 2, s. 6, ch. 5).

113 "We acknowledge," says John of St. Thomas (in 1-2, q. 70, disp. 18, a. 3, 15), "that these gifts are sometimes perfected and increase from a certain illumination given in the form of rapture or prophecy. But this is not because they claim of their nature to excel, but from the abundance of light. For it is the gifts in themselves that are required for salvation, not the lights."

114 When the servant of God, M. Marie Dominique Claire de la Croix, O.P. (*Vie*, 1910, ch. 10, p. 129), begged Him not to lead her by ways so unfrequented and even so extraordinary as hers were, He replied: "I want to finish what I have begun in you.... I am your Master and I can do what I will in your soul; and you ought not to place obstacles in my way.... So long as you seek me alone and sincerely try to do my will, there is no danger for you in these unfrequented ways."

115 St. Paul, Bácuez points out (*Manual Bibl.*, IV, n. 699), "does not hesitate to put the gift of inspiration—or prophecy—first, before all the others; for there is none so useful to the Church or so apt to convert and edify souls."

116 "Wisdom is glorious and never fadeth away, and is easily seen by them that love her, and is found by them that seek her. She preventeth them that covet her, so that she first sheweth herself unto them.... To think therefore upon her, is perfect understanding" (Wisd. 6:13-14, 16).

117 "As there is no remaining stationary in children, who naturally can but grow or die, similarly the soul, either has to die in its sin or always grow in grace until it rises to God and enjoys him in his Kingdom, where it is to enter upon its *perfect age*" (Ven. Ángela de la Concepción, *Life*, bk. 2, ch. 8).

118 "Do not become *children in sense*: but in malice be children, and *in sense be perfect*" (1 Cor. 14:20).

119 "It is a thing to be wondered at," remarks Bl. John of Ávila (*Audi filia*, ch. 4), "that there should be people so grudging in the service of our Lord that if they are told to do something, although it is something very good, go considering and turning over in their minds whether it is a thing which obliges them under pain of mortal sin, in order to avoid doing it. For they say they are weak and don't want to meddle in high things and those belonging to perfection, but to go along the level road, as they express it. Such souls on the one hand are cowardly in seeking perfect virtue for themselves—which with the Lord's grace it would be easy for them to attain to—and on the other, they are forward enough in concerning themselves with high office authority and honours, to use which well and without harm to oneself, perfect or proved virtue is needed. This they give you to understand they possess, and that they will give good account of the exalted position, without danger to

their consciences. In this many have fallen into peril. So greatly does the desire for domination and honour and human interests blind, that it makes those who do not dare to tackle what is easy and safe, tackle that which is full of dangers and difficulty. And those who do not trust God to help them in good works which concern themselves alone, promise themselves with great temerity that God will lead them by the hand in what concerns the government of others....

"Experience has shown us that dignities and places of honour have very seldom made bad men good, but have very often made good men bad; because to bear the weight of the honour and of the opportunities that come with it, great strength of virtue is necessary."

120 "The more a soul is favoured with sublime contemplation, with all the greater ardour does it devote itself to action. Only in beginners and the imperfect can the one harm the other.... In the perfect, this opposition disappears" (St. Gregory, *In I Reg.*, ch. 2, n. 10).

"A mark of good prayer," observed the Ven. Mary of Agreda (*Escala*, 17), "is that it is never idle, and as prayer is wholly love or in love, this fits in well with what is commonly said, that love cannot be idle. By this will be known whether the prayer is genuine, for perfect prayer *is always working*, urging and showing us how to work much" (Cf. St. Bernard, *Serm.* 5, 7, *in Cant.*).

"Those whom the Holy Spirit has filled, he makes both fervent and eloquent" (St. Greg., M., *In Evang.*, Hom. 30, 5).

121 Cf. *Exposición mística del Cantar de los Cantares*, ch. 2, 4, 14.

122 Cf. St. Bonaventure, *In III Sent.*, D. 35, a. 1, q. 1.

123 Cf. St. Thomas, 2-2, q. 45, a. 2 and 5.

124 Cf. Lallemant, *Doctrine spirituelle*, pr. 5, ch. 3, a. 1. "The contemplative life ... moves and directs the active life" (St. Thomas, 2-2ae, q. 182, a. 4).

"Action, if it is to be fruitful," remarks Dom Chautard (*L'âme de tout apostolat*, p. 61 [Paris, 1917]), "needs contemplation. When the latter reaches a certain degree of intensity it spreads over the first something of its superabundance, and through this the soul draws directly from the heart of God the graces which it is the function of action to distribute. That is why in the soul of a saint, since action and contemplation are fused in perfect harmony, they give perfect unity to his life—as, for instance, in the case of St. Bernard, the most contemplative and at the same time most active man of his age."

125 "Just as a man, in spite of the good food he may eat, if he does not have the rest of sleep will be weak and even run the risk of losing his senses; so it will happen to the man who works well but does not pray well; for prayer is to the soul as sleep to the body. There is no business, however large it be, that does not come to an end if there is continual outgoings and no incomings; nor

can good works last without prayer; for in it we reach the light and strength with which we recover what our fervour loses of charity and interior devotion by occupations, even good ones" (Bl. John of Ávila, *Audi filia*, ch. 70).

Prayer, said the Bl. Francisco Posadas (*Carta del esposo*, 20), is "food that sustains, conversation that delights, intercourse that entertains and sweet sleep in which the soul rests. Why then do you not take advantage of it? What are you without prayer? Your works will answer, for they turn out to be without sense, like those of a man who neither eats nor sleeps."

126 "It behoves every Christian who is in the state of salvation to have some hare in contemplation (*In III Sent.*, D. 36, q. 1, a. 3, ad. 5).

127 "Of its own nature," says St. Thomas (2-2, q. 183, a. 2), "the contemplative life is of greater merit than the active." "External labour," he adds (ibid., ad. 1), "is carried out for the increase of an accidental reward; but the increase of merit in respect of the essential reward consists chiefly in charity; one sign of which is external difficulties borne for Christ. But a much clearer sign of it is when someone, setting aside all the things that pertain to this life, takes delight in giving himself up to divine contemplation."

"Active life is prior to contemplative in time, for from good works men tend to contemplation.... But the contemplative [life] is greater in merit than the active life, for the latter works for the usefulness of present things, the former, however, already enjoys the future rest in an intimate delight" (St. Greg. M., *Hom. 13 in Ezech.*).

128 Cf. St. Thomas, *In III Sent.*, d. 35, q. 1, a. 3, sol. 3; 2-2, q. 182, a. 4, c. and ad. 3. "He in fact passes to the contemplative life, who in the active life has not changed [the covering of] his intention to worse things" (St. Gregory the Great, *Hom. 3 in Ezech.*).

129 "And so peaceful men are called by God to contemplation, and the ungentle are also called and not only once, that in the former he may show the sweetness of his rule and in the latter the power of his grace to dominate nature" (Álvarez de Paz, *De inquisit. pads*, bk. 5, p. 1, ch. 2).

"Therefore," as St. Francis de Sales observes and points out, "progress in the love of God does not depend on one's natural complexion." – "As God our Lord," remarks Fr. La Puente (*Guía*, tr. 3, ch. 1, 1), "at the beginning of the world, when the works of the six days were finished, rested on the seventh day and sanctified it; willing that it should be devoted to quiet contemplation ...; so also to those who have exercised themselves in the works of the active life, he indicates the sabbath day and rest, on which the works of the contemplative life are practised and such men share to some extent in the eternal rest; for, as the Apostle says (Heb. 4:9), also 'there remaineth therefore a day of rest for the people of God,' and they enter to enjoy their leisure, resting in him who is the centre and final end of our soul."

130 Cf. *Evolución mística*, p. 424, ed. 5*; Blosius, *Institutio spiritualis*, ch. 1; Lallemant, *Doctrine spirituelle*, pt. 2, sect. 2, ch. 6, a. 2; ch. 4, a. 4; Sauvé, *États mystiques*, pp. 60–63, etc.

131 Cf. *La vie contemplative: Son rôle apostolique*, par un Religieux Chartreux, IV–XI.

132 "With all watchfulness keep thy heart, because life issueth out from it" (Prov. 4:23). "Then a certain requisite fervour of action is present whenever we thus apply ourselves to the work, so that with a quiet heart we may see him to whom we are trying to consecrate our works. . . . The disposer and receiver of our works declares, then, that one thing is necessary, lest the mind be dispersed on many things, so that, being unified through tranquillity, it may rise in strength to the intuition of the highest good" (St. Gregory the Great, *In I Regum*, Lib. V, cap. 15).

133 All active souls should believe me," said Juan de los Ángeles (*Conquista*, dial. 8º, 3), "that if Mary does not help them, they will weary and fail in what they have begun, however fervently they may begin, and even fall into deep troubles. . . . 'Be instant in prayer,' says St. Paul (Rom. 12), 'communicating to the necessities of the saints.' If then, having to deal with holy people, it is necessary to be instant in prayer, will not a double measure of prayer be necessary to deal with sinners? . . . Believe me, to work one hour with our neighbours to their profit and not to our harm, eight hours of converse with God are necessary."

It can be seen from the valuable little book by Dom Chautard, *L'âme de tout apostolat*, how meagre and barren the fruit of the most brilliant works of zeal and propaganda usually is today when they are not inspired by and rooted in the interior life, and how exposed to deplorable falls are the many lovers of activity who neglect to temper their souls in prayer and mortification.

St. Teresa herself (*Life*, ch. 13) for her part declares that so long as she did not give herself sufficiently to prayer, after being exposed to many dangers, she scarcely succeeded in gaining a few souls to God, however much she liked speaking of Him; while afterwards, almost without realizing it, she attracted innumerable ones.

"Those who are very active then, should here note, though they think to encompass the world with their preachings and external works," says St. John of the Cross (*Spiritual Canticle*, note to cant. 29), "that they would bring much more profit to the Church and please God much more (leaving aside the good example that would be given) if they were to spend perhaps half this time in being with God in prayer. . . . It is certain that they would then do more and with less effort, and more with one work than with a thousand [now], for their prayer would merit this and they would have gathered spiritual strength for it; for otherwise, everything is hard hammering and they do little more than nothing, and at times nothing; and they even sometimes do harm. God deliver us from the salt when it begins to lose its savour."

"We are to be pitied," exclaimed Bellarmine in a sermon (July 31, 1599), "if our life is purely active. For however much we may profit others, we shall harm ourselves, if we do not harm them also."

"Man," says St. Catherine of Siena (*Dialogue*, ch. 1), "cannot bring to his neighbours truly useful doctrine, example, and prayer, if he has not taken advantage of it himself beforehand." On the other hand, "the soul that is in love with my truth," the Eternal Father then tells her (ch. 7), "never fails to profit the whole world."

"He cannot profit others," similarly observed St. Lawrence Justinian (*De casto connubio*, ch. 12), "who is worthless in himself.... No one, unless he is very holy, busies himself with the care of his neighbours without detriment to himself.... When he sets out to obtain his neighbour's profit he becomes a diligent guardian of himself.... He has faithfully performed the work enjoined, carried it out fervently, and taken care to return to himself; thus he hastens with great joy into the embrace of the word.... He is resplendent with glory and languishes with love.... For the more he forgets himself, the more he inheres in the footsteps of the Word."

134 "When we live in this union with our Lord," said Margaret Mary Doëns (1842–1884; cf. *Vie*, 1910, ch. 11), "we are called to do good as in the manner of another sacrament.... This good we spread and filter into our surroundings without noticing. Just as the Holy Eucharist works in us gradually, so we, in our turn, go to Jesus.... As he, in the days of his mortal life, communicated himself to all those around him, so he still wishes to communicate himself through us to those who are around us. At times it seems to me that I hear him say in the depths of my soul: 'Take, daughter, and give me wholly to those souls, it is for this I am wholly at your disposal: give me in a smile, in a good word, in an act of charity.'"

"Our mission," the Discalced Carmelite Sr. Elizabeth of the Trinity (1880–1906), remarked (cf. *Souvenirs*, p. 137), "is to prepare the ways of the Lord by our union with him whom the Apostle calls 'consuming fire.' At his contact our soul will come to be like a flame of love which extends over all the members of the Mystical Body. Then we shall console the Heart of Jesus ... and he will be able to say, showing us the Father: 'Now I am glorified in them ...' Since our Lord dwells in our hearts, his prayer is ours; and I should like to share in it unceasingly, holding myself like a pitcher at the fountain, to be able then to communicate life, allowing these waves of infinite charity to overflow.... Yes, let us sanctify ourselves for souls; and since we are members of one body, in the measure in which we abound in divine life, we shall be able to make it circulate through the great organism of the Church."

135 "In an acceptable time I have heard thee, and in the day of salvation I have helped thee ... that thou mightest say to them that are bound: Come forth: and to them that are in darkness: Shew yourselves. They shall feed in the ways, and their pastures shall be in every plain. They shall not hunger, nor thirst, neither shall the heat nor the sun strike them: for he that is merciful to them shall be their shepherd, and at the fountains of waters he shall give them drink" (Isa. 49:8–10).

136 Donoso Cortés rightly said that those who pray do more for the world than combatants on the field of battle, and that if the world goes from bad to worse, it is because it trusts more in battles than in prayers.

"A short but fervent prayer," wrote Dom Chautard (*L'âme de tout apostolat*, pt. 1, p. 37), "will usually advance a conversion much more than long discussions and fine speeches.... Ten Carmelites *praying*, said a bishop of Cochin-China to the governor of Saigon, will be more use to me than twenty missionaries *preaching*.... The Bl. Anna Maria Taigi in her capacity as a poor housewife was an apostle, as was also the beggar St. Benedict Labré....

"M. Dupont, the Holy Man of Tours, Colonel Paqueron, consumed by the same fervour, were mighty in their works, because they were interior men. — Through the union he had with God, Général de Sonis found the secret of the apostolate between two battles."

137 "The lips of the just teach many: but they that are ignorant shall die in the want of understanding" (Prov. 10:21). Let us consider, for instance, a teacher in a religious school. If he is not fairly devout and a lover of recollection and prayer, as Dom Chautard so rightly says (*L'âme de tout apostolat*, pt. 4), "he will think he has done his whole duty if he keeps exclusively to the examination programme. But if he were an interior soul, a phrase escaping his lips and his heart, deep feeling clearly shown in his face, an expressive gesture, how shall I put it? — his very manner of praying after or before a lesson even if it be a mathematics class — could have greater influence on his pupils than a sermon.... How mighty is the external radiance of a soul united with God.... The apostle comes to be an accumulator of supernatural life and condenses in himself a divine fluid which is diversified and adapted to all the needs of the medium in which he is and works. — 'Virtue went out from him, and healed all' (Luke 6:19). In him words and works are only the outflow of this latent strength which is sovereign in breaking down obstacles, obtaining conversions and increasing fervour."

138 "Can a man hide fire in his bosom, and his garments not burn?" (Prov. 6:27).

139 "Rest and glory for me?" exclaimed the Ven. Ángela María de la Concepción (*Vida*, 32). "Enjoyment for me, when I see Holy Church in such great tribulation, and the world full of wretchedness, sin and calamities? My God, I want to live to suffer and co-operate in your work of redemption, although it be

until the end of the world and although it be in hell so far as the cruelty of its torments is concerned, willingly depriving myself of enjoying you and of all the happiness you offer me in the possession of glory." "Ah, Lord, how can I rest?" exclaimed St. Catherine of Siena much earlier (*Life* by Bl. Raymond of Capua, Prol. 15), "while a single soul created in your image is in danger of being lost. Would it not be better that all should be saved and I alone condemned, provided I could continue to love you?" St. Magdalene of Pazzi said the same thing in substance, as did the Ven. Sr. Barbara de Santo Domingo (cf. *Evolución mística*, p. 582).

140 The Ven. Ángela María de la Concepción, already quoted—she was born in Asturias and died in high odor of sanctity at the age of seventy-eight, in 1746, with the Bernardines of Valladolid (cf. *Life* 31, in *Medula historica Cisterciense*, by Fr. Muñiz, vol. 4, 1785, p. 261)—says of herself: "On great days my soul was usually carried up to heaven, seeing beauty that I cannot express. I saw that I was being carried along until I entered the choir of the seraphim. The Lord said to me: 'I want you to take possession of what I have to give you; for this, I am carrying you by the love corresponding to the state of the seraphim; for that is your state on earth. *And I regard the city where you are with much consideration for your sake*; for your love holds the arm of my justice bound and in your soul I find rest from the evil treatment they give me in the world.'"

"I have chosen you," our Lord said to St. Veronica Juliani (*Life*, bk. 3, ch. 1), "as intermediary between sinners and myself. I now confirm and give you this office by my own lips.... Let your business be to save souls, being ready to give your life and blood for my glory and their salvation.... I want you to be wholly transformed into me: my passion, my merits and all I suffered and did in the space of thirty-three years I give and make over to you, so that you may work with my works: you will suffer with my suffering and work with my labour. Do all in conformity with my will: strip yourself of everything so that you may truly say: 'With Christ I am nailed to the cross.'"

"Our Lord made me see," similarly wrote Sr. Bernarda Ezpelosín, on June 16, 1882 (*Life*, p. 222), "that he has done, does and will do much good through me wherever I serve him: this I know, see and believe because it is the Lord himself who tells me and assures me of it.... A short time ago ... I seemed clearly to hear our Lord saying to me: 'Yes, a generous soul giving itself wholly to me in sacrifice, is sufficient not only to sanctify one household, but also to save a nation and even the entire world.' It seemed to me that God our Lord—who wants something very big from me—was asking me, by means of an absolute sacrifice of all my being—for the salvation of the whole world.... The Heart of Jesus suffers and it seems the world is being lost: I see the multitude of souls who are casting themselves into hell and, what is more painful, how those chosen among thousands, do not know him, are ungrateful to him and many of them are damned. This sight causes me inexpressible suffering."

141 "The blessings which make the ministry fruitful," observed Chautard (*L'âme de tout apostolat*, pt. 4), "are reserved for the supplications of the *man of prayer*.... For restoring all things in Christ through the apostolate of works, divine grace is necessary, and the apostle only receives it on condition of being united with Christ. When we have formed Jesus Christ in ourselves, then only can we give him back to families and societies in forming them with his spirit.... We are the salt of the earth in the measure in which we are holy."

142 It was on this account, to teach us by His own example, that our Lord prayed so much and spent so many nights in prayer. "An example is given to us, that those we instruct by our words, we should help by the suffrage of our prayers; for the divine word bears very great fruit in the hearts of its hearers, when it is supported by prayer" (St. Thomas, *In Joan.* 17, lect. 1).

143 Cf. St. Thomas, *In III Sent.*, D. 35, q. 1, a. 1, ad. 5; a. 3, sol. 3; 2-2, q. 182, a. 1. "It is not sufficient," says St. Gregory, "that one should have much speculative knowledge of virtue and much knowledge of theology or scripture: For if one only knows the examples of good men, or even if one is learned in Sacred Scripture and lacks the revelation *given by contemplation, he will not be a perfect man in the field of preaching.* For contemplation is the virtue through which not only what is stored up in Scripture is called to mind, but through which these things not yet fully understood may be established: and through which the things stored up are daily at the disposal of the will of God" (St. Gregory, *In I Regum*, lib. 3, cap. 7). "Preachers are holy," he adds (ibid., lib. 5, ch. 14), "and are *most exalted*, not only through their work, but *also through contemplation.*"

"The excellence and perfection of the sacred ministers," says Fr. La Puente (*Perf. est. ecles.*, tr. 4, ch. 2), "is founded jointly in the works of the two lives, active and contemplative, united together in this form. The contemplative, as St. Thomas says (2-2, q. 180, a. 3, ad. 4), performs three acts: the first is to receive the doctrine of others, hearing it in sermons and discourses about God, or reading it in sacred books and works of devotion; the second is to pray and meditate on the divine mysteries, receiving light from God through prayer, and working for our part through the knowledge and love of truth through meditation; the third is the contemplation of the supreme Truth, which is God, and of his perfections and wonderful works, looking at them with a gentle, quiet and loving gaze, full of admiration at their excellence. The active life embraces three other kinds of works: the first are ordained to our own perfection...; and in this way all the moral virtues are the work of the active life, although in so far as they dispose us to contemplation they pertain in some manner to the contemplative life. But more properly the works of the active life, as St. Gregory says (*Hom.* 14 *in Ezech.*), are ordered to the profit of our neighbours, and for this reason include two principal works: one sort, external and purely material, as to visit the sick ..., and the other, external and spiritual, arising from the inwardness of *contemplation.*... Such are the mysteries ... of teaching, preaching and governing."

144 "Certain people," says St. Thomas (*Qs. disp., q. unica de caritate*, a. 11, ad. 6), "take so much delight in practising divine contemplation that they are unwilling to leave it, even to abandon divine praise for the salvation of their neighbours. Some, however, rise to the highest point of charity, for they even set aside divine contemplation, which legitimately in itself they delight in most, that they may serve God in the salvation of their neighbours.... And this perfection is proper to *prelates and preachers and all those others who are concerned with procuring the salvation of souls*: hence by the angels ascending Jacob's ladder are typified those rising upwards by contemplation, by the descending angels, men who come down to earth moved by the solicitude they have for the salvation of their neighbours."

"A property of true, chaste contemplation," says St. Bernard (*Serm.* 57 *in Cant.*), "is this, that it enkindles the mind, as it were, with so much zeal and desire of acquiring for God souls who will similarly love him in like manner, that a man will most willingly interrupt the leisure of contemplation for the labour of preaching; and again having done what he set out to do will return to the same [i.e., the leisure of contemplation] so much the more fervently as he reflects that the interval was a profitable one: and again having resumed the pleasurable experience of contemplation, he will return with alacrity and with greater courage to the quest for his customary gains [i.e., of souls].... You have these three things, that is, preaching, prayer and contemplation, commended and indicated in three words. For rightly do we use the term *beloved* for one who diligently and faithfully, by preaching, counselling and the ministry, seeks the advantage of the Bridegroom. Deservedly do we use the term *dove* for one who while he groans and supplicates in prayer for his sins, does not cease to conciliate the divine mercy for himself. Deservedly also do we use the term *comely* for one who, shining with heavenly desire, puts on the garment of heavenly contemplation."

145 "The work of the active life is two-fold: one aspect indeed is derived from contemplation—such as *teaching* and *preaching*: Hence St. Gregory says (*Hom.* 5 *in Ezech.*) that of perfect men returning after their contemplation, it is said (Ps. 144:7): 'They shall publish the memory of the abundance of thy sweetness.' This surpasses simple contemplation. For as it is greater to give light than merely to be light oneself, so it is a greater thing to hand on to others the fruits of contemplation than merely to contemplate, The work of

the active life is different for it consists wholly of external occupations such as the giving of alms, the bestowing of hospitality and other things of this kind, which are lesser in importance than the works of contemplation" (St. Thomas, 2-2, q. 188, a. 6).

146 "I will give you pastors according to my own heart, and they shall feed you with knowledge and doctrine" (Jer. 3:15). "As those who give refreshment to others heed a double light which they must have firmly in their hand and at the right time, so they stand in need of a double measure of prayer, and to be so expert in it that they practise it without difficulty. In this way they will know the Lord's will as to what they have to do in detail, and will acquire strength to fulfil it. This knowledge that is acquired thus surpasses that we acquire by our reasoning and speculation. It is like the difference between the man who directs his steps to something that is sure and certain and the man who goes along, as they say, feeling for the wall. The good resolutions and strength which souls thus gather are usually incomparably deeper and truer than those which are obtained outside prayer.... Not to weary you I do not say more except that the supreme Truth said (Luke 11) that the heavenly Father will give his good spirit to those who ask, with whom come all good things" (Bl. John of Ávila, *Audi filia*, ch. 70). "Prayer is the source whence the water of the wisdom of salvation is drawn" (St. Thomas, *In Joan*. 6, lect. 2).

147 Cf. *Living Flame of Love*, cant. 3, v. 3, § 7-12; *Evolución mística*, pp. 254, 357-358.

148 "The director," said the Ven. Mary of Agreda (*Escala*, § 6), "needs to be learned and experienced.... In this there is a lack ... a very great lack. And God's Majesty complains very much of the ministers of his Church, for there are few who come to learn in this school; and thus there are few masters." Hence the painful hunger and thirst which innocent and pure souls so often feel, especially the virgins of the Lord, to hear the true divine word, the true spiritual doctrine, until they faint away through not finding anyone who will administer it to them properly."

"I will send forth a famine into the land: not a famine of bread, nor a thirst of water, but of hearing the word of the Lord. And they shall move from sea to sea ...; they shall go about seeking the word of the Lord, and shall not find it. In that day the fair virgins, and the young men shall faint for thirst" (Amos 8:11-13).

149 "Where there is no knowledge of the soul, there is no good" (Prov. 19:2). But for this knowledge of the soul, a purely speculative study is not sufficient. As in medicine, theoretical knowledge is not enough but practice is necessary, without which lamentable mistakes would be made, "so also in spiritual and mystical things," remarks the Ven. Falconi (*Camino*, bk. 4, ch. 5), "theologians will have to know the speculative points of meditation and contemplation

...; but in coming to deal with how contemplation is practised and the manner in which souls enter into it and at what time, with what dispositions, and the different modes and diversity of means through which God leads them, they lose their foothold and never succeed in understanding it, nor in believing that similar and such secret interior converse passes between God and the soul. They say that prayer is to be idle and do nothing and that it is wasting time. With this they destroy many souls and cause them to be lost. This particularly happens with some who are very learned, who want to cling closely to the definitions and arguments of theology, which do not extend to the special and supernatural ways by which God leads souls. And as on the other hand they have ... no experience of this ..., they do not know what to think except that it cannot be good, for theological reasoning and speculation does not cover it; as if God were tied to schema and the art of theological speculation, to communicate himself to souls with love and secret familiarity.... There is, then, no need to be astonished at anything unless it runs counter to the faith and good morals. The rest would be to fall into the fault which St. James mentions, that what they do not know, they blaspheme. Let them do what Fr. Bartolomé of the Martyrs teaches in his *Compendio espiritual* (pt. 2, ch. 26): 'When those who are learned but have no experience [he says], see what is happening in certain devout souls and do not understand what the latter tell them and that their mode of prayer surpasses their speculation and reasoning, and that, moreover, it is not against faith and good morals, let them hand over such souls to others more experienced in the matter, and not discredit what they hear nor trouble and disturb these poor souls.'"

St. John of the Cross says the same (loc. cit.), adding that otherwise they will have to render a very strict account to God of the harm they cause.

"Certain learned men whom the Lord does not lead by this way of prayer, nor have they even a beginning of its spirit," says St. Teresa in turn (*Concepts of Love*, ch. 6), "want to conduct things so much according to discursive reason and so much according to their understanding, that it appears as if only they with their learning understood all the greatness of God. If only they could have something of the humility of the most Blessed Virgin!"

150 "Whoever wants to exclude mysticism, that is, Christianity in its full development, either from practical life, private moral activity or public activity, or from the direction of the business of the Church and a participation in secular matters, such a man," says Fr Weiss (*Apologia*, vol. 9, conf. n. 5-7), "would do better to say frankly that he wants separation between Christianity and the world.... Mysticism is the concern of all those who want to accept Christianity in its fullness.... There should be no fear that certain rich qualities or certain legitimate aspirations of humanity will suffer prejudice. Mysticism will not lower or diminish in any way either intelligence, heart,

will, knowledge, energy, justice, charity, Church, state, school or family.... Only when mysticism receives the place that is due to it will the sublime designs which God had in creating the world and saving it through his Son, be accomplished. Then heaven and earth, the natural and the supernatural, the divine and the human will form a single whole, that is: the true kingdom of God among men."

"Retirement and contemplation," he then aptly remarks (*Conference* 12, n. 11), "did not prevent St. Rose of Lima, as the bull of canonization indicates, from being a strongminded woman who understood the difficult art of avoiding domestic upsets, who did the work of others before they got up and surpassed the most skilful in the good government of her household.... For the saints, place, time and occupations mattered little, for they found God everywhere and in him they did all things. Often the most meritorious works, the most intimate conversations with God and the most sublime communications of the Holy Spirit have taken place in the kitchen, the stable, on the staircase, carrying up water, guarding cattle."

Thus we see St. Francis de Sales, as Dom Mackey points out (Introduction to *Works*, IV, pp. xxxv–xlix) "recommending the reading of the *Treatise on the Love of God* to people in the world.... What he had done with regard to devotion, he does with regard to the mystical life: he shows it to be attractive, simple, desirable and even easy. It is an error, he would say, and almost a heresy, to want to exclude the ranks of soldiers, the shops of craftsmen, the palaces of princes and the families of married people from high forms of prayer" (cf. *Devout Life*, pt. 1, ch. 3).

151 Cf. Wisd. 7:11. "Counsel and equity is mine, prudence is mine, strength is mine. By me kings reign, and lawgivers decree just things.... With me are riches and glory" (Prov. 8:14–18).

152 That is, as criticize the prayer described. – Tr.

153 That is, the faculties of the soul. – Tr.

154 The Spanish text is here obscure. The above would seem to be the sense. – Tr.

155 The poem of M. María de San Alberto, O.C.D., is very apposite (cf. *Works of St. John of the Cross*, critical edition, vol. 3, p. 241):
Sleeping restfully,
The dwellers left her free.
The Bridegroom opened and went in;
But when they awoke
They complained at seeing themselves already awake.

Sophia Institute

Sophia Institute is a nonprofit institution that seeks to nurture the spiritual, moral, and cultural life of souls and to spread the gospel of Christ in conformity with the authentic teachings of the Roman Catholic Church.

Sophia Institute Press fulfills this mission by offering translations, reprints, and new publications that afford readers a rich source of the enduring wisdom of mankind.

Sophia Institute also operates the popular online resource CatholicExchange.com. *Catholic Exchange* provides world news from a Catholic perspective as well as daily devotionals and articles that will help readers to grow in holiness and live a life consistent with the teachings of the Church.

In 2013, Sophia Institute launched Sophia Institute for Teachers to renew and rebuild Catholic culture through service to Catholic education. With the goal of nurturing the spiritual, moral, and cultural life of souls, and an abiding respect for the role and work of teachers, we strive to provide materials and programs that are at once enlightening to the mind and ennobling to the heart; faithful and complete, as well as useful and practical.

Sophia Institute gratefully recognizes the Solidarity Association for preserving and encouraging the growth of our apostolate over the course of many years. Without their generous and timely support, this book would not be in your hands.

www.SophiaInstitute.com
www.CatholicExchange.com
www.SophiaInstituteforTeachers.org

Sophia Institute Press is a registered trademark of Sophia Institute.
Sophia Institute is a tax-exempt institution as defined by the
Internal Revenue Code, Section 501(c)(3). Tax ID 22-2548708.